THE KISSINGER
LEGACY

THE KISSINGER LEGACY

American–Middle East Policy

Ishaq I. Ghanayem
and
Alden H. Voth

PRAEGER SPECIAL STUDIES • PRAEGER SCIENTIFIC

New York • Philadelphia • Eastbourne, UK
Toronto • Hong Kong • Tokyo • Sydney

Library of Congress Cataloging in Publication Data

Ghanayem, Ishaq I.
    The Kissinger legacy.

    Bibliography: p.
    Includes index.
    1. Near East–Foreign relations–United States.
2. United States–Foreign relations–Near East.
3. Kissinger, Henry, 1923–   . 4. United States–
Foreign relations–1969–1974. I. Voth, Alden H.,
1926–   . II. Title.
DS63.2.U5G47   1984   327.73056   83-24512
ISBN 0-03-069752-2 (alk. paper)

Published in 1984 by Praeger Publishers
CBS Educational and Professional Publishing
a Division of CBS Inc.
521 Fifth Avenue, New York, NY 10175 USA

456789 052 987654321

Printed in the United States of America
on acid-free paper

To my mother, Naimeh Ghanayem

—I.I.G.

To youth—South, East, West—
who deserve something better than World War III

—A.H.V.

Doomed humanity teeters on the nuclear abyss,
Yet from within, the spirit casts aside the spell of night—
N'er to contain the self.

For out from the maze of our inventions' self-entrapment,
The soul emerges—free at last.

Preface

No one could have predicted the momentous changes that have occurred in the Middle East since Henry Kissinger left Middle East policy to others in the political game of musical chairs. Change, in all its dimensions, seems to be the permanent feature of the area. From this writer's personal experience in the Middle East, both Arabs and Jews seem to agree on one point: Henry Kissinger left his imprint on the political order of the region. It would be interesting to speculate on the changes the next decade will bring. Projecting changes in American Middle East policy during the same period might be equally interesting. One of my students captured the spirit of the times when he suggested final examinations in the Middle East course never need changing because the answers always change.

In any case, the potential for great triumph as well as great tragedy in the Middle East is very real. At this writing the recreation of Lebanon as a sovereign state and the future of the Palestinians are very much in doubt. Another one of my students, this one from the Persian Gulf area, was recently freed from prison and allowed to return to San José State University. His cellmate was not so lucky; without fanfare or ceremony—such as a trial—he was simply taken out and shot.

The Kissinger Legacy, like the real world of politics, had its moments of both discipline and joy. Working with my coauthor, Dr. Ishaq I. Ghanayem, has been an especially pleasant and worthwhile experience. He was my student at San José State, then continued his graduate studies at the University of California (Santa Barbara), and became a recognized scholar in American foreign policy.

Both of us appreciated the many contributions others have made in bringing the project to a successful conclusion. I want to especially thank professors and colleagues Charles Burdick, Roy Young, Kent Schellenger, Robert Harmon, and Milton Loventhal, at San José State University, for reading parts of the manuscript, providing suggestions, serving as a sounding board for ideas, and helping, in general, to get the book "into orbit." There were others who helped sustain the project and bring it to a successful conclusion; my thanks go to Mary-Lynne Bainbridge, Farid Rahimi, and Jaleh Rahimi.

Finally, I want to pay special tribute to my dear wife, Norma, who shared her skills as an established author, whose patience knew no bounds, and whose encouragement extended far above and beyond the call of duty. Thanks also to Susan and Tom for their patience in postponing "family times" so that the manuscript could grow and finally see the light of day.

Alden H. Voth

Table of Contents

Henry Kissinger

1

INTRODUCTION

Henry Kissinger, however controversial, left his imprint on American foreign policy. It was an imprint based on and guided by his conceptualization of international relations. Any assessment of the Nixon administration's foreign policy, whether global or in reference to the Middle East, should proceed on two levels: Not only is it important to probe the international and domestic milieu to which the foreign policy was adapted, it is also imperative to analyze the conceptual framework that Kissinger applied to its formulation.

In a variety of ways, the Nixon-Kissinger foreign-policy system represented innovative changes from previous American approaches to foreign affairs. First, and contrary to what happened in the cold-war era, Kissinger did not emphasize the role of ideology in diplomatic transactions. As William Fulbright characterized it, "The Nixon-Kissinger policy . . . represented a significant departure from the ideological anti-Communism which so strongly influenced the foreign policy of American presidents from Truman to Johnson."[1] Under Kissinger's influence, the Nixon administration placed more emphasis upon the role of classical power politics and upon the priority of pragmatically defined national interests.

Second, the Nixon-Kissinger foreign policy frankly acknowledged the basic political role of diplomacy in this international environment of power and interest.[2] The Nixon-Kissinger approach to diplomacy has been referred to as "creative diplomacy," in contrast to what might be called "routine diplomacy." The innovative aspect of this creative diplomacy led to a "diplomatic revolution"[3] yielding a new grid of national ties and group cleavages. The Kissinger approach emphasized concrete interests rather than legal and formalized obligations. In contrast to the cold-war era, Nixon and Kissinger de-emphasized American nuclear predominance in their diplomatic transactions; they were willing to acknowledge approximate nuclear parity (or sufficiency) vis-à-vis the Soviet Union, in the interests of

1

their overall political objectives. The political approach increased the diplomatic maneuverability of American foreign policy, especially in the Middle East, an area which threatened to undermine the entire Nixon-Kissinger foreign-policy approach—particularly during the October War of 1973.

Third, the Nixon-Kissinger foreign-policy approach placed more emphasis on secrecy and on centralized decision making than had previous American administrations.[4] Secrecy was one of the major aspects of the Nixon-Kissinger National Security Council (NSC) structure. In addition, centralization was deemed essential to avoid bureaucratic haggling over foreign-policy formation. Kissinger believed the national security bureaucracy lacked the imagination to initiate policy.[5] The White House's fait accompli replaced the State Department's normal channels in dealing with major foreign-policy issues—particularly those confrontations requiring new policy directions. Kissinger's trip to China and his secret meetings in 1973 with Hafez Ismail, President Anwar Sadat's national security advisor, are good examples of the "back channel."

The central figure of the Nixon National Security Council was, of course, Kissinger himself. He preempted the role from his position as President Nixon's assistant for national security affairs. Beginning as director of the National Security Council (NSC), and later (after September 1973) as secretary of state, Kissinger played a multiple role in dealing with defense and foreign-policy problems.[6] Both the State Department and the Department of Defense were unhappy with Kissinger's commanding role and the secrecy of his operations.[7]

The new channels represented a significant departure in American foreign-policy procedures from previous American administrations. Impetus for that departure should be attributed to the Vietnam War and to the "intellectual failure" that characterized previous American foreign policy, especially during the Johnson administration.[8] Furthermore, the Nixon-Kissinger era coincided with certain fundamental changes in the international setting, most notably the advent of detente and increasing global interdependence. Nixon and Kissinger recognized the need for a fresh look in American foreign policy that would match this changing world. The search for new policies, in turn, sparked a debate, inside and outside the United States, on the American role in the world arena. George Kennan, for one, did not see retrenchment from world politics as the answer to the compelling problems of American foreign policy. With the end of the cold war, the United States should, in his view, move to preserve the natural environment on a global scale and to play a positive role in developing the full potential of the United Nations.[9]

Zbigniew Brzezinski was another prominent scholar who criticized American foreign policy because the involvement in Vietnam had undermined the domestic consensus in the United States and America's position in international affairs.[10] As a solution to the problem, Brzezinski recommended American acceptance of greater global interdependence with primary emphasis upon trilateral cooperation between the United States, Japan, and Europe.[11]

Another prominent critic, G. A. Arbatov, opposed America's aggrandizement in its self-appointed role as a world policeman—a short-sighted policy of previous administrations that reacted to events, rather than anticipating the future and thereby being able to modify what would be encountered downstream. Arbatov spoke of the imperative need to reduce U.S. commitments abroad.[12] He noted the irony of an American foreign policy dependent less on the objective challenges abroad than on the outcome of political infighting in the United States.[13]

In the period from 1969 to 1974, the direction of American foreign policy was monopolized by two men, Richard Nixon and Henry Kissinger. Though Nixon was weakened by Watergate after 1972, he retained a veto over every major initiative in the field of foreign affairs until his departure from office in August 1974. Cooperation between the two luminaries was therefore essential to American foreign policy during the five-and-a-half crucial years. As a former Kissinger assistant put it, "The relationship between the two men is complex, contradictory, and momentous. In its impact on world politics and American government, their collaboration may be the most important event of the century."[14] Both men wanted to reassess and energize American foreign policy in the early days of the new Republican administration. A common observation was that the Washington scene had neglected Europe and the Middle East. Other pundits lamented Washington's failure to get a handle on the foreign-policy opportunities related to the escalating conflict between the Soviet Union and China in 1969. Additionally, the complex arms-control negotiations needed attention. Yet attention to these issues could not be allowed to distract the administration from the need to revitalize relations with Japan, and from the most pressing challenge of all—the ruinous war in Indochina.

Conceptually, the Nixon-Kissinger foreign policy rested on three basic principles: global détente with the Soviet Union and China; a new structure of peace that extended cooperation to all major powers; and the Nixon Doctrine as a selective "guideline" at the regional level. Kissinger viewed détente as involving peaceful co-existence and the avoidance of nuclear war—but not at any price. The Washington administration insisted the United States would oppose efforts by the Soviet Union to use détente for the purpose of achieving global predominance; it also affirmed America would not buy détente at the cost of good relations with its major allies in Europe and elsewhere. The United

States, furthermore, would refuse to accept attempts by either the Soviet Union or China to exploit détente during crisis situations.[15] As long as these conditions were satisfied, Kissinger was willing to push détente to achieve a relaxation of tensions at the global and regional levels. Kissinger saw this as an essential strategy for managing the new triangular power relationship between the United States, the Soviet Union, and China. Indeed, the introduction of China to the new international setting (after 1969) was the most significant difference between the cold-war era and the détente years.[16] To Nixon and Kissinger, the American-Chinese rapprochement was crucial for building a stable international order. In their opinion, a revolutionary power like China (with its growing military capability) would be a destabilizing influence in the world arena if it were left outside the family of nations; therefore, the logic of the situation called for the normalization of American-Chinese relations on the assumption that China itself would develop (in time) a stake in preserving peace both globally and regionally. Equally important, Nixon and Kissinger considered this rapprochement as added leverage in their dealings with the Soviets. Nor was that all; they hoped the Chinese (as well as the Soviets) would help them in negotiating an early settlement of the war in Vietnam.[17]

Détente, however, was not an end in itself in the Nixon-Kissinger conceptual framework. It constituted the bedrock of a larger orientation that President Nixon liked to call "a structure of peace."[18] This structure was intended to be neither a balance-of-power system (in the classical sense) nor a community of nations operating through collective security.[19] Instead, the Nixonian structure entailed a model of great power interaction that was inspired by the European concert of the post-Napoleonic era.[20] The Nixon-Kissinger concert stressed a pentagonal power relationship in which the United States, the Soviet Union, China, Western Europe, and Japan would be the major actors.[21] Even though Nixon and Kissinger recognized the discrepancy in the nature and the pattern of the power relationship among these countries—a relationship in which the United States and the Soviet Union still retained military bipolarity—the emphasis was on the equilibrium of national interests rather than on the predominance of one actor or of a combination of actors.[22] The emphasis was to be on political and economic issues rather than on the military aspect of that equilibrium. At times, the equilibrium might exert the image of a superpower condominium in the form of spheres of influence. In practice, such a condominium was vigorously resisted by Western Europe, Japan, China, and, most importantly, the Third World (including the Middle East), where most of the competition between the United States and the Soviet Union had taken place in the 1950s and 1960s. The Middle East, in particular, was a good example of neither superpower being able to establish a dominant sphere of influence.[23] Yet Kissinger believed a limited détente between the United States and the Soviet Union was possible in the Middle East.

Next, Nixon and Kissinger hoped to utilize the theory of "linkage" in sustaining détente at the global level, especially with the Soviet Union.[24] This theory stressed the interrelationships of the issues arising between the United States and the Soviet Union (and, to a limited degree, China as well). Thus, Middle East negotiations between the two superpowers would invariably affect the negotiations on other outstanding issues, e.g., Vietnam and the Strategic Arms Limitation Talks (SALT).[25] They regarded economic interdependence as a supplement to their political strategy by exploiting the Soviet Union's desire for Western trade and technology.[26] By adroit use of linkages, the Nixon administration hoped to entangle the Soviet Union in a web of interlocking relationships, making it harder for Moscow to pursue anti-U.S. interests anywhere, in view of the costs linked to other Soviet objectives. In short, Nixon and Kissinger sought to use the American advantages in economic power and technological superiority to further their political objectives vis-à-vis both the Soviet Union and China.

Did the Soviets understand détente in these terms? For the Soviets, détente meant several things: It would permit easier access to Western trade and technology, yet they were not going to pay an excessive price for these objectives. The Soviets were against any outside interference in their internal affairs. Détente would slow down the arms race, which was a significant economic burden for the Soviet Union; but the Soviets would not abandon their efforts to further communism by non-military means. Détente would relax tensions, especially in Europe; however, the Soviets would refuse any action threatening to undermine their dominant position in Eastern Europe. Finally, détente would allow the Soviets to concentrate more on China, especially in the light of the American-Chinese rapprochement in 1971 and 1972; it would help keep this rapprochement from going too far.

The Republican administration in Washington also pushed other related policy options in its "strategy for peace." First, President Nixon stressed the principle of strength vis-à-vis the adversaries of the United States. In truth, despite the notion of strategic nuclear parity, the Nixon administration continued the policy of Soviet containment while, at the same time, trying to preserve American supremacy in world politics.[27] Clearly, Washington sought to demonstrate to its allies in Europe and to Japan that its dealings with Moscow (and Peking) would emanate from a position of strength rather than from retrenchment—a policy of considerable importance in view of what was happening to America in Indochina.

Second, the Nixon administration was willing to negotiate with all nations, including adversaries. To Nixon and Kissinger, the overriding concern—avoiding a nuclear war—necessitated the downplay of the ideological rivalry between the United States and its Communist adversaries. In their view, the containment of the main adversaries (the Soviet Union and China) had to be pursued via the route of negotiations, rather than in the context of confrontation as characterized by the previous administration. [28]

Third, the Nixon administration sought partnerships with friendly nations through the Nixon Doctrine. Where détente was the central theme of the Nixon-Kissinger foreign policy at the global level, the Nixon Doctrine represented the cornerstone of that policy at the regional level. In explaining the Nixon Doctrine, the president said:

> Its central thesis is that the United States will participate in the defense and development of allies and friends, but that America cannot—and will not— conceive all plans, design all the programs, execute all the decisions and undertake all the defense of the free nations of the world. We will help where it makes a real difference and it is considered in our interests. [29]

The doctrine was based on two premises. First, it assumed American interventionism would be less essential in an era of détente. Rather than relying on overt military intervention, Nixon and Kissinger shifted the emphasis to covert operations (e.g., in Chile), arms transfers (e.g., Iran), and proxy actions (e.g., Israel during the Jordanian civil war) to preserve American regional predominance, especially in the Third World. [30] Second, the doctrine assumed regional challenges could be met by regional allies through the mobilization of their forces equipped with U.S.-supplied weapons. Accompanying these two assumptions was the expectation of reduced Soviet-instigated threats due to détente. [31]

The doctrine sought to come to grips with an era of changed balances of power and of polycentric communism. [32] By the application of the Nixon Doctrine, the United States would retain a central role in world affairs and a predominance regionally. At the same time, though other nations assumed greater responsibility for their own defense, the United States was the final judge in the selective process of mutual defense. Henceforth, the first emphasis would be on efforts to define American global interests. American commitments anywhere in the world were to be calculated on the basis of previously and comprehensively defined national interests, with specific commitments having to be measured more rationally against cost and risk factors. [33]

Did the Nixon Doctrine signify neoisolationism? The administration did sometimes link the Nixon Doctrine to withdrawal of American military forces from Vietnam, but this primarily served as a public-relations move. Domestic opponents of the Vietnam War wanted to hear phrases like "American withdrawal" and "getting out of Vietnam." Yet, in reality, the doctrine should not be defined as a return to American isolationism. In fact, Nixon and Kissinger never accepted the "no-more-Vietmans" syndrome as pointing the Nixon Doctrine toward isolationism. [34] Neither did the limited attention Kissinger gave to the problems of the Third World point to a withdrawal from world politics. The Third World's political and economic dilemmas were deemphasized, yet Kissinger stressed the importance of the developing world in the international politics of the great powers. [35]

The Middle East was considered exceptional because of its proximity to the Soviet Union, oil resources, and the Arab-Israeli dispute. Interestingly enough, the Middle Eastern situation provided an easier operational arena for applying the Nixon Doctrine than did other Third World regions, precisely because there were key states in the Middle East, such as Iran and Israel, that American policy makers believed they could rely on in crises. The U.S.-Israeli cooperation during the Jordanian civil war (and later in Lebanon) was a case in point.

The Nixon administration's Middle East policy provided an excellent example of America's refusing to return to the isolationism of the 1930s. Kissinger had no delusions about the important role the United States ought to assume in the area. It was important for the United States to guide and influence world politics so as to serve American interests. Always, however, those interests should be pragmatically, rationally, and responsibly defined and measured against their costs. Kissinger was surprised by the October War because Egypt's action hardly fit the pragmatic rationalism of his own conceptualization of politics. The war forced American involvement beyond the original intentions of the Nixon Doctrine. [36]

The linkage between the global level (détente) and the regional level (the Nixon Doctrine) in the Nixon-Kissinger grand design required U.S.-Soviet cooperation in regional crises. [37] In the Middle East this meant, first, enhancing the already existing limited détente between the two countries in the area. At the same time, under the umbrella of the Nixon Doctrine, Nixon and Kissinger aimed at preserving American predominance there while trimming American commitments and denying the Soviet Union any gains.

American Middle East policy, under the initiative of Kissinger, sought to build the image of Middle East cooperation with the Soviet Union in the wider context of détente. In reality, Kissinger's strategy was essentially a superpower strategy designed to provide a global background within which the administration could pursue resolutions of local conflicts there. An analysis of the Middle East conflict that neglected the Soviet interest and the Soviet capacity to help or to hinder a resolution of the local conflict would be inadequate, in turn, for understanding American policy.

The Nixon-Kissinger strategy had a number of ingredients. First, from 1969 until the October War of 1973, the two leaders supported a Middle Eastern policy based, in many ways, on the same perceptions that characterized former American administrations. The chief difference was the greater concern about the Soviets' presence in the region. Also, the administration set its Middle East policy on the conceptual foundations of the Nixon Doctrine in dealing with regional issues. This meant supporting key states in the area, such as Israel, Iran, and Jordan, to protect stability from internal and external threats.

Second, the two-power and the four-power talks, the Rogers Plan, and, to a lesser degree, the Jarring mission were intended (by the State Department) to provide a framework that could guide the parties in the Middle East toward a peaceful settlement. These efforts, however, were not directed at the crux of the Arab-Israeli conflict— the Palestinian issue. Nevertheless, Nixon and Kissinger recognized the need for any comprehensive settlement to include the interests of the Palestinians.

Third, Kissinger's shuttle diplomacy (the step-by-step efforts) after the 1973 October War resulted in the realization that the post-1973 war situation was conducive only to an interim disengagement. Kissinger was determined to make the disengagement function as a first step toward a final settlement.

Fourth, unlike the Kennedy-Rostow Third World policy of promoting economic development as the answer to the political problems of the developing world in general and of the Middle East in particular, the Nixon administration used economic aid, trade, and technology in its strategy for realizing political objectives.

Finally, the Nixon-Kissinger Middle Eastern policy was designed to save détente, which was almost shattered by the 1970 civil war in Jordan and the Arab-Israeli war of 1973. As a regional policy, it was aimed at resolving the Arab-Israeli conflict after the October War, provided the local parties and the Soviets were ready for a settlement. In short, Kissinger realized it would be necessary to include the Soviet Union in any comprehensive and lasting settlement of the Arab-Israeli dispute.

NOTES

1. William Fulbright, The Crippled Giant: American Foreign Policy and Its Domestic Consequences (New York: Random House, 1972), p. 4.

2. Norman A. Graebner, "Henry Kissinger and American Foreign Policy: A Contemporary Appraisal," The Australian Journal of Politics and History 22 (April 1976): 21.

3. George Liska, Beyond Kissinger: Ways of Conservative Statecraft (Baltimore: Johns Hopkins University Press, 1975), p. 25.

4. Anthony Hartley, American Foreign Policy in the Nixon Era, Adelphi Papers, No. 110 (Winter 1974/75), p. 9.

5. Henry Kissinger, "Bureaucracy and Policy Making: The Effect of Insiders and Outsiders on the Policy Process," in Bureaucracy, Politics, and Strategy, ed. Henry Kissinger and Bernard Brodie (Los Angeles: University of California, 1968), pp. 3-6 (Security Studies Paper Number 17); also see Wilfred Kohl, "The Nixon-Kissinger Foreign Policy System and U.S.-European Relations: Patterns of Policy Making," World Politics 27 (October 1975): 7.

6. I. M. Destler, Presidents, Bureaucrats and Foreign Policy: the Politics of Organizational Reform (Princeton: Princeton University Press, 1972), p. 118.

7. Ibid., pp. 118-32.

8. For an expanded discussion of this problem of intellectual failure, see the statement by Stanley Hoffman in No More Vietnams: The War and the Future of American Foreign Policy, ed. Richard M. Pfeffer, (New York: Harper and Row, 1968), pp. 115-37.

9. George F. Kennan, "After the Cold War: American Foreign Policy in the 1970s," Foreign Affairs 51 (October 1972): 226-27.

10. Zbigniew Brzezinski, "U.S. Foreign Policy: The Search for Focus," Foreign Affairs 51 (July 1973): 714.

11. Ibid., p. 723.

12. G. A. Arbatov, "American Foreign Policy on the Threshold of the 1970s," Orbis 15 (Spring 1971): 135-53.

13. Ibid., p. 153.

14. Roger Morris, Uncertain Greatness: Henry Kissinger and American Foreign Policy (New York: Harper and Row, 1977), p. 3.

15. Henry Kissinger, "The Nature of the National Dialogue on Foreign Policy," in The Nixon-Kissinger Foreign Policy: Opportunities and Contradictions, ed. Fred Warner Neal and Mary Kersey Harvey (Santa Barbara: Center for the Study of Democratic Institutions, 1974), p. 11.

16. Coral Bell, The Diplomacy of Détente: the Kissinger Era (New York: St. Martin's Press, 1977), pp. 1-6.

17. Dan E. Caldwell, "American-Soviet Détente and the Nixon-Kissinger Grand Strategy and Grand Design" (Ph.D. diss., Stanford University, 1978), pp. 174-75.

18. Stephen A. Garrett, "Nixonian Foreign Policy: A New Balance of Power or a Revised Concert," Polity VII (Spring 1976): 412.

19. Ibid.

20. Ibid., pp. 393-94.

21. James Chace, "The Five-Power World of Richard Nixon," New York Times Magazine, February 20, 1973, pp. 42-43.

22. Ibid., p. 43.

23. James Chace, A World Elsewhere: The New American Foreign Policy (New York: Charles Scribner's Sons, 1973), p. 43.

24. Ibid., p. 42.

25. Ibid.

26. Franklyn D. Holzman and Robert Legvold, "The Economics and Politics of East-West Relations," in World Politics and International Economics, ed. C. Fred Bergsten and Lawrence B. Krause (Washington, D.C.: Brookings Institution, 1975), pp. 293-94.

27. Stanley Hoffman, Primacy or World Order: American Foreign Policy since the Cold War (New York: McGraw-Hill Book Co., 1978), p. 43.

28. Ibid.

29. Richard Nixon, U.S. Foreign Policy for the 1970s: A New Strategy for Peace, A Report to the Congress by Richard Nixon, President of the United States, February 18, 1970 (Washington, D.C.: Government Printing Office, 1970), p. 6.

30. Hoffman, Primacy or World Order: American Foreign Policy since the Cold War, p. 43.

31. Michael J. Brenner, "The Problem of Innovation and the Nixon-Kissinger Foreign Policy," International Studies Quarterly 17 (September 1973): 264.

32. U.S. President, U.S. Foreign Policy for the 1970s: Building for Peace, A Report to the Congress by Richard Nixon, President of the United States, February 25, 1971 (Washington, D.C.: Government Printing Office, 1971), p. 11. ✱

33. Nixon, U.S. Foreign Policy for the 1970s: A Strategy for Peace, p. 7.

34. Brenner, "The Problem of Innovation and the Nixon-Kissinger Foreign Policy," p. 282.

35. Brenner, "The Problem of Innovation and the Nixon-Kissinger Foreign Policy," p. 285.

36. Hartley, American Foreign Policy in the Nixon Era, p. 32.

37. Liska, Beyond Kissinger: Ways of Conservative Statecraft, p. 53.

2

U.S. MIDDLE EAST POLICY FROM 1948 TO 1969: AN OVERVIEW

The Arab-Israeli conflict has been a central problem of American Middle Eastern policy since the establishment of Israel in 1948. Other important aspects of American Middle East policy include the problem of securing oil for the Western world and, of course, the East-West rivalry in the cold war, with its sensitivity to territorial expansion in power vacuums—particularly in the Middle East, the strategic crossroads of the three continents.

From the outset, American Middle Eastern policy was marked by competing objectives, contradictions, and ambiguities. The U.S. objective of preventing Soviet advancements was undermined in the Middle East by the extension of the cold war to the region. Rather than decreasing Soviet influence, the cold war facilitated the increase of Soviet power in the Arab world. The need for securing oil for the Western world was complicated by American support for Israel. This support created problems in American relations with the Arab states and later created problems between the United States and its own allies.

THE TRUMAN ADMINISTRATION

The Truman administration supported the UN plan of 1947 for the partitioning of Palestine between the Arabs and the Jews. Also, it supported the establishment of the state of Israel in 1948 and its admission to the United Nations the following year. Nevertheless, some American policy makers did oppose the idea of supporting the establishment of a Jewish state in Palestine. Various State Department projections cautioned against the adverse impact a Jewish state in Palestine might have on the future of the Middle East. Secretary of State Dean Acheson thought the establishment of Israel would not only hurt American interests in the Middle East; it would also undermine the interests of the whole Western world.[1] George Kennan, then head

of the Policy Planning Council at the State Department, presented to
Secretary of State Marshall, in February 1948, two strategic papers
regarding American global policy; the second paper bluntly stated that
the creation of Israel would increase Soviet and Communist influence
in the Middle East.[2] He urged American policy makers to negotiate
with the Soviet leadership for a reduction of tension not only in Europe,
but also in the Middle East.[3] Other officials in the national security
bureaucracy (the State and Defense Departments and the Joint Chiefs
of Staff) were also opposed to the idea of active American support for
Israel. Again, they feared it would threaten Western oil supplies.

In summary, there were strong voices in the American foreign-
policy organization that pointed to the dangers of creating a Jewish
state in Palestine. The strong Arab opposition to Israel would create
grave problems for future Western objectives in the Middle East.

Once the United States had committed itself to the creation of
Israel, the course for additional commitments tended to be set. Washington joined Paris and London in the Tripartite Declaration of May
25, 1950. This declaration sought to maintain Israel's existence by
maintaining a balance of power and preserving the status quo defined
in terms of the existing de facto national boundaries. It sought to
stabilize the arms race between the Arab states and Israel. By maintaining political stability in the region, the Western powers excluded
the Soviet Union from the area.

As the cold war gathered momentum—particularly after the
North Korean strike across the thirty-eighth parallel—the Western
powers developed a sense of urgency to build a containment structure
in the Middle East. The West overplayed its hand and the effort became counterproductive. The pressure gave rise to Arab anti-Western
hostility resulting in a move by Middle East states "to invite into the
area the very Soviet presence the West sought so vigorously to exclude."[4] The initial source of this hostility, however, was the United
States' role in the creation and maintenance of Israel.

The Arab states were not happy with the Tripartite Declaration.
Britain, France, and the United States never consulted the Arab states
or Israel before announcing the policy. Egypt soon rejected the declaration as a Western attempt to perpetuate the British military bases
in that country. Israel accepted the statement with some reservations.
Nevertheless, the declaration represented a dilemma for Israel. On
the one hand, acceptance might anger the Soviets, who had supported
the establishment of Israel; on the other hand, acceptance also represented security—a border guarantee by the maintaining of the balance
of power in the area. While Israel finally declared its support for the
policy, it emphasized its right, as a sovereign state, to acquire
weapons from any available alternative source if it chose to do
so.

THE EISENHOWER ADMINISTRATION

From 1951 until 1958, American policy was dominated by two ideas: to resolve the Arab-Israeli conflict and to defend the area against possible Soviet encroachments.[5] American policy makers tried to contain, and, at times, even attempted to resolve, the Arab-Israeli dispute through aid to the countries in the area. Regional cooperation was encouraged, for example, by the Eric Johnston plan for the equitable sharing of the Jordan Valley's water. The failure of these efforts to promote regional cooperation was probably inevitable without prior reconciliation of the Arab-Israeli confrontation; regional cooperation in the absence of peace was totally unrealistic. Yet peace was elusive. The Arab-Israeli antagonisms involved irreconcilable issues such as the right of Israel's very existence in the Middle East. No pragmatic approach to regional stability and development could be successful in the long run because of intractable positions on such vital interests. Thus, American economic aid and the use of the Eisenhower administration's good offices could not overcome the deep antagonisms, and resulted in failure.

The second idea dominating American Middle Eastern policy was the defense of the region through military alliances. In 1951 the United States proposed the Middle East Defense Organization (MEDO). The MEDO plan was unsuccessful because countries in the area, including especially Egypt and Israel, resisted it. Nevertheless, the proposed alliance indicated the underlying desire of American policy makers and planners to pursue some sort of alliance system. In essence, the MEDO plan represented a tendency by American policy makers to extend a successful model (e.g., NATO, 1949) to an area characterized by entirely different political realities.[6] The Truman administration had initially contacted Egypt inasmuch as that country was considered the key to success. Nationalism was already a volatile political issue in Egypt, and it was important to defer to Cairo's sensitivities by approaching Egypt first in the attempt to organize a Middle East alliance to contain the USSR. Egypt, with its large population, its educated, sophisticated elite, and its strategic location astride the Suez Canal, was the key link. But Egypt had become antagonistic toward Britain over the latter's continued presence in the sprawling military base on the banks of the Suez Canal. Egypt had failed in its unilateral de-colonization efforts via the Sidqi-Bevin Treaty of 1946 and at the UN Security Council in the summer of 1947. Egypt considered Western containment of the Soviet Union in the Middle East as decidedly secondary in priority to its complete independence from Western colonialism. Egypt insisted the Arab League was the appropriate organization for Middle East regional defense.

In 1953 Secretary of State Dulles decided on a renewed effort to bring Egypt into a Soviet-containment alliance.[7] The United States, Dulles told Gamal Abdel Nasser, would help Egypt obtain arms and would assist it diplomatically in negotiations with Britain. Nasser agreed with Dulles regarding the need to contain communism, but he argued that the threat was internal rather than external.[8] Dulles's mission was doomed from the outset. In short, the Arabs felt the primary danger to the Middle East was from Israel and its Western supporters, and not from the Soviet Union.

The reluctance of Egypt and other Arab states to join Western-sponsored Soviet-containment alliances did not, however, divert American policy makers from pursuing regional alliances against the Soviet Union. A revealing National Security Council study of October 30, 1953, emphasized the Communist threat to the United States. The study, "Basic National Security Policy," prescribed the acquisition of a network of overseas bases in countries adjacent to the Soviet Union. American strategic air power should then be integrated with these bases to create new options, and thereby enhance U.S. strategic capabilities.[9] Regional alliances would supplement the expanded primary focus on the air force. In reference to the Middle East, the National Security Council document (which President Eisenhower approved as representing official policy) stated:

> In the Middle East, a strong regional grouping is not
> feasible. In order to assure during peacetime for the
> United States and its allies the resources (especially
> oil) and the strategic position of the area and their
> denial to the Soviet bloc, the United States should build
> on Turkey, Pakistan and if possible, Iran, and assist in
> achieving stability in the Middle East by political actions
> and limited military and economic assistance, and tech-
> nical assistance, to other countries in the area.[10]

After the failure of the MEDO plan, American policy makers continued their efforts to organize the region in terms of Eisenhower's New Look policy as it applied to the strategy of containment. The renewed alliance-building attempt involved a northern-tier emphasis. It was initially to include the Middle East states near the southern borders of the Soviet Union; once the alliance was created, other Arab states would be encouraged to join. The proposal was noteworthy in that it bypassed Nasser's Egypt. This new Middle East pact came into existence in 1955, with the four northern-tier states of Turkey, Iraq, Iran, and Pakistan plus the Western state of Britain as members. Nevertheless, the Baghdad Pact (as the alliance was called) proved disappointing to American planners since only one Arab state, Iraq, joined.

The Baghdad Pact was generally not welcomed by either the Arab states or Israel. The pact also generated extreme Soviet opposition. From an Arab perspective, the alliance led to inter-Arab conflicts; it polarized the Arab states around the contending positions of Egypt and Iraq. Egypt's opposition to the pact boosted Nasser's prestige as the leader of Arab nationalism and the defender of the area against Western designs.[11] On March 31, 1955, Nasser gave a major foreign-policy speech in which he denounced the Baghdad Pact as an attempt to undermine Arab independence and freedom;[12] defense of the Middle East, he stressed, should emanate from the Arab countries, and not from foreign countries. The proposed Western-initiated alliance would tend toward foreign domination, including Communist domination.[13] Nasser's speech was aimed not only at Dulles, but also at the Soviet leadership; it emphasized the desire of Egypt (and of the Arabs in general) to stay neutral in the East-West conflict.

Israel was also unhappy to have an antagonistic Arab state, Iraq, receiving Western arms that might well be used against her. For the Jewish state, the most immediate threat came from the Arabs, not the Soviet Union. American and British reassurances were not convincing: Israel did not accept the idea that Arabs would be less dangerous within a Western alliance rather than outside it.[14] Subsequently, Israel tried to join NATO, but without success. It then initiated efforts to conclude a bilateral defense treaty with the United States; but the United States was not ready for such a move, which would inevitably damage its influence in the Arab world.[15]

The Soviet Union interpreted the Western attempts to organize a Middle East containment alliance as a serious liability to its national interests. Moscow condemned the U.S.-initiated cold-war move creating a coalition of Muslim states on its immediate southern border—with Soviet Muslim minorities residing on the common boundary. The Soviets opposed adding a Middle East enemy alliance to the already adverse situation of NATO and SEATO (the 1954 South-East Asia Treaty Organization). Moscow's Ministry of Foreign Affairs reiterated its position in an April 16, 1955, statement:

> It goes without saying that the Soviet Union cannot be indifferent to the situation taking shape in the Near and Middle East, since the formation of blocs and the creation of military bases in Near and Middle East countries have a direct bearing on the security of the U.S.S.R. The Soviet government's position should be all the more understandable because the U.S.S.R. is situated in close proximity to these countries, which cannot be said of other foreign powers, such as the U.S.A., which is thousands of kilometers away from this area.

> Nonparticipation by Near and Middle Eastern coun-
> tries in aggressive military blocs would be an important
> prerequisite for ensuring their security and the best
> guarantee against their involvement in dangerous military
> ventures.[16]

Gradually the Soviet and Arab opposition to Western proposals for defense alliances in the Middle East led to a Soviet-Arab rapprochement culminating in the September 1955 arms deal between the Soviet Union and Egypt. Soviet arms shipped to Egypt were intended mainly for Egyptian defensive purposes, i.e., to deter any Israeli threat against Egypt and the other front-line Arab states. By this bold stroke of foreign policy, Moscow seized a brilliant opportunity to expand its influence in the Middle East. Now it would also be easier for the Soviets to expand their interests across the broad range of the Third World. Washington saw this as a major effort by Soviet leaders to make expansion into the Third World a top priority of foreign policy.

The Soviet-Arab rapprochement was not due to Soviet initiatives alone, but to Arab efforts as well. Rising Arab nationalism, with its anti-Western antagonism, helped produce this new affinity with the East. Israel's political situation, both domestic and international, favored the West. Israel could not maneuver its foreign policy to head off the pro-Arab movement of Soviet policy because it could not negate itself—the country's very political culture would not allow the breaking of vital ties with the West in the ideological struggle. Moreover, the Arab nationalist movement was gaining strength and turning more anti-Western as it grew. With Israel inevitably locked into a pro-Western position, the Soviet-Arab rapprochement created an entirely new situation for the United States. Henceforth, American policy makers viewed the Soviet presence in the Middle East as a dominant factor in shaping American policy toward the region. U.S. preoccupation with Soviet Middle East expansion could become a serious liability because it distracted Washington's attention from the region's local political needs.

The cold war, now introduced into the Middle East, further destabilized the political systems of the area. Ironically, the American global policy of building containment alliances actually weakened American influence in the Middle East. The Baghdad Pact created more problems for American foreign policy, rather than solving them.[17]

With Soviet influence increasing in the region, the Eisenhower administration decided to play a greater role in the Arab-Israeli conflict. In early 1956, President Eisenhower sent his personal envoy, Robert Anderson, to Cairo with a message emphasizing the urgency of resolving the Arab-Israeli conflict.[18] Anderson soon realized the impossible nature of his mission. President Nasser's irreducible position demanded a reduction in Israeli territory, at least to the original boundaries of the UN partition plan.[19] The United States was in no position to push Israel into that kind of retrenchment. Consequently, the Anderson mission failed.[20]

On May 16, 1956, Egypt recognized Communist China—a step which aroused animosity in the United States and contributed, later, to the American decision to cancel its offer to build the Aswan Dam. Initially, the Soviets had been apprehensive about a possible rapprochement stemming from the American-Egyptian negotiations for U.S. funding of the dam, but the deliberately abrupt American cancellation provided the Soviets with an excellent opportunity to escalate their penetration into the Middle East by substituting Soviet funds for the original American offer.

Egypt's nationalization of the Suez Canal in July of 1956 was a retaliation against the West for its refusal to help fund the Aswan Dam. The bold Egyptian initiative created a crisis that culminated in the combined Israeli-British-French attack on Egypt in late 1956. In the United Nations, an overwhelming majority of states, including the United States and the Soviet Union, condemned the military strike. The international community's action in the United Nations, together with the failure of Britain and France to seize the canal quickly and completely, transformed Egypt's military defeat into Nasser's political victory. At the same time, the Suez affair gave the Soviet Union an excellent pretext to appear as the champion of the Arab cause. From a Western perspective, the Suez war was a costly political setback that threatened to split the NATO alliance. The United States justified its action against its allies, Britain and France, on the grounds that its commitments in the NATO alliance were mainly directed at Soviet actions in Europe and did not extend to other regions. Furthermore, the United States would not tolerate unilateral adventurism that could lead to a confrontation with the Soviet Union.

These events convinced American policy makers of the need for more direct American involvement in Middle East affairs. Such involvement would not only help curb Soviet influence and contain the Arab-Israeli conflict; it would, above all, help to protect and preserve American interests in the area after the collapse of the French and British influence. Accordingly, in January 1957, the United States announced the Eisenhower Doctrine—a unilateral presidential policy statement regarding the security of the Middle East. The Eisenhower Doctrine not only intended to deter possible Soviet domination of the area and to protect the region against what was termed "international communism"; it also attempted to slow the tempo of President Nasser's ambitions in the Arab world by bolstering local pro-Western governments. Indeed, the Eisenhower administration believed the economic and strategic interests of the Western world were at stake in Nasser's threatened expansion in the Middle East. Economically, the United

States felt the interests of Western Europe coincided with its own; any threat to West European interests (e.g., oil) would mean a threat to the United States and the entire NATO alliance. Strategically, the United States considered the collapse of French and British prestige after October 1956 as creating a dangerous power vacuum that would inevitably be an invitation for Soviet expansion unless the United States acted to stop it. [21]

The Eisenhower Doctrine could be viewed as a logical extension of American alliance policy. As Secretary of State Dulles asserted, "In the Middle East, the Baghdad Pact and the Eisenhower Doctrine assume collective response to Communist aggression at points of special danger or weakness."[22] Thus, Soviet threats and Communist threats in general would be resisted by regional as well as global policies. A critical assessment of the Eisenhower Doctrine would have to conclude that it was only a limited success in realizing its original objectives. Lebanon was the only Arab country to ever invoke the doctrine, when, in 1958, it asked the United States for troops to help the government maintain law and order—especially against the threat of Syrian infiltrators serving as the vanguard of Pan-Arab imperialism and emanating from the recently created United Arab Republic.

There were a number of reasons for the Eisenhower Doctrine's inadequacies. First, the doctrine failed to reflect the political realities of the situation since it overlooked the regional sources of the Middle East crisis. In essence, the United States tried to extend its global containment strategy, vis-à-vis the Soviet Union, to the Middle East, an unstable area in which strategic deterrence was largely irrelevant to the regional equation.[23] Also, it attempted to substitute a global containment strategy for a coherent policy appropriate to the political sensitivities of those states the doctrine intended to protect. The doctrine was a purely military solution for a political situation.

Second, with the exception of Lebanon, the Arab states did not support the Eisenhower Doctrine. The U.S. policy failed to prevent the Soviet Union from extending economic and military aid to Arab states. To the Arabs, the traditional enemy was Western imperialism, not communism or even the Soviet Union.[24] The Soviets, in turn, viewed the doctrine as an integral part of American cold-war strategy. Furthermore, Third World states such as India and Yugoslavia opposed the policy; it was irrelevant to their political experience.[25]

Third, even Western European countries responded to the doctrine with apprehension. They viewed it as a unilateral attempt by the United States to replace their interests in the region with American domination;[26] the United States had failed to consult its European allies before proclaiming the expanded American role in the area. Europe was unhappy about the independent course and the enhanced role the United States assumed in the Middle East, [27] even though the doctrine resisted Soviet expansion in the region. Indeed, on the whole, Europeans felt America had cashed in on their misfortune by taking the occasion to replace their long history of hegemony with its own. Britain and France felt they still might have maneuvered a comeback in the area after the Suez debacle faded. [28] They also doubted America's ability to handle the complex political problems of the Middle East, especially in the light of increased Soviet power in the post-Suez era.

Washington considered the post-1956 war situation similar to the 1947 Greek and Turkish experience, under the Truman Doctrine, when U.S. power had replaced the fading British influence due to the latter's severe economic plight. This 1947 policy, in deterring the Soviet Union in the Balkans, served as a model for the Eisenhower Doctrine seeking to deter the Soviet Union in the Middle East. On balance, then, the Eisenhower Doctrine was part of a global policy geared to stabilizing the Middle East, Africa, and Southeast Asia— areas perceived to be either weak, or vulnerable to Soviet domination, or a threat to regional stability. Critics of the policy noted the liability of extending superpower rivalry to the Middle East. It involved the United States in inter-Arab politics by supporting the pro-Western regimes against their local rivals; it polarized the Arab-Israeli conflict by considering the Middle East as an adjunct to American global containment policy.

But if the Eisenhower Doctrine weakened the overall American position in the area, the Soviets hardly fared better. The assumed advantage for the Soviet Union also failed to materialize. Soviet economic and military aid to several Arab countries failed to produce the glittering advantages the Soviet leaders had hoped for. Moscow was confronted with choices between competing objectives and multiple interests; almost every policy decision suffered from the trade-off syndrome. [29] For instance, in their quest to improve relations with the Arab world, the Soviets found it easier and quicker to concentrate efforts in the radical Arab states, instead of curbing American influence with the conservative Arab regimes. [30] Moreover, though the Soviets tried to maintain good relations with all the radical Arab states, this was done at the expense of the local Communist parties within these states; note the hard choices the Soviets had to make concerning pro-Soviet Communist party members who were citizens, respectively, of Egypt, Iraq, and Syria. Soviet Russia's national interests usually won out over Soviet ideological interests supporting local Communist parties in foreign states. This tarnished the Soviet Union's image as leader of the world Communist movement.

THE KENNEDY ADMINISTRATION

The Kennedy administration, which took power in 1961, represented a fresh outlook in American global and regional policies. President Kennedy's Middle East policy emphasized aid to promote economic and political development. The greatest Western opportunity to promote peace and stability lay in economic and technical assistance; at the same time, Third World states should be encouraged to reduce military expenditures—resources should be transferred from the military to social programs and economic development. President Kennedy urged Egypt to withdraw from military involvement in the Yemen civil war and concentrate on its economic development.[31] Nasser objected. He informed Kennedy that Egyptian withdrawal from Yemen would not be feasible as long as Saudi Arabia, an American client, supported the royalist forces in the civil conflict.[32] Nevertheless, Nasser continued to receive massive economic aid from the United States. Washington assumed the aid would undermine Soviet and Communist appeal in the Arab world.[33]

President Kennedy's approach to Egypt produced disappointing results. Nasser questioned Kennedy's motives. He detected duplicity in American policy: On the one hand, Kennedy sent Ellsworth Bunker to Cairo for peace talks; at the same time, he sent American intelligence officers to handle the military situation on behalf of Egypt's enemies in the Yemen civil war.[34] Nasser also objected to Kennedy's decision to sell defensive Hawk missiles to Israel.[35] He insisted it would only escalate the arms race in the Middle East. Simultaneously, Kennedy pressured West Germany to sell arms to Israel. This further alienated Nasser.[36]

Kennedy also assumed an active role in the Arab-Israeli conflict, especially with regard to the Palestine refugees.[37] He revived efforts to solve the problem by working through the United Nations Conciliation Commission for Palestine (UNCCP). Joseph E. Johnson went to the Middle East as a special representative of the UNCCP. The United States contacted both sides, urging each to make concessions.[38] As it turned out, neither Israel nor the Arabs found Johnson's proposals acceptable. Israel insisted that the Palestinian refugees should be permanently settled in the Arab countries. The Arab states, on the other hand, were not ready to accept a partial solution. They insisted the issue could be dealt with only in the context of a comprehensive settlement of the Arab-Israeli dispute.[39] In brief, they were opposed to assimilating the Palestinian refugees in their own states. They wanted to keep the Palestinian issue alive. It was important to their interests to preserve the Palestinian identity. Equally important, the Palestinians themselves were against the idea of abandoning their own homeland. But as it turned out, the Arab states used the Palestinian problem to further their own political objectives.

In the spring of 1964, renewed Middle East efforts by the administration did produce some limited diplomatic achievements. After Lyndon Johnson assumed the presidency upon the death of Kennedy (November 22, 1963), Washington renewed its determination to see what could be done about the conflict in Yemen. On April 13, 1964, Egypt and Saudi Arabia reached an agreement to restrain their military objectives in the Yemeni conflict. This accord would have been highly unlikely without the good offices of, and even the diplomatic pressure from, the United States.[40] The American-sponsored interim agreement, however, was primarily designed to protect the Saudi regime. The withdrawal of military forces from Yemen was a secondary objective.[41]

Washington helped stabilize the region and reduced the tempo of Soviet expansion. American policy did not, however, prevent the Soviet Union from extending military aid to the radical Arab regimes, especially Egypt. Despite the limited success of the Kennedy term in Middle East peace efforts, some important changes were occurring in American foreign policy. The United States found it imperative to redefine its Middle East interests. Avoiding a direct confrontation with the Soviet Union that could lead to a nuclear war became the dominant concern. There was thus an urgent need to keep the Arab-Israeli conflict from escalating into a conflict between the superpowers. Kennedy's death put a damper on the natural evolution of these changes.

In summary, President Kennedy initially made Arab leaders optimistic about expecting forward movement in the seemingly intractable Arab-Israeli confrontation. The high Arab expectations received from the vigorous new president, however, soured quickly and ended with Lyndon Johnson finishing the presidential term with less-than-expected results—at least so it seemed to the Arabs.

THE JOHNSON ADMINISTRATION

The Johnson administration, after mid-1964, was primarily concerned with domestic issues and, of course, the escalation of the Vietnam War. In the light of these developments, American policy makers reduced the priority of Middle East problems. President Johnson was reluctant to open another dialogue with the Arabs in the midst of growing hostility toward the United States. In private he expressed concern about the explosive nature of the Arab-Israeli conflict. In a letter to President Nasser about American policy, Johnson stressed the American determination to maintain the balance of power in the area and to restrain arms deliveries to the conflicting parties.[42] A State Department document attached to the letter further explained American objectives on arms supply:

> It is important to understand that impartiality and re-
> straint remain the basis of the United States' arms
> policy. Any United States sales of weapons to Arab
> states or to Israel will be the minimum dictated by
> the circumstances.[43]

Nasser, on the other hand, was unhappy with Johnson's policy on supplying arms to Israel. Even though the United States was not Israel's main supplier of arms before the 1967 war, the Arab states were dissatisfied with American rationalizations on the issue. The United States was supplying limited amounts of arms to Jordan and Saudi Arabia in order to appear evenhanded. American arms to the Arab side, to "balance" the arms sent to Israel, went to conservative-moderate Arab governments. The radical Arab states felt the impact of discrimination.

The decline in American–Egyptian relations after 1964 reached a climax in May 1967, when Nasser mobilized his armed forces with (initial) Soviet encouragement and closed the Strait of Tiran. In addition, he ordered a partial withdrawal of the United Nations Emergency Force (UNEF) from Sinai. U Thant, the UN secretary general, responded by withdrawing the entire force. President Johnson considered Nasser's actions a challenge to American policy in the region and a threat to Israel's security. Nasser miscalculated the positions of both Israel and the United States. He believed Israel would not act without American support. Israel, in turn, considered Nasser's moves a direct threat to its survival. The Egyptian head of state recalled the 1956 war, and he optimistically assumed the United States would force Israel to withdraw if war occurred and the Egyptian military forces were defeated.[44]

In Washington, the Johnson administration worried about the deteriorating situation in the Middle East. The increased Soviet influence in the Mediterranean added to the president's concern. Six months earlier, President Johnson had asked former Ambassador Julius Holmes to direct a study of Soviet penetration into the region. Holmes's research revealed "a pattern of serious Soviet advances, sparked in large part by emotions generated in the Arab-Israeli confrontation and including the active expansion of Soviet power and missile capability."[45] On the basis of the study, he considered the Arab-Israeli conflict a manifestation of the larger global confrontation between the Soviet Union and the United States with its NATO allies.[46]

In early 1967 the Johnson administration encountered a crisis-management problem in the deteriorating Middle East situation. Johnson relied on an interdepartmental group from the national security bureaucracy to advise him on how to handle the crisis.[47] He was well aware of a possible Israeli preemptive strike against the front-line

Arab states; this, in turn, might escalate the local conflict into a larger confrontation between the two superpowers. He realized the impact Nasser's closing of the Strait of Tiran had on Israeli vital interests. With American forces tied down in Vietnam, the United States faced a precarious situation if the Soviets moved into the Middle East.

President Johnson cautioned Israel about relying on U.S. military forces should war occur and the battle turn against Israel. Any action by the United States needed congressional approval. The United States wanted to build multilateral support by taking the matter to the United Nations.[48] Johnson basically faced two options: either to let the situation take its natural course, which would most likely result in a war, or to act with other nations in order to challenge Nasser's closure of the Strait of Tiran.[49] Consequently, his strategy was simple: to restrain the Israelis while exploring the second option.

Despite the Johnson administration's diplomatic maneuverings, including use of UN channels, Israel felt neither the United States nor the United Nations would take action—unilaterally or multilaterally—to challenge Nasser's actions or, for that matter, come up with a diplomatic solution. On June 5, 1967, Israel moved militarily to resolve the crisis; in five days the Jewish forces shattered the armies of Egypt, Syria, and Jordan. The Arab armies proved incapable of stopping the well-organized and sharply honed Israeli forces; yet another dimension of the crisis must be noted—Arab weakness. The Arabs lacked a military-deterrence strategy due largely to inter-Arab conflicts, and to domestic political instability resulting from internal divisiveness and, in some cases, from very mediocre political leadership. Thus, the Arabs proved incapable of agreeing on long-term objectives and on a negotiating posture in relation to Israel.[50] In brief, Nasser's adventurism had not only resulted in a general defeat for the Arabs; it also contributed to the polarization of the Middle East between the two superpowers.

After the war, the Arab states convened a summit meeting at Khartoum, in August 1967, to discuss postwar strategy. They agreed on a common approach to Israel—no recognition, no negotiations, no peace agreement, and no abandonment of Palestinian rights.[51]

Generally speaking, the Johnson administration opposed unilateral Israeli military action to resolve the crisis. However, he was grateful to see Nasser's challenge being met by a regional power (Israel) without the need for American intervention—an intervention which would have undermined Washington's position in the entire region. Ironically, the 1967 war contributed to the drastic increase of Soviet influence in the area—the very thing the United States had been trying to prevent. Nevertheless, the administration felt expanded Soviet influence might be utilized to restrain the behavior of radical

Arab states. The 1967 war demonstrated the failure of global powers to control regional events; in a bipolar world, regional conflict posed serious escalation problems. Soviet leadership drew important lessons from the war: Military and economic aid could not readily be translated into political control over client states.[52] In spite of the Arab disaster, Moscow resumed arms transfers to the Middle East in an effort to maintain and enhance its political influence with the radical Arab regimes.

If the Soviets had badly misjudged the dynamics of the 1967 crisis in initially supporting Nasser's action, American perceptions of the crisis were even worse. American Middle East policy vacillated between two approaches to the containment of the Soviet Union in the region: the great-power approach and the commitment approach.[53] From 1948 until 1957, American policy makers emphasized the first; the Middle East conflict, as a local dispute, should not be allowed to escalate into a global conflict. In this view, containment of the Soviet Union could be achieved by depriving the Soviets of the opportunity to exploit the Arabs' hostility toward Israel. After 1957, the second approach dominated American strategy. It developed as a response to Soviet support for the Arabs against Israel and followed a policy that had proved successful in other parts of the world.[54] Viewed from this angle, containment of the Soviet Union could be achieved by raising the costs and risks of exploiting the Arab-Israeli conflict. Neither approach, however, was pursued to the point of excluding the other, and the vacillation between the two failed both to contain the Soviet Union and to produce a concrete American policy for crisis situations in the Middle East.

Next, many American policy makers, in the aftermath of the 1967 war, viewed the Middle East conflict as a "zero-sum" relationship between the United States and the Soviet Union. This view can be seen in a statement made by the under secretary of state for political affairs, Eugene Rostow:

> The protracted conflict between Israel and some of her
> Arab neighbors is not the cause of the Middle Eastern
> crisis but its symptom and its consequences. The heart
> of the crisis is the process of Soviet penetration in North
> Africa and the Near East. Without Soviet influence, Soviet
> support, and Soviet arms, there would have been peace
> long ago between Israel and her neighbors. The Arab
> states would have had no alternative but to accept Israel's
> right to exist.[55]

Rostow's assessment mirrored the "strategy-of-commitment" approach; he viewed the Middle East crisis primarily in terms of the East-West conflict rather than as a regional dispute. Rostow stated:

> The Middle Eastern crisis is a NATO crisis, not an Arab-
> Israeli quarrel. It is a fissure in the foundation of world
> politics—a Soviet challenge to the relationship of Western
> Europe and the United States, and therefore to the balance
> of power on which the possibility of general peace through-
> out the world depends.[56]

Even though Rostow viewed the problem in global terms, he recognized
both levels of the crisis: the global and regional.[57] American emphasis
on the global level, however, tended to overshadow complex political
realities at the regional level. In point of historical fact, the Arab-
Jewish conflict over Palestine had existed long before the Soviet Middle
East thrust of the mid-1950s. Rostow's views made an accurate assessment of the crisis difficult. But more importantly, the failure to grasp
the sharp Arab-Israeli hatred created a misperception of reality,
making an appropriate American policy even less likely.

At the Glassboro, New Jersey, summit meeting in June 1967,
President Johnson and Soviet Premier Kosygin were unable to reach
a common understanding on the urgent Middle East issues. The Soviets
disagreed with American proposals to limit arms shipments to the
area.[58] Arms shipments, argued the Soviets, should be limited after
a political settlement of the Arab-Israeli conflict. Soviet reasoning
was simple: Any arms limitations before reaching a comprehensive
settlement would only ensure continued Israeli military superiority,
placing severe pressure on both Soviet and Arab options in the region.

On June 19, 1967, President Johnson presented his Five Great
Principles of peace for the Middle East.[59] He recognized the right
of national life (peaceful co-existence) for both the Arab states and
Israel. He sought justice for both the Arab states and Israel. He
sought justice for the Palestinian refugees. He advocated innocent
maritime passage (freedom of navigation). He wanted limits on the
wasteful and destructive arms races. Finally, he called for the political independence and territorial integrity of all states in the area.
Johnson's policy was designed to satisfy the minimum demands of all
concerned parties. His five principles were eventually incorporated
into UN Security Council Resolution 242 of November 22, 1967.

UN Resolution 242 was a Soviet-American compromise revision
of a British proposal submitted to the Security Council. It became the
most important UN resolution on the Middle East since the UN Pales-
tine-partition resolution of 1947. The UN action called for the withdrawal of "Israeli armed forces from territories occupied in the recent
conflict"; it advocated the "termination of all states of belligerency"
and the "acknowledgement of sovereignty, territorial integrity and
political independence of every state in the area"; it affirmed "freedom
of navigation through the international waterways in the area"; it rec-

ognized the need for "a just settlement of the refugee problem"; and it affirmed the right of every state "to live in peace within secure and recognized boundaries free from threats or acts of force." The resolution also empowered the UN secretary general to designate a special representative to proceed to the Middle East in order to help local governments achieve a peaceful settlement.[60]

Resolution 242, however, had important limitations:[61] It did not call for an Israeli withdrawal from all the occupied territories; it did not oblige the Arabs to make full peace with Israel; and it did not specify what "secure" boundaries for Israel would be. These were deliberate omissions because the Security Council proved incapable of reaching agreements on the respective issues. Without resorting to ambiguity in the text, no resolution would have been possible. Indeed, a great deal of public commentary has dealt with the unfortunate omissions in the 1967 resolution. The Johnson (after 1967), Nixon, and Ford administrations expended a great deal of diplomatic effort haggling with the concerned parties over the exact meaning of the resolution's operative clauses. In fact, most of the criticism was misdirected. It should properly have lamented the failure of the Security Council to reach an agreement; the lack of precision was really deliberate ambiguity necessary to get any resolution on the Middle East war passed in the Security Council.

The UN resolution was intended to be a framework within which the parties would try to achieve a political solution. Israel interpreted Resolution 242 as a comprehensive package deal in which the withdrawal from occupied territories was only one part of the total settlement; the withdrawal, furthermore, did not mean a withdrawal to the pre-1967 boundaries. Israel also wanted direct negotiations with the Arabs to achieve permanent peace.[62] On the other hand, the Arabs interpreted Resolution 242 differently and were also divided over its meaning. Though Egypt and Jordan viewed the resolution as a package, they were not inclined to face the Israelis in direct negotiations.[63] The Palestinians increasingly opposed the resolution because it failed to mention their right to statehood. Especially galling was the reference to them, not as a nation, but only as a "refugee problem" needing a "just settlement." Syria and the Palestine Liberation Organization (PLO) announced their complete rejection of the resolution.[64]

In this situation, President Johnson was not anxious to pursue the active role in the Arab-Israeli conflict that Secretary of State Dulles had pursued in the Eisenhower administration after the 1956 Suez war. He believed a resolution of the conflict was properly the responsibility of the parties to the dispute. American efforts would only serve as an opportunity for each side to avoid necessary compromises. America would become the targeted scapegoat. Johnson and his advisors were against pressuring Israel to withdraw from the occupied territories without a final peace agreement. However, the president hoped Israel would exchange the occupied territories for a final settlement that provided for its security and its right to exist.[65] But this idea was not rigorously pushed by American policy makers. The Arabs, after the humiliation of the June 1967 war, found the American mediation position unacceptable. In Washington, urgency in dealing with the Middle East conflict tended to fade as the new demands of the Vietnam struggle competed for attention. Not surprisingly, the coordination of American policy in the aftermath of the 1967 war was largely left to two non-Middle East experts, McGeorge Bundy and Eugene Rostow.[66]

Johnson's policy toward the Middle East after the June war could be described as "quiet diplomacy"; the efforts were now channeled through the United Nations or linked to occasional contacts with the Soviet Union.[67] American Middle East policy presented an appearance of concern and activity. In reality, Middle East efforts were eased into a "holding pattern" providing time for the local parties to reassess their negotiating positions. Note Walt W. Rostow's description of American Middle East policy:

> It is not up to Moscow or Washington. It is up to the leaders of the Middle East. That means, of course, getting a settlement [with Israel], which they regard as honorable and dignified. And it means that Israel will emerge with a sense of confidence that it is living in an environment of peace and not an environment of belligerency.
>
> We have bought time for the natural forces of the Middle East to find their way to the judgment that the only realistic, decent option for them all is to make peace and get on with the job of development.[68]

On the whole, then, it was unrealistic to expect a movement in American Middle East policy in 1968; it was a presidential-election year; both presidential candidates announced their full and uncritical support for Israel and its negotiating position. But if the election-year politics made it inappropriate for the United States to appear as the honest broker between Israel and the Arab states, the front-line Arab states, nevertheless, knew that the United States alone, through its military and economic aid, had the power to pressure Israel into a more moderate position.

In January 1968, Israel asked the Johnson administration for F-4 Phantom jets; in December of that year, the American-Israeli arms deal was signed, providing for 50 F-4s.[69] After 1967, the United States became Israel's main supplier of arms because France

embargoed arms shipments to Israel after the Six-Day War. Originally
(after the 1967 war), the foreign-policy bureaucracy in Washington
was divided on an arms policy toward Israel. Some felt any major
supply of arms to Israel should be accompanied by Israeli concessions, such as the promise of a full withdrawal in return for a comprehensive peace agreement. [70] Other advisors wanted Israel, before
receiving arms, to sign the Nuclear Nonproliferation Treaty. Israel's
growing nuclear capability—since the Kennedy administration—was a
constant source of friction with Washington; however, in the light of
mounting domestic political pressure (especially from Congress),
Johnson ordered the bureaucracy to end its search for concessions
from Israel. [71]

In a broader perspective, the June war of 1967 marked a watershed not only in the relationship between the United States and Middle
Eastern countries, but also in that between the United States and its
European allies. The Western European countries gradually initiated
a more assertive role including an occasional independent course in
Middle East affairs. The French position was a marked example of
this independence. President de Gaulle preferred a four-power conference to deal with the Middle East crisis. [72] An effective concert
of big powers, de Gaulle pointed out, would be the only way the Middle East conflict could be settled. The French position seemed to
support the Soviet position (at least in the UN debates) on the Middle
East; in reality, the French proposal sought to provide an independent
European relationship with the Arab world and then, in turn, to use
that relationship as a counterweight against both Soviet and American
influence in the area. [73] The French supported UN Resolution 242,
which incorporated the views of both the United States and the Soviet
Union. To the Arabs, the new French position marked a change away
from the previous anti-Arab policy resulting from the Suez crisis and
the Algerian conflict; French policy was now seen as easing toward
neutrality. [74] To Israel, the French change from a policy of informal
alliance to one of neutrality   implied both a pro-Soviet and a pro-Arab
stand. [75]

In conclusion, the inability of the Johnson administration to deal
effectively with the Arab-Israeli conflict could be explained on several
grounds. First, the political environment in the region was not conducive to a negotiated settlement because of the humiliating Arab military defeat. The Arab states were not ready to negotiate from a position of weakness or to accept Israeli terms for a final settlement.
Second, the global dimension of the Arab-Israeli conflict, complicated
now by increased Soviet influence, had further polarized the positions
of the two superpowers. Third, the Vietnam War still received policy-
making priority. Fourth, 1968 was a presidential-election year and
the powerful Jewish vote could not be ignored. Finally, the administra-

tion objected to the principle of "imposing" a settlement in the Middle East. Israel, for its own reasons, joined in support of that principle. When Richard Nixon took office on January 20, 1969, the need for a new look at Middle East policy had become obvious.

NOTES

1. Dean Acheson, Present at the Creation: My Years in the State Department (New York: W. W. Norton and Co., 1969), p. 169.

2. George F. Kennan, Memoirs, 1925-1950 (Boston: Little, Brown and Co., 1967), p. 380.

3. Ibid., p. 379.

4. A. L. Horelick, "Soviet Policy in the Middle East, 1955-1969," in A. S. Becker and A. L. Horelick, "Soviet Policy in the Middle East," Rand Memorandum, R-504-FF (Santa Monica, September 1970), p. 20.

5. William Quandt, "United States Policy in the Middle East: Constraints and Choices," Rand Memorandum, R-1864-ISA (May 1976), pp. 16-17.

6. Ibid., p. 19.

7. Mohammed Hassanein Heikal, The Cairo Documents (Garden City, N.Y.: Doubleday and Co., 1973), p. 31.

8. Ibid., pp. 41-42.

9. See Document 18 in The Pentagon Papers, vol. 1 (Boston: Beacon Press, 1971; Senator Gravel ed.), p. 417.

10. Ibid., p. 425.

11. Horelick, "Soviet Policy in the Middle East, 1955-1969," p. 22.

12. Al-Ahram (Cairo), April 1, 1955, p. 1.

13. Ibid.

14. Nadav Safran, From War to War: The Arab-Israeli Confrontation 1948-1967 (New York: Pegasus, 1969), p. 105.

15. Ibid.

16. Pravda (Moscow), April 17, 1955, p. 1, cited in the Current Digest of the Soviet Press 7, no. 16 (June 1, 1955): 19.

17. Michael Yizhar, "Origins of the American Involvement in the Middle East," International Problems (Israel) 13 (January 1974): 340.

18. Heikal, The Cairo Documents, p. 55.

19. Ibid., pp. 55-56.

20. Ibid., pp. 56-57.

21. Alexander L. George and Richard Smoke, Deterrence in American Foreign Policy: Theory and Practice (New York: Columbia University Press, 1974), p. 320.

22. John Foster Dulles, "Challenge and Response in the United States Policy," Foreign Affairs 36 (October 1957): 30.

23. George and Smoke, Deterrence in American Foreign Policy: Theory and Practice, p. 357.

24. Ibid.

25. Michael Yizhar, "The United States Middle East Resolution as Viewed by Foreign Powers," International Problems (Israel) 12 (June 1973): 76.

26. Ibid., p. 60.

27. Ibid., p. 69.

28. Ibid., p. 75.

29. Horelick, "Soviet Policy in the Middle East, 1955-1969," p. 31.

30. Ibid., p. 29.

31. Heikal, The Cairo Documents, p. 219; also see William R. Polk, The United States and the Arab World, rev. ed. (Cambridge: Harvard University Press, 1969), pp. 285-87.

32. Heikal, The Cairo Documents, p. 219.

33. Safran, From War to War: The Arab-Israeli Confrontation, 1948-1967, p. 132.

34. Heikal, The Cairo Documents, pp. 219-20.

35. Ibid., p. 222.

36. Ibid., p. 193.

37. Don Peretz, "The United States, The Arabs, and Israel: Peace Efforts of Kennedy, Johnson, and Nixon," The Annals of the American Academy of Political and Social Science 401 (May 1972): 119.

38. Ibid.

39. Ibid., pp. 119-20.

40. John Badeau, The American Approach to the Arab World (New York: Harper and Row, 1968), p. 143.

41. Ibid., p. 145.

42. Heikal, The Cairo Documents, p. 233.

43. Ibid., p. 235.

44. Malcolm H. Kerr, The Middle East Conflict, Headline Series, No. 191, (New York: Foreign Policy Association, 1968), p. 21.

45. Lyndon B. Johnson, The Vantage Point: Perspective of the Presidency (New York: Holt, Rinehart and Winston, 1971), p. 288.

46. Eugene V. Rostow, Peace in the Balance: The Future of American Foreign Policy (New York: Simon and Shuster, 1972), p. 250.

47. Ibid., p. 255.

48. William B. Quandt, Decade of Decisions: American Policy Toward the Arab-Israeli Conflict, 1967-76 (Berkeley and Los Angeles:

University of California Press, 1977), p. 53; also see Johnson, The Vantage Point, p. 292.

49. Rostow, Peace in the Balance, p. 260.

50. Malcolm H. Kerr, "Regional Arab Politics and the Conflict with Israel," Rand Memorandum, RM-5966-FF (October 1969), p. 31.

51. Quandt, Decade of Decisions, p. 65.

52. Malcolm Mackintosh, "Soviet Mediterranean Policy," vol. 2, The Atlantic Papers (Lexington, Mass.: Lexington Books, 1972), p. 22.

53. Stanley Hoffmann, "France, the U.S. and the Middle East," Middle East Information Series 21 (December 1972): 4.

54. Ibid.

55. Rostow, Peace in the Balance, p. 250.

56. Ibid.

57. Eugene V. Rostow, "The Middle Eastern Crisis in the Perspective of World Politics," International Affairs 47 (April 1971): 278.

58. Walt W. Rostow, The Diffusion of Power: An Essay in Recent History (New York: Macmillan Co., 1972), p. 419.

59. Johnson, The Vantage Point, p. 404.

60. United Nations, Security Council, Resolution and Decisions of the Security Council, 1967 (New York: Security Council Official Records, 1968), pp. 8-9.

61. Quandt, Decade of Decisions, p. 65.

62. Kerr, The Middle East Conflict (Headline Series), pp. 34-35.

63. Ibid., p. 35.

64. Ibid., pp. 36-39.

65. Quandt, Decade of Decisions, p. 63.

66. Quandt, "United States Policy in the Middle East: Constraints and Choices," p. 40.

67. See data on the news conference held by Secretary of State Dean Rusk, January 3, 1969, in Department of State Bulletin 60, no. 1543 (January 20, 1969): 45-46.

68. New York Times, January 5, 1969, p. 14.

69. Quandt, Decade of Decisions, pp. 66-67.

70. Ibid.

71. Ibid., p. 67.

72. Naseer H. Aruri and Natalie Hevener, "France and the Middle East, 1967-68," The Middle East Journal 23 (Autumn 1969): 492.

73. Hoffmann,"France, the U.S. and the Middle East," p. 4.

74. Aruri and Hevener, "France and the Middle East," pp. 497-98.

75. Ibid., p. 498.

3

KISSINGER AND NIXON'S INITIAL REASSESSMENT, 1969–70

Richard Nixon's inaugural in January 1969 represented a watershed in U.S. foreign policy. American supremacy in world politics was now being challenged by other centers of power, such as the Soviet Union and China as well as Western Europe and Japan. In this setting, the United States felt obliged to consider the national interests not only of its adversaries, but also of its allies, in planning foreign policy. Détente became increasingly relevant to the new era of foreign relations.

A sense of renewal sparked an early effort to reappraise national interests. Urgently up for review were a wide range of foreign-policy challenges: The protracted, seemingly endless war in Vietnam had already ruined one president; arms negotiations with the Soviet Union needed attention; American national interests needed defining for the threatened escalation of violence along the Sino-Soviet border; there was the confrontation related to the new international economic order being pushed by the Third World; and, finally, a Middle East polarized between East and West needed to be defused.

From the beginning of 1969, the Nixon administration moved the Middle East conflict up the priority ladder. Realizing the deteriorating situation in that region, American policy makers gathered resources for a new strategy. According to Secretary of State William P. Rogers, President Nixon instructed his foreign-policy advisors to "pursue a more active strategy, putting forward our own ideas, consulting actively with other outside powers having interests in the area, and employing a broad range of tactics."[1] Nixon's initial multi-faceted approach to the Middle East conflict represented a symbolic as well as a substantive departure from American policy immediately after the June war of 1967. The new approach emphasized five dimensions.[2] The United States would support the Jarring mission and the promotion of peaceful settlements based on UN Resolution 242 of November 22, 1967; conduct bilateral talks with the Soviet Union regarding an overall framework for a peaceful settlement; participate in the four-power talks at the United Nations that would include the Soviet Union, France, and Britain; engage in direct talks with the parties to the Middle East conflict; and, finally, promote the long-range economic development of the region by a plan similar to the Eisenhower-Strauss Middle East development plan of the 1950s. In summary, the Nixon administration wanted to be involved in any negotiating process regarding the area. The objective was not only to achieve stability and a peaceful settlement, but, above all, to preserve American interests in the region. Only by active involvement could the United States ensure the protection of its vital interests against the challenges of global politics and a break in Western access to Middle East oil.

Before advancing any concrete proposals for a peaceful settlement, Nixon sent his special envoy, William Scranton, on a fact-finding tour of the Middle East. The mission sought to improve the American image in the Arab world—an image which had seriously eroded during the 1967 war when the Arabs officially proclaimed the Americans were bombing Arab targets and providing air support for the Israeli ground forces. In addition, Scranton wanted to reassure Israel by affirming the new administration's commitment to Israel's security and vital interests in any negotiating process. However, Scranton's comments regarding the American policy of "evenhandedness" in the region caused some consternation and worry in Israel; in fact, Jerusalem became concerned about the incoming administration's intentions.[3] Nixon's enthusiasm for his new approach to the Arab-Israeli conflict could also be seen in his appointment of Joseph Sisco, a State Department official with extensive UN experience, as assistant secretary of state for Near Eastern and South Asian affairs. Charles Yost, a career diplomat with experience in and expertise on the Middle East, was appointed ambassador to the United Nations.

AN INITIAL ASSESSMENT BY THE
NATIONAL SECURITY COUNCIL

The new National Security Council initiated a review and assessment of American Middle East policy, as one of the first substantive items on its agenda. A specific focus on the Arab-Israeli conflict was included. NSC background memorandums made an analysis of the Middle East situation and outlined U.S. policy options, integrating them into the global perspective of the administration's foreign policy.

The NSC deliberations involved policy alternatives, principles, and diplomatic strategies. On February 1 the council considered three Middle East alternatives.[4] One alternative would leave the responsibility for a settlement largely to the conflicting parties in the Middle

East—with outside influence being limited basically to the mediating role of UN Representative Gunnar Jarring. There was a second alternative for the United States: Pursue an active strategy with a special emphasis on American-Soviet talks. Until increased Soviet-American cooperation could be achieved, it was unrealistic to expect a peace settlement.[5] Yet a peace settlement would frustrate Moscow's strategy for exploiting the tensions in the region; a balanced peace proposal would test Moscow's intentions there.[6] Finally, one could accept the alternative that an overall settlement would be impossible; in this case, American Middle East policy would have to concentrate on limited, short-range objectives. The Nixon administration decided to pursue the second alternative, designating the third alternative as a backup in case of failure.

Next, the NSC discussed principles for guiding American policy in the Middle East.[7] An effort should be made to bring the major antagonists into the negotiating process; the United States wanted to avoid an imposed settlement. At the same time, limited initial steps in a time sequence of reciprocity would probably be essential as a prelude to a full peace treaty. A scenario for the step-by-step approach was postulated: Israeli withdrawal from the occupied Arab territories, with only minor border changes for security reasons, some areas to be demilitarized, and Jordan to have an administrative role within a unified city of Jerusalem; and a satisfactory settlement of the Palestinian-refugee problem. In public statements, the State Department ruled out an imposed settlement; privately, the department always felt the United States would have to apply pressure on Israel to "encourage" that government to make the necessary concessions if a peace agreement with the Arabs were ever to be realized.[8]

The National Security Council also discussed diplomatic strategies.[9] One was a unilateral peace plan implemented by the United States. Such a plan would probably not be acceptable to the Soviets or to the involved states of the region, especially to Israel. The proposal was rejected. Another proposed strategy was a step-by-step approach in which the Soviet Union joined in establishing guidelines for its implementation. Once the superpowers agreed on a plan, it would be submitted for approval to the four-power group (the United States, France, Britain, and the Soviet Union). A four-power agreement could then be given to UN mediator Jarring as the basis for a negotiated settlement among the regional parties.

Kissinger had reservations about this strategy. The State Department's push for a more active American peace initiative in the Middle East would sooner or later call for Washington to present its own solution, which would obviously not be acceptable to both parties. The United States would then be seen as weak and ineffective in the Middle East unless it was prepared to force Israel into an acceptance of a pro-Arab settlement. This would be a repeat performance of the American diplomatic disaster of the post-1956 war situation in which the Soviets received the credit resulting from the thankless American opposition to its own NATO partners, Britain and France. Furthermore, a U.S.-pressured settlement would most certainly require an American guarantee of that peace—a situation with all the potential for long-term U.S. involvement, with America being the long-term scapegoat.

President Nixon felt he could not reject outright either the two-power confidential negotiations between the United States and the USSR, or the four-power strategy among the United States, the USSR, Britain, and France. In the first case, he wanted to build leverage with the USSR to help the United States extract itself from the Vietnam conflict; in the four-power strategy, Nixon felt it important not to unnecessarily alienate President de Gaulle, with whom he would have to work in the years ahead. Thus, Nixon tentatively adopted Kissinger's recommendation on how to meet the problem: Play for time by proposing to utilize both the two-power and the four-power forums. By making progress in the four-power talks dependent upon progress in the two-power arrangement, the tempo could be slowed down to allow for the development of Soviet cooperation on Vietnam. Furthermore, the State Department's impatience could be blunted so as to avoid the inevitably thankless development of an American substantive resolution of the Arab-Israeli conflict. Washington's efforts would be incapable of bridging the gap and would thus result in pressure for another thankless step—i.e., forcing Israel's acceptance of the American proposal.

Kissinger felt the passing of time would help the United States, not the Soviet Union. Therefore, American strategy ought to procrastinate with a time-consuming exploration of the issues. Kissinger believed Israel and the Arabs were simply too far apart to be able to successfully bridge the gap at this time. Pushing for a resolution of the conflict now would be counterproductive to American interests. In contrast to the State Department's position of urgency, insisting on seizing the present opportunity before the Middle East became a major crisis area for the new Nixon administration, Kissinger felt "a continuing deadlock was in our interest. . . ." He believed the lack of diplomatic movement "would persuade Egypt to face the reality that Soviet tutelage and a radical foreign policy were obstacles to progress and that only the United States could bring about a settlement; it would demonstrate Soviet impotence and in time might impel a fundamental reconstruction of Arab, and especially of Egyptian, foreign policies."[10]

To summarize, Kissinger considered an active American strategy at this time inadvisable. It would not achieve a lasting peace settlement. Alternatively, the administration's strategy should be directed toward two goals: One should try to reduce Soviet influence in the region; a second, simultaneously, should seek to gain some maneuverability for the moderate Arab states vis-à-vis their radical rivals in the Middle East. This did not mean Kissinger was totally opposed to any American initiative in the Arab-Israeli conflict. In fact, he favored a partial settlement on the Israeli-Jordanian front.[11] Such a settlement would benefit the West rather than Soviet clients, i.e., Egypt and Syria. But in the absence of peace, he stressed the need for the local parties to reassess each other's negotiating posture; it was important for each to keep in mind the constraints and limitations of the other's policy predicament.[12] He wanted to use American power and diplomacy in support of moderate Arab states at the regional level and, at the same time, use it to restrain the Soviet Union at the global level.

To Kissinger's regret, the State Department's efficiency moved the diplomatic game to the substantive dimension much faster than the national security advisor had hoped for. Secretary of State Rogers had seen an opportunity to preempt foreign-policy initiatives, and he took it. As Kissinger had predicted, Rogers now pushed Nixon for "new instructions" and "clarifications" to the point where the Rogers people won the competition for the president's response.

The drama unfolded as Rogers gambled to go public with the Rogers Plan the day before President Nixon had scheduled an important National Security Council meeting to get a handle on Middle East policy. Rogers, on December 9, 1969, made his move in a major foreign-policy address that implied American pressure on Israel to return to its pre-1967 boundaries, in exchange for a peace settlement from the Arabs.

The tactic worked, with the media launching the Rogers Plan. Tactics sometimes create their own momentum. American Middle East policy now surfaced as the Rogers Plan. President Nixon even asked Kissinger to leave the Middle East to the State Department.[13]

These events did not, however, prevent Kissinger, in his capacity as director of the National Security Council, from conducting his own NSC studies regarding a settlement. In early 1969 the planning group of the NSC initiated a study on how to bring Israel and Jordan together to negotiate a peace settlement. Nevertheless, before the research was completed, Kissinger changed his mind and ordered a halt to the study.[14]

Although Kissinger was primarily busy with Vietnam and Far East policy at this time, he participated in every major decision regarding the Arab-Israeli conflict.

THE TWO-POWER AND FOUR-POWER TALKS

By the end of 1968, the Soviet leadership recognized the predicament of the Arab states; the level of rearmament attained after
the defeat in the 1967 June war could not alone change the status quo
in the region. Even though there were sporadic contacts between the
Soviets and the Americans in 1968 regarding the Middle East, the
Soviets felt that a more sustained movement on the political front was
necessary to supplement the military option for the front-line Arab
states.

Before presenting any specific proposals to the United States,
the Soviet leadership discussed Egyptian goals with President Nasser,
during his trip to the Soviet Union in July 1968. As related by Mohammed Hassanein Heikal, Nasser outlined the Egyptian view of the options
in the Arab-Israeli dispute. War to avenge the humiliation of defeat
in 1967 was not an absolute requirement; still, a capacity to threaten
war might be an essential element predisposing Israel to make the
necessary concessions Egypt could accept, short of another actual
trial by combat. [15] Heikal confirmed Moscow's agreement with
Nasser's guidelines for a peaceful settlement: The Arabs would not
accept direct negotiations with Israel, especially while Israel was
occupying Arab lands; there would be no alternative to complete
Israeli withdrawal to the lines of June 4, 1967; and, finally, the
rights of the Palestinians should be asserted—these could not be
compromised. [16]

On December 22, 1968, the Soviet Union presented a note to the
American government regarding the Middle East. Basically, the Soviet
note called for the implementation of UN Resolution 242, over a three-
stage period of several months, with the help of UN Representative
Jarring. [17] In the first stage, Israel and the Arab states would agree
to end the state of war between them, and Israel would be asked to
announce a time-table for withdrawal, under UN auspices, from lands
occupied as a result of the 1967 war. Once that was done, then Israel
should partially withdraw her forces on the Egyptian, Jordanian, and
Syrian fronts. In the end, Israel would have to withdraw to the border
of June 4, 1967, in a final peace settlement. In guaranteeing these
borders, the Security Council would undertake the major responsibility.

On January 15, 1969, the Johnson administration replied to the
Soviet note. It agreed that a Middle Eastern settlement should be based
on UN Resolution 242. Israel had supported the UN resolution, and
President Johnson assumed the Jewish state was thereby committed
to negotiate with the Arabs. The Johnson administration, however,
took the position that the 1949 armistice borders would have to be
modified for mutual security reasons. In addition, the administration

rejected the Soviet position requiring Israel to withdraw from the occupied territories, unless the Arabs also agreed to an overall settlement of the Arab-Israeli dispute. President Johnson also disagreed with the Soviet assumption concerning the partial demilitarization of the Sinai. He did not believe it would necessarily lead to a final Arab-Israeli peace settlement.[18]

Despite these Soviet-American difficulties, the administration, nonetheless, indicated its willingness to join the Soviets in aiding the Jarring mission. Additionally, the exchange of diplomatic notes helped to clarify each superpower's positions. But the main problem for the United States and the Soviet Union remained unsolved: how to have the Middle East client states of each agree to a common formula which could be used for an eventual peace settlement.

Both local parties were unhappy with these diplomatic notes. The Israelis simply rejected the Soviet proposals; they implied an imposed settlement, and Israel publicly criticized the threat of outside pressures.[19] What it wanted was a direct agreement with the Arabs. Egypt, for its part, dismissed the American proposals as pro-Israel; this led the Johnson administration—aware of the extreme dissatisfaction with which Nasser viewed the U.S. position—to subsequently inform Cairo that these proposals should be considered tentative only.[20]

Despite the Israeli and Egyptian differences, the Nixon administration decided to continue the dialogue with the Soviet Union. The exchange would at least help clarify the individual issues contained in the earlier notes. But more importantly, this format was consistent with the administration's general outlook on foreign policy, which stressed the importance of negotiations with adversaries as well as allies.

The four-power talks—whose origins went back to de Gaulle's idea in the aftermath of the 1967 war—got underway at the United Nations in March 1969. They lasted for nearly a year and focused on the Jordanian front, Jerusalem, the Palestinians, and related issues.[21] While these were going on, the United States and the Soviet Union continued their bilateral talks—this time between Soviet Ambassador Anatoly Dobrynin and Sisco. The new administration clearly attached more importance to these bilateral talks than it did to the UN negotiations.[22] Their agenda, too, was different—they dealt mainly with the Egyptian-Israeli front.

Even though Kissinger, as director of the National Security Council, did not personally participate in the four-power talks, he was getting regular briefings on their progress. In addition to close consultations with Sisco, Kissinger had several discussions with Charles Yost on the progress of the UN negotiations throughout 1969.[23] Kissinger viewed both sets of talks with considerable skepticism, although he did not oppose them publicly since Nixon supported the talks. Kissinger favored a reduction, as previously mentioned, of both diplomatic conversations because he believed that neither the Soviets nor the local parties were ready for a comprehensive settlement. [24]

Despite Kissinger's reservations, other advisors in the Nixon administration pushed the four-power talks, hoping they would clarify the conditions for a settlement based on UN Resolution 242. In this way, the Jarring mission could count on renewed support in negotiations with the regional parties. [25] The Soviets pushed these four-power talks toward developing guidelines for the negotiation of an Arab-Israeli agreement. [26] Moscow looked upon the two-power talks as a forum for narrowing the difference the superpowers had on these guidelines. [27]

From the Nixon administration's perspective, the two sets of talks represented a new tactical approach, for several reasons. First, the administration began these talks on the assumption that the Soviet Union would be anxious to stabilize the superpower rivalry in the region. [28] It assumed both superpowers wanted to avoid a direct confrontation in the Middle East. There was always the danger of a Middle East "Sarajevo" triggering World War III. Thus, any degree of cooperation with the Soviets was viewed as a plus for the overall Nixon-Kissinger foreign policy. Beyond that, they hoped to link the progress of these talks to other outstanding problems between the Soviet Union and the United States. Nixon, in particular, thought in terms of trading American cooperation in the Middle East for Soviet reciprocal cooperation in matters such as the SALT negotiations, Berlin, and the Vietnam conflict. [29]

Second, in agreeing to the four-power talks, the Nixon administration switched to a position similar to de Gaulle's after the 1967 June war. De Gaulle preferred an international solution implemented by the big powers through some kind of concerted action. [30] In essence, the administration encouraged French and British participation in the talks to broaden the European support for its policies and, in general, to narrow the American-European differences over the Middle East. At the same time, it would impress upon Israel and the Arabs that there existed broader international support for the superpowers' initiatives. [31]

Third, the Nixon administration believed the Arab leaders would eventually realize the inability of the Soviet Union to achieve, through diplomacy, what it had failed to deliver through arms. Kissinger envisaged, during these talks, a Soviet-Arab split over the ramifications of the Arab-Israeli conflict. In this case, Soviet influence with the Arabs would decrease and American influence would thereby increase.

Finally, in talking to Moscow, the Nixon administration hoped to restrain Soviet arms deliveries to the region. This would de-escalate the "war of attrition" that was raging between Israel and Egypt during the summer of 1969.

In reference to the Soviet perspectives, the two sets of talks would serve as a forum for gaining insight into the American, Israeli, and Arab positions. From the outset, the Soviets insisted on success, in both sets of talks, as a prerequisite of a final agreement on the Middle East.[32] The Arabs, however, remained suspicious of Soviet motives in these big-power contacts. Subsequently, the Soviets found it necessary to reassure the Arabs of their earlier commitments. Moscow reaffirmed its previous promises made to the Arabs, and agreed to maintain its position unless prior consultation with the Arabs took place.[33] The reasoning behind these Soviet tactics was apparently threefold: First, the Soviets wanted to assure themselves a certain degree of influence over any eventual Middle Eastern settlement. Second, even though the Soviets were skeptical about the outcome of the talks, they regarded them as a political supplement to their growing military power in the region. Third, the Soviets hoped the talks would move the United States to pressure Israel into something the Arabs could accept. Moscow was in no position to influence Israel at this time.

Israel and Egypt were both unhappy with these talks—but for different reasons. Israel feared any imposed settlement as harmful to its security.[34] But the specter of an imposed settlement was not the major concern; Israel feared even more the expansion of great-power participation in the Middle East conflict.[35] Communications with Washington included this sense of an urgent need to head off great-power political manipulation at Israel's expense, or the even more dangerous threat of superpower confrontation embodying a threat to Israel's vital interests.

The United States now found itself caught in an untenable middle position between Jerusalem's pressure for American support in maintaining the status quo, and the Soviet demand for action to defuse the "powder keg" of Middle East tensions.[36] Israel began to lend greater support to the Jarring mission as a substitute for the four-power talks, because the Jarring effort represented what Israeli Foreign Minister Abba Eban called "the international interest" rather than the separate interests of the four big powers.[37]

Egypt, on the other hand, wanted the negotiations channeled directly through the United Nations, even though it acknowledged that a lasting Middle East settlement could only be achieved by arrangements between the superpowers. The Soviets in this case disagreed with Egypt. They thought UN Representative Jarring did not have the power to implement any general agreement; the two sets of talks would have to supplement his mission. President Nasser, in the end, felt it expedient to support the Soviet policy; Egypt urgently needed additional economic and military aid from the Soviet Union.[38]

Nasser believed the Soviets would eventually realize the limitations of their proposed diplomatic route. At least, having received Egyptian support in their efforts, the Soviets would now increase their military and economic aid to Egypt. Moreover, the diplomatic exchanges between the big powers would give Nasser time to improve the Egyptian front against Israel. Time was indeed important to improve Cairo's international position: After the debacle of the 1967 war, Cairo needed time to improve its situation with regard to rebuilding its military forces, restoring confidence in Soviet-Egyptian relations, and recreating the Arab coalition.[39] In short, Egypt valued the talks between the big powers as an extra opportunity to exert more pressure on Israel and to move the United States toward a more even-handed policy in reference to the Arab-Israeli dispute.

At the beginning of these talks, William Rogers emphasized the need for an active American role—bilaterally and multilaterally—in reversing the deteriorating situation in the Middle East.[40] He reasserted the United States' firm adherence to UN Resolution 242 as the basis for a just and lasting peace in the area.[41] Both the four-power and the two-power talks, complemented by the Jarring mission, would help to implement that resolution. Secretary of State Rogers also stressed the problem of mutual security between Israel and the Arab states:

> Clearly withdrawal should take place to establish boundaries which define the areas where Israel and its neighbors may live in peace and sovereign independence. Equally, there can be no secure and recognized boundaries without withdrawal. In our view rectifications from pre-existing lines should be confined to those required for mutual security and should not reflect the weight of conquest.[42]

Rogers's statement stressed the importance of striking a balance between Israel's claim for maximum security and the Arab states' demand for a full Israeli withdrawal from the occupied territories. In essence, the United States was advancing a formula that would provide a sense of balanced "unhappiness" (or a balance of discomfort) between the regional parties.[43] The idea seemed to be in line with Kissinger's "balanced-insecurity" theory that he applied to deterrence. One Israeli strategist, in particular, considered such an idea to be a misapplication of Kissinger's strategic theories in that the Middle East conflict could not be treated like the superpower conflict.[44]

But despite the administration's new active strategy, the Arab-Israeli impasse deepened as the war of attrition on the Suez Canal front escalated. This created insurmountable difficulties for the

superpowers' reconciliation efforts. In late April 1969, the State
Department submitted to President Nixon a detailed Arab-Israeli
peace proposal. It emphasized only moderate changes from the pre-
June 5, 1967, boundaries. Kissinger, however, had two reservations
about the proposal: It would be unacceptable to the local parties; and
it would strengthen the Soviet position in Egypt—i.e., because it would
not be acceptable to Israel, the United States would need either to
force Israel to accept it or accept the proposal's failure. Without
controlling the negotiating situation in terms of a compromise on both
sides, it would be futile to attempt to get concessions from Israel
only. Alternatively, accepting failure would create gains for the
Soviet Union in the Middle East since the Arab states would now be
convinced the United States could not help them.[45] The proposal was
discussed at the April 25 NSC meeting, but Nixon avoided making a
decision because of the conflicting views between the State Department
and Kissinger. Nonetheless, the president, after balancing several
viewpoints, approved a revised version of the proposal on May 5. The
new proposal differed in two ways: The total plan would not be presented to the Soviets (in the two-power talks), but, rather, in a piece-
meal fashion; and the United States would not initially commit itself
to call for a full Israeli withdrawal from Sinai.[46] Kissinger hoped
these changes would delay the State Department's active strategy for
a negotiated settlement in the Middle East.

Immediately after Nixon approved the new proposal, Sisco presented it to Dobrynin as a basis for negotiations. The Soviets expressed
dissatisfaction with the American proposal, and, as Kissinger had
feared, their stand reaffirmed the earlier support for the Arab position. Moreover, the Soviets were clearing everything with the Arabs,
while the United States informed Israel ex post facto.[47] The Soviet
response did, however, contain positive elements: the desire to seek
a binding agreement and to secure the Arabs' recognition of Israel.
The State Department felt the Soviets' reply indicated enough "forward
movement" to warrant another proposal. Secretary Rogers thus decided to send Sisco to Moscow to discuss the new proposal. In his
view, Sisco should present Moscow with what was dubbed the American
"fallback position"—an explicit American commitment to the pre-1967-
war borders—if Moscow were forthcoming on key issues such as commitment to a peace treaty, security arrangements, and direct negotiations.[48] Kissinger disagreed with Rogers's strategy of revealing the
American fallback position at this point. In contrast, he believed the
Soviet reply showed no significant concessions that would warrant
further American compromises. Besides disagreeing with Rogers's
strategy, Kissinger insisted the Soviets must pay a price—the strain-
ing of Arab-Soviet relations—for their reluctance to pressure their
Arab clients in a manner equivalent to that expected from the United

States in relation to its local client, Israel.[49] Consequently, he advised Nixon to go along with the proposed Sisco trip to Moscow, but not to offer any new ideas to the Soviets. Nixon agreed with Kissinger's recommendations.[50]

Against this background, Sisco visited Moscow from July 14 to 17 (1969). Without new proposals (the fallback position), Sisco failed to obtain any concessions from the Soviets regarding a settlement. Yet Sisco's unproductive mission had stalled the negotiating process for two more months.

On September 11, the NSC met to discuss the Middle East. The State Department repeated its desire to advance the American fallback position as a basis for a negotiated settlement. Again, Kissinger objected to this tactic. He felt that a continuing stalemate in the negotiating process would ultimately convince the Soviets and the Arabs to make their positions less rigid.[51] In the course of the meeting, Nixon inquired about the possible Israeli reaction to all of this; Rogers and Sisco assured him that the Israelis would be happy with a package deal—presumably, the deal itself would contain some elements of the Israeli definition of peace. But Nixon and Kissinger still remained unconvinced by the State Department's argument. Worried about confronting the Israelis and their domestic supporters, Nixon instructed the State Department not to advance any new ideas, but to keep the talks with the Soviets at the exploratory level.[52] He also ordered a study of what terms Egypt, Jordan, and Syria might accept in a package settlement. All in all, Kissinger succeeded in delaying the negotiations for the next few weeks.

At the end of September, Dobrynin contacted Kissinger and suggested a joint Soviet-American position for providing guidelines to the Jarring mission. Kissinger, however, was unwilling to cooperate with the Soviet ambassador on the Middle East. Dobrynin, for his part, turned to Sisco for talks. In mid-October, Sisco reported to the White House that there was enough agreement on the procedural issues—under the Rhodes formula—to warrant substantive discussions. The "Rhodes formula" referred to the procedure used by the UN acting mediator, Ralph Bunche, to achieve the Arab-Israeli armistice in the 1948 war: Since the Arabs refused to meet Israeli officials face-to-face, the UN mediator organized a procedure for achieving the armistice, whereby he shuttled back and forth between the Arab rooms and the Israeli room on the island of Rhodes. Now, in October, Sisco sought to deepen the American diplomatic involvement and to submit to the Soviets the administration's fallback position (the American commitment to have Israel accept the pre-1967-war boundaries) as the basis for a settlement on the Egyptian front. Balancing Kissinger's arguments against those of the State Department, Nixon felt he had little choice but to reluctantly accept the latter's position.[53] Not surprisingly, Nixon hinted strongly to the leaders of the American Jewish community that nothing would come out of this new American proposal.[54]

On the whole, the United States and the Soviet Union appeared to be open to a compromise, especially in reference to the Rhodes formula as a means of advancing the Arab-Israeli peace negotiations.[55] The United States, in particular, liked the Rhodes formula because it would be a move in the direction of satisfying Israel's demands. For the Arabs, it would maintain the facade of indirect negotiations.[56] The Soviets, in turn, agreed to the formula.

In the end, however, the Egyptians changed their minds. In effect, the Egyptians pulled the rug from under the Soviets at the point where the superpowers had reached a considerable agreement on principles for the settlement of the Arab-Israeli dispute—the closest the two powers had come to an agreement since the June war.[57]

Ultimately, the failure of the four-power and the two-power talks in 1969-70 could be attributed to several causes. First, the four-power talks failed because the more important two-power talks proved incapable of producing an agreement.[58] Hardly any coordination of the two sets of talks was done by the Nixon administration.[59]

Second, there was some domestic political opposition to these talks, mostly from pro-Israeli elements in Congress. For instance, in April 1969, 226 members of Congress signed a "Declaration for Peace in the Middle East," which called for direct negotiations between Israel and the Arab states, rather than a settlement under the sponsorship of the big outside powers.[60]

Third, the United States and the Soviet Union interpreted Resolution 242 in different ways. The United States viewed the resolution as a compromise, while the Soviet Union interpreted the resolution as a UN demand for a complete Israeli withdrawal from the occupied Arab territories.[61] Equally important, the same conflicting interpretation of Resolution 242 prevailed between Israel and the Arab states.

Fourth, the Soviet Union and the United States were not willing to pressure their regional clients, especially during 1969, to accept what the superpowers might find to be a mutually acceptable compromise.[62] Note, however, that the U.S. position at the beginning of these talks was more carefully developed than the Soviet position—a position it rigidly maintained without pressuring its client Arab states to be more flexible. Later the United States—despite Kissinger's objections—moved unilaterally toward Moscow's position without demanding reciprocal modifications.[63] This explains in part the Nixon administration's lack of enthusiasm for the Middle East problem at the end of 1969. The Soviets were in complete control of their diplomatic position, while the United States was not. Thus, the United States felt handicapped by the ill-prepared negotiating strategy. In addition, it had no direct diplomatic relations with Egypt and no prior consultations with Israel.[64]

Finally, the events in the Middle East made it difficult for both
the United States and Israel to trust either Soviet or Arab motives.
The war of attrition on the Egyptian front, which began in April 1969,
and the PLO activity launched against Israel from Jordan and Lebanon
created severe liabilities—insurmountable liabilities for the kind of
sustained negotiations and compromise solutions necessary for settlement of a conflict as intractable as the Arab-Israeli dispute.

THE NIXON-KISSINGER IMAGES AND
PERCEPTIONS OF THE MIDDLE EAST

Decision makers' images of international politics always play
an important role in foreign policy. The Nixon-Kissinger Middle East
policy was no exception. It is important to view these perceptions at
two levels—the regional and the global—relative to the crucial years
from 1969 to 1974.

At the regional level, Nixon and Kissinger did not consider the
Middle East a typical Third World area because of its oil-rich resources, its strategic importance, and the American-Israeli "special
relationship." The importance of the Middle East was stressed by
President Nixon on July 1, 1970, when he stated:

> The Mideast is important. We all know that 80 percent of
> Europe's oil and 90 percent of Japan's oil comes from the
> Mideast. We know that the Mideast, this area, this is the
> gateway to the Mediterranean; it's the hinge of NATO; and
> it is the gateway through the Suez Canal down into the
> Indian Ocean. [65]

The Nixon administration was especially concerned about the
stability of the moderate regimes in the area, the inter-Arab rivalries,
Israeli security, and the problem of growing Soviet influence in the
region. An appropriate Middle East strategy would require policies
considerably different from those pursued by the Johnson presidency.
The Nixon administration pointedly switched from an emphasis on promoting stability in general to a renewed, specific effort at reconciling
the Arab-Israeli conflict. [66] In 1970 the Republican administration
moved away from President Johnson's five peace principles to the
new focus—a change stemming from the crucial reassessment of
overall American interests in the Middle East. [67]

The new Middle East policy reflected two aspects of the Nixon
Doctrine. First, the Nixon administration wanted to pursue a Middle
East policy measured on the basis of a realistic appraisal of American
national interests. As President Nixon put it, "The more that policy

is based on a realistic assessment of ours and others' interests, the more effective our role in the world can be."[68] Henceforth, the emphasis would not be on the formal alliances or moral commitments stressed before 1969.

Second, the Nixon administration sought to dispel the image of neoisolationism in American foreign policy—neoisolationism had become popular as a result of the Vietnam War and American over-extension elsewhere. The Middle East conflict, therefore, served as an arena in which to test the Nixon administration's determination to promote local participation, negotiations, and partnership. As Nixon stated:

> In the Middle East, we shall continue to work with others
> to establish a possible framework within which the parties
> to the Arab-Israeli conflict can negotiate the complicated
> and difficult question at issue. Others must join us in
> recognizing that a settlement will require sacrifices and
> restraints by all concerned.[69]

The Nixon administration wanted to demonstrate to the local parties of the region, to the European allies, and, most importantly, to the Soviet Union that it had no intention of withdrawing from its global commitments. Kissinger's emphasis on the issues of participation and partnership was designed, in part, to preserve American influence, as well as to minimize the need for American intervention in regional crises, especially in a volatile area like the Middle East.

From the very creation of Israel in 1948, the American military objective in the Middle East was to preserve the balance of power between Israel and the adjacent Arab states. In view of Israel's success in building an effective military force, there was little need for direct American intervention to protect the Jewish nation's security against the Arab threat, especially in the light of Israel's victory over the Arabs in June of 1967. But, after 1967, American policy makers had to consider two new, major developments in the region: Israeli nuclear capabilities, and the increased Soviet military involvement in the Mediterranean area—particularly the Kremlin's success in Syria.

Beginning with the Kennedy administration, the Israeli nuclear program functioned as a source of constant concern to American policy makers. France had provided the foundation for the Israeli nuclear program, yet it was the United States that supplied Israel with its first nuclear reactor (Nahal Soreq), under a 1955 agreement.[70] The major issues between Israel and the United States now centered around two points: The Israelis were reluctant to sign the Nuclear Non-Proliferation Treaty, and they refused to open the Dimona nuclear reactor to international inspection.[71]

Kissinger pointed out the dramatic political and military implications for American policy that would occur if Middle East regional powers acquired nuclear weapons. In this case, the United States would face the increased danger of a local war escalating into a global confrontation;[72] and the enhanced unpredictability of regional threats and responses would create a greater threat to American Middle East interests. One could also assume a decrease in the predictability of Soviet Middle East foreign policy that might well erode the prevailing American bipolar advantage there. Finally, the introduction of nuclear weapons would have a destabilizing effect on the balance of power between Israel and the Arab states. The American-Soviet "balance of terror" would be the least suitable model for the region,[73] because the stabilizing factors—such as a carefully nurtured second-strike capability and the relatively satisfactory status quo of the superpowers (particularly of the United States)—would be missing.[74] In the Middle East, the destabilizing effect might induce the Israeli leaders to launch a preemptive strike on the strategic centers in Egypt and Syria, or it might tempt the Arab leaders to launch a preventive war against Israel.[75]

Given these concerns, Kissinger initiated, in early 1969, an intelligence-community (CIA, Defense, and State) study dealing with the nuclear possibilities for several near-nuclear countries including Israel.[76] The research, however, did not deal with the diplomatic implications of Israel's atomic capability; it only examined the state of technology in that country.[77] Nonetheless, the fact that Kissinger initiated the study indicated his anxiety about bringing nuclear weapons into the Middle East. This apprehension can be seen in the Nixon administration's recommendation, early in 1969, to cancel (eliminate from the budget) President Johnson's proposed nuclear desalting plant for Israel.[78] In the end, even though Israel's nuclear capability was not a major factor in the administration's 1969 assessment of necessary negotiating procedures for achieving a Middle East peace,[79] Kissinger concluded "nuclear understandings" with Israel and Egypt in the summer of 1974. These supplemented the step-by-step diplomacy and increased American influence in the region.

At the global level, Kissinger considered the Middle East more dangerous than the Vietnam problem. There was a greater danger of direct Soviet-American confrontation in the Levant, with its intractable Arab-Israeli dispute.[80] Both the United States and the Soviet Union had client states in the area that were of vital mineral and great strategic importance. Under these circumstances, the Middle East was a powder keg for escalation in a superpower confrontation. Interestingly, the Harvard professor turned statesman considered the problem of American involvement in Vietnam an "intellectual failure," whereas the Middle East was seen "more as a tactical than a philosophical problem."[81] President Nixon also addressed the problem in his foreign-policy report to Congress on February 18, 1970:

> If the Arab-Israeli conflict cannot be finally resolved, at least its scope must be contained and the direct engagement of the major powers limited. For this is a second dimension of the conflict in the Middle East—the rivalries and interests of the major powers themselves.[82]

Above all, the Nixon administration sought to avoid a direct confrontation with the Soviet Union in the Middle East;[83] it remained the continuing top priority in American Middle East policy. Both American and Soviet foreign-policy decision makers had seen this as the priority item during the Suez war of 1956 and the Arab-Israeli war of June 1967. Each side sought the cooperation of the other in order to defuse the explosive situation and limit the conflict to the region. By 1969 this important objective had assumed even greater importance, for many reasons. The relationship between the regional states and the big powers had now changed; there was a significant growth of Soviet power in the Mediterranean region and within the Arab world. Furthermore, the relationship between the superpowers had changed, especially in regard to strategic parity and détente.[84] The Nixon administration anticipated a favorable Soviet response to an American détente initiative. Hopefully, Moscow would respond by cooperating in the Middle East as well as in Vietnam.[85] To carry the reasoning one step further, Nixon and Kissinger assumed American-Soviet cooperation in the Middle East would encourage the Soviets to develop a sense of shared responsibility for preserving peace and stability worldwide. Alternatively, Kissinger insisted it would be intolerable for the Soviet Union to push for predominance in the Middle East. He reminded Moscow of its greater benefit from détente than from aspiring to superiority in the Arab world. In short, the Nixon administration wanted to convince the USSR of détente's mutual benefits. Yet the benefits required responsibilities including the very essential one of practicing restraint in the Middle East.

Given its global interests, Soviet actions in the Arab world would be expected to transcend regional concerns. Yet, by the end of 1970, the Nixon administration had viewed the Middle East conflict as a test of strength between the two superpowers—a situation challenging the above assumptions about Soviet policy.[86] Kissinger's doubts about the rational priorities of Soviet global policy stemmed from the recent Soviet activities during the Jordanian civil war and from the attempt to build a nuclear-submarine base in Cuba. Additionally, the administration worried about the southern flank of NATO, the role the U.S. Sixth Fleet might have to play, and the amount of Israeli military power needed to prevent Soviet hegemony in the Middle East.

In sum, the Soviet factor played a critical role in the Nixon-Kissinger perceptions at the two levels of the Middle East conflict, especially during the Jordanian civil war of 1970 and the October war of 1973. Kissinger still remained hopeful that a Middle East accommodation with the Soviet Union might be achieved—an accommodation built upon détente at the global level and on the Nixon Doctrine at the regional level.

DOMESTIC FACTORS INFLUENCING AMERICAN POLICY

The Arab-Israeli conflict could be described as a unique problem for American foreign policy in at least one overriding respect: in the domestic support for Israel in American politics. Since 1948 this support came from consecutive American governments and varied little, regardless of which political party controlled the White House. As Assistant Secretary Sisco put it, "The United States has supported the security and well-being of Israel for two decades, with a constancy rarely surpassed in the history of relations between nations."[87] This solid governmental (White House) support for Israel—the State Department excepted—tended to reflect the overwhelming internal support for that state in the mass media, in the intellectual and scientific communities, in the liberal establishment (especially within the ranks of the Democratic party), in the American intelligence community, and in the American Congress. In short, this domestic support could be regarded as one of the main ingredients of the "special relationship" between Israel and the United States.

Beginning with President Nixon's inaugural, the administration realized that an evenhanded, active strategy in the Middle East would alienate the powerful pro-Israel (Zionist) lobby. In fact, the administration found itself in a more maneuverable position than had the Johnson administration. President Nixon felt less indebted to the Jewish vote in the 1968 presidential campaign since he only received 17 percent of the Jewish vote as compared to the 81 percent support for the Democratic candidate.[88] There was also a widespread feeling in America, in the light of Vietnam, that it should stay out of regional conflicts. A Gallup poll in January 1969 found that 52 percent of the American people felt the United States should stay out of the Middle East conflict, while only 41 percent had felt this way in 1967.[89] The same poll found that in 1967, 5 percent of the American people favored sending American troops to help Israel; in 1969 the figure had shrunk to 1 percent.[90] In May 1969, a Time-Harris poll revealed a widespread skepticism on the part of the American public regarding the uses of military power.[91] In the poll, 44 percent of the American people favored aid to Israel if it were threatened by Soviet-supported

Arab regimes, while 39 percent of the Americans opposed aid. However, only 9 percent of the people favored sending troops to Israel.[92] As Louis Harris observed, "The American people are not prepared to make to Israel anything like the commitment that we have made to South Vietnam."[93] This apparent decline in support for direct American intervention on behalf of Israel made it easier for the Nixon administration to withstand the Israeli/Zionist pressure as it sought to formulate its policy at the United Nations in the context of the four-power talks on the Arab-Israeli dispute. Israel strongly objected to the UN connection of these great-power talks. By choosing the UN route, Washington was trying to blend the American position with the various positions of the other big powers in order to make it difficult for the Israeli/Zionist lobby to single out the American position for criticism.

Unlike the powerful Zionist lobby, the pro-Arab lobby had a very modest effect on American policy. The latter included various fragmented, pro-Arab groups scattered throughout the United States, plus the multinational oil corporations operating in the Arab world. The lobbies pursued contrasting strategies toward the policy-making apparatus in Washington. Whereas the pro-Israeli strategy sought to influence key structures within the American governmental process— e.g., public opinion, the labor-union hierarchies, Congress, and the White House—the oil companies usually pursued a low-key strategy in explaining to the American government the importance of the economic and related political interests of the United States in the Arab world.[94] But as demonstrated by William Quandt's study of domestic influences on American policy, the above lobbies, especially the pro-Israeli lobby, were more effective in restraining American policy makers than in dictating new initiatives.[95] After the 1973 oil embargo and the 1973-74 oil crisis, however, there was a definite linkage between politics and economics in American policy toward the Arab-Israeli conflict. This linkage provided the Arab states with a psychological weapon for challenging the largely uncontested power of the pro-Israel lobby in American domestic politics.

Even though there were no diplomatic relations between the United States and several Arab states, the Nixon administration preferred to keep contacts with the radical Arab regimes through the economic field.[96] This "pragmatic business approach" in 1969 served to keep the political dialogue alive between the United States and the Arab states, but it had only a minor impact on the Nixon-Kissinger assessment of American policy toward the Arab-Israeli conflict.

EVENTS IN THE MIDDLE EAST:
IMPLICATIONS FOR U.S. POLICY

One of the most important consequences of the 1967 June war
was the emergence of Israel as the dominant military power in the
region. The Johnson administration felt a sense of relief because the
Israeli victory meant predominance by an American ally rather than
by a Soviet client (Egypt). Furthermore, this military predominance
in the Middle East would demonstrate to the Arab states the inability
of the Soviet Union to change the existing balance; thus, the Arabs
would have no alternative except to negotiate with Israel.

This American assessment forged a common American-Israeli
political strategy concerning a peaceful settlement in the years 1967
and 1968.[97] In clarifying this strategy, Israeli Foreign Minister Abba
Eban noted: "If we are not for the same thing, we are against the same
things—against a return to the previous fragile situation, a fragmented
approach to peace, and in favor of a solid, contractual peace agreement."[98] But by late 1969, the regional balance had been dramatically
changed by three major events: the rise of the Palestinian resistance
movement, increased Soviet political and military involvement, and
the war of attrition between Israel and Egypt in 1969 and 1970.

The Palestinian Resistance Movement

One significant consequence of the June 1967 war was the emergence of the Palestine liberation movement as a decisive challenge to
the existing power relations in the region. In the 1950s and 1960s, the
Palestinians viewed their struggle as an integral part of the overall
Arab conflict with Israel. The Arab League's establishment of the
Palestine Liberation Organization in 1964 was designed, in part, to
keep the Palestinian activities under the control of the Arab states.[99]
But the Arab defeat in 1967 discredited the Arab regimes and their
strategy; it provided the PLO with an opportunity to gain an independent
status within the Arab world. The PLO strategy against Israel emphasized the concept of protracted warfare and the notion of a popular
war.[100] The Palestinians saw their struggle against Israel as similar
to the Vietnamese struggle against the United States.

By 1969, the PLO had gained recognition within the Arab world,
as well as having received increasing recognition internationally—
especially after the battle of Karameh on March 21, 1968, in which
Israel suffered unexpected losses.[101] But the PLO's impact on the
Arab world during these years was primarily the result of its political
efforts in promoting its revolutionary ideology; the PLO had little
military effectiveness against Israel.[102] Equally important, the PLO

kept the Palestinian problem at the center of inter-Arab politics.[103] By November 1969, the PLO had gained an autonomous presence in Lebanon as a result of the Cairo Agreement between itself and the Lebanese government.[104] This agreement did not signify an alliance against Israel; rather, it was an uneasy modus vivendi between the two parties—one enjoying popular support in the Arab world and the other suffering from relative weakness.

In Jordan, the PLO enjoyed a semi-autonomous presence. But the Jordanian regime, fearing heavy Israeli reprisals, was less tolerant than the Lebanese government in regard to the PLO's activities within the country. Even more importantly, King Hussein of Jordan was worried about the collapse of his regime as a result of the PLO activities inside the country. Major clashes between the Jordanian regime and the PLO took place in November 1968, in February 1970, and in the decisive showdown during the civil war in September 1970.[105] By the summer of 1971, King Hussein's army had achieved a complete victory over the Palestinian fedayeen.

To summarize, even though the role of the PLO was not a central factor in the Nixon-Kissinger assessment of the Arab-Israeli conflict of 1969-70,[106] the emergence of the Palestinian resistance movement, as a new factor on the Middle East scene, had major implications for American policy toward the region. Washington considered the PLO as a threat to Israel and to the moderate Arab regimes, e.g., Lebanon and Jordan. The Nixon administration feared commando activities might impede the peace negotiations taking place at the two-power and four-power talks.[107] For the PLO was vehemently opposed to those Arab states that accepted UN Resolution 242 of November 22, 1967. In fact, the PLO opposed any diplomatic solution to the Arab-Israeli problem.[108] Anything less than a military solution was considered hopeless.

Another crucial aspect of Middle East politics was the internal transformation of the PLO. In February 1969, Al Fatah, the largest commando group, took control of the organization.[109] Fatah sought to bring some degree of unity and organization to the badly fragmented resistance movement. In April 1969, the newly created Palestine Armed Struggle Command (PASC) sought to unite all the major commando groups.[110] But this transformation did not end the internal debate concerning the most suitable strategy for combating Israel. Fatah was ready to coexist with the various Arab regimes as long as those regimes provided protection and aid to the resistance movement.[111] The other major commando groups, such as the Popular Front for the Liberation of Palestine (PFLP) and the Popular Democratic Front for the Liberation of Palestine (PDFLP), assumed a position of less tolerance toward the existing Arab governments. They pushed hard for an internal political and social revolution within the

Arab states as the best means of achieving their goals for the Arab world. [112]

In this situation, the Nixon administration feared a radicalization of the region that could drastically harm American economic interests, especially the supply of oil to Western Europe. On the other hand, the PLO viewed the United States as a champion of world imperialism, Zionism, and Arab reaction. [113] The Palestinian goals hindered Kissinger's effort to improve American prestige in the region—a prestige already at a low ebb since the June war of 1967.

The Nixon administration also worried about the PLO's relations with China and the Soviet Union. This concern was justified by the PLO's growing importance not only within the Arab world, but also at the international level. Both Moscow and Peking considered the PLO a part of the national liberation movements in the Third World. [114] They were in competition with each other to increase their influence in the PLO. China, not the Soviet Union, was the first major power and non-Arab state to recognize the PLO as a national entity. [115] The Chinese viewed it as an alternative to the national-bourgeois and pro-Soviet regimes, Egypt and Syria. [116] But China's support for the Palestinian cause and for the overall Arab position against Israel did not mean that it favored the dismantling of Israel. [117] China only favored the return of the occupied territories to the Arab states and the establishment of a Palestinian entity on the West Bank.

The Soviet Union considered the PLO as an extra vehicle for extending its influence in the Middle East. The PLO was not regarded as representing an alternative to the established Arab states, however. [118] The Soviet Union approached the PLO cautiously with considerably more subtlety than did the Chinese. Moscow regarded the PLO as a destabilizing element in the Arab-Israeli conflict. [119] The Soviets wanted to restrain the activities of the PLO against Israel, a country whose right to exist was already recognized by the Soviet Union. [120] In all, the Soviets, vis-à-vis the PLO, wanted to avoid another tactical fiasco similar to their miscalculated assessment of and premature support for Israel in 1948.

The PLO, in turn, strove for independence from the two Communist superpowers. It used a pragmatic, not an ideological, approach to China and the Soviet Union. The PLO viewed the Communist countries in terms of their economic and military aid, rather than in terms of a shared ideological bond. [121]

Despite the PLO's reservations about its ties to the Soviet Union and China, the Nixon administration continued to worry about the spread of Communist ideology throughout the Middle East, especially by the major Communist factions within the PLO, the PFLP, and the PDFLP. [122] In short, the radicalization of the area might threaten the stability of the pro-Western regimes and, ultimately, lead to a change in the configuration of power there. On the other hand, there was the possibility of a favorable development for American foreign policy; the expansion of Chinese influence into the Middle East conflict might increase American maneuverability with the Soviet Union.[123] This would not, however, necessarily secure Soviet cooperation in the search for a Middle East settlement.

The Soviet Politico-Military Involvement in the Region

By 1969, the Soviet Union had expanded its naval squadron to the point where it could be of concern to the Sixth Fleet, and ultimately pose a danger to the southern flank of NATO, Yugoslavia, and the Middle East. It had also acquired some concessions from several Arab countries, such as land-based naval and air facilities for providing an air cover for its Mediterranean squadron. This development affected American planning toward the area in a variety of ways.

First, the expansion of Soviet forces in the Mediterranean caused apprehension in Washington and Jerusalem. Israel saw this as an added threat to its national security. An effective Soviet military force in the Mediterranean reduced the certainty of American military effectiveness in determining the outcome of Middle East crises, as had occurred, for instance, in the 1958 direct military intervention in Lebanon.

Second, Soviet forces in the Mediterranean posed a direct threat to the oil-rich Persian Gulf region, especially in the light of the recent British decision (announced in 1968) to withdraw its military presence from east of Suez by the end of 1971. In terms of the Nixon Doctrine, the administration wanted regional powers such as Iran and Saudi Arabia to fill the political (and military) vacuum after the British withdrawal from the Persian Gulf.

Third, the Soviet military presence in the Mediterranean was considered by American policy makers as a supplement to the growing Soviet political and military influences in the Indian Ocean and the surrounding areas. This development could adversely affect the global military balance between the United States and the Soviet Union; the superpower competition in the Indian Ocean was a new destabilizing factor in the world arena.

Finally, from the foregoing developments in Soviet Mediterranean policy, a bolder Soviet policy in the Middle East and on the African continent could be expected in the future. This Soviet policy could have grave implications for the Arab-Israeli conflict. The Soviets could encourage the Arabs to expand use of the oil weapon against the Western countries that supported Israel, especially the

United States.[124] In addition, the Soviet involvement in the internal affairs of the Arab states, especially in Syria and Egypt, could result in an irreversible Soviet presence in the Arab world that, in turn, could destabilize the whole region. Kissinger felt the Soviets might urge the Arab states to take a tougher stand against Israel, such as that exemplified by the Egyptian war of attrition against Israel in 1969-70.

The War of Attrition: 1969

From the Egyptian standpoint, the reactivation of the front against Israel in April 1969 was based on several considerations. President Nasser insisted the Egyptian-Israeli front must not be allowed to become deactivated, because the status quo would demonstrate to the world, and especially to the United States, that Israel was in command of the political and military situations.[125] He also wanted to discredit the Israeli strategy of consolidating the status quo. He would do this by exploiting the Israeli weakness in manpower and in defense spending that, together, defined Israel's Achilles' heel— the inability to sustain a state of protracted warfare. Furthermore, Nasser wanted to demonstrate to the Egyptian people and to the rest of the Arab world, including the PLO, that Egypt was still the leader of the Arab nationalist movement as well as the main bulwark against Israel. Additionally, Nasser's decision to reactivate the front coincided with the ongoing two-power and four-power talks between the big powers; military activities along the Suez Canal were intended to pressure the United States and the other powers to avoid a settlement based on the results of the June 1967 war.[126]

In summary, the overriding purpose of the war of attrition was to keep the Israeli military presence at the Suez Canal from becoming a recognized status quo. Egypt sought to make it too costly for Israel, with its limited resources in both manpower and revenues, to maintain the territorial conquests of the 1967 war. Egypt intended to send a message to the Nixon administration: The United States must switch to a more balanced policy and provide other alternatives to the Egyptian dependency on the Soviet Union;[127] the United States needed to re-examine its policy of supplying F-4 Phantom jets to Israel;[128] additionally, the Egyptians were anxious to know what Israel was saying to the United States concerning negotiations.[129] In short, Nasser preferred to keep some political contacts with the United States because he realized it was the only country capable of effectively pressuring Israel to modify its negotiating posture.[130]

From the American standpoint, the war of attrition was a very disturbing development in the Middle East; it raised the prospect of a direct confrontation with the Soviet Union. The Nixon administration saw this as a dangerous escalatory situation caused by each super-power's backing of its local clients. The war of attrition might also undermine the American objective of détente. The survival of détente in the Middle East, Kissinger insisted, would ultimately depend on keeping the Soviet political influence and military presence within tolerable bounds. In essence, the confrontation created a dilemma in American policy. On the one hand, the United States was trying to promote a peaceful settlement through the two-power and the four-power talks with the Soviet Union and other countries; and, on the other hand, it was stepping up the arms race—increasing the possibility of a major war in the region by delivering Phantom jets to Israel to ensure Israeli air superiority.[131]

The Soviets found themselves in an equally difficult situation in the limited conflict, but they hoped the continued polarization would further increase Arab dependency on the Soviet Union and, at the same time, alienate the Arab world from the United States.

In all, as the cycle of violence escalated in the region, espe-cially with the heavy Israeli air strikes against targets near Egyptian population centers, the Nixon administration felt the fighting had altered the political and military environment and brought the nego-tiating process to a standstill. In this situation, President Nixon allowed the State Department, through the initiative of Secretary of State Rogers, to present the American proposals for breaking the diplomatic deadlock. This effort was made on December 9, 1969, and was known as the Rogers Plan.

NOTES

1. U.S. Department of State, United States Foreign Policy, 1969-1970: A Report of the Secretary of State, William Rogers, Department of State Publication No. 8575 (Washington, D.C.: Gov-ernment Printing Office, 1971), p. 72.

2. See President Nixon's News Conference of February 6, 1969, in U.S., President, Public Papers of the Presidents of the United States (Washington, D.C.: Government Printing Office, 1971), Richard Nixon, 1969, p. 69.

3. Marvin Kalb and Bernard Kalb, Kissinger (Boston: Little, Brown and Co., 1974), pp. 187-88.

4. William B. Quandt, Decade of Decisions: American Policy Toward the Arab-Israeli Conflict, 1967-1976 (Berkeley and Los Angeles: University of California Press, 1977), pp. 82-83; also see William B. Quandt, The Middle East Conflict in U.S. Strategy, 1970-71," Journal of Palestine Studies 1 (Autumn 1971): 41-42.

5. Interview with Walter B. Smith II, Department of State, Washington, D.C., July 25, 1977; also see Kalb and Kalb, Kissinger, pp. 187-88.

6. Henry Kissinger, White House Years (Boston: Little, Brown and Co., 1979), p. 350.

7. Quandt, Decade of Decisions, pp. 82-83.

8. Kissinger, White House Years, pp. 350-51.

9. Quandt, Decade of Decisions, p. 83.

10. Kissinger, White House Years, p. 353.

11. Ibid., p. 351.

12. Kalb and Kalb, Kissinger, p. 188.

13. Ibid.

14. Interview with Morton Halperin, NSC, 1969 (Planning Group), Washington, D.C., March 16, 1977.

15. See Mohammed Heikal's weekly column in Al-Ahram, January 10, 1969, p. 3.

16. See Heikal's weekly column in Al-Ahram, June 20, 1969, p. 3.

17. For complete details, see Al-Ahram, January 19, 1969, p. 3. U.S. government officials confirmed that Al-Ahram has printed an accurate version of the UN note to the Soviet Union; see the article by Hedrick Smith in the New York Times, January 21, 1969, p. 14.

18. Ibid.

19. Jersualem Post, January 6, 1969, p. 1.

20. Al-Ahram, January 27, 1969, p. 1.

21. Interview with Walter B. Smith II.

22. Interview with Charles Yost, Aspen, Colo., August 9, 1977.

23. Ibid.

24. Interview with Walter B. Smith II; also see Kissinger, White House Years, pp. 353-57.

25. U.S. Department of State, United States Foreign Policy 1969-1970: A Report of the Secretary of State William Rogers, p. 72.

26. Ibid.

27. Ibid., pp. 72-73.

28. Robert J. Pranger, American Policy for Peace in the Middle East, 1969-1971: Problems of Principle, Manoeuvre, and Time (Washington, D.C.: American Enterprise Institute for Public Policy Research, 1971), p. 10.

29. Richard Nixon, RN: The Memoirs of Richard Nixon (New York: Grosset and Dunlap, 1978), pp. 369-70, 391; Kissinger, White House Years, p. 352.

30. Jerusalem Post, January 1, 1969, p. 1.

31. See the article by I. L. Kenen in the Jerusalem Post, February 11, 1969, p. 3.

32. Interview with Walter B. Smith II.

33. Lawrence L. Whetten, The Canal War: Four-Power Conflict in the Middle East (Cambridge: Massachusetts Institute of Technology Press, 1974), pp. 73-74.

34. Jerusalem Post, March 31, 1969, p. 1.

35. Bernard Reich, Quest for Peace: United States-Israel Relations and the Arab-Israeli Conflict (New Brunswick, N.J.: Transaction Books, 1977), pp. 102-3.

36. Ibid., pp. 103-04; also see the Jersualem Post, January 27, 1969, p. 8.

37. Jerusalem Post, March 6, 1969, p. 2.

38. Mohammed Heikal, The Road to Ramadan (New York: Quadrangle, 1975), p. 57.

39. Ibid.

40. U.S., Congress, Senate, Committee on Foreign Relations, Briefings By Secretary of State William Rogers, Hearings before the Committee on Foreign Relations, 91st Cong. 1st sess., 1969, pp. 10-11.

41. Ibid., p. 10.

42. Ibid.

43. See the article by I. L. Kenen in the Jerusalem Post, March 13, 1969; also see Kissinger, White House Years, p. 358.

44. Haim Herzog, "Kissinger, Heikal, and Israel," Jerusalem Post Week-End Magazine, March 21, 1969, p. 4.

45. Kissinger, White House Years, pp. 364-65.

46. Ibid., p. 365.

47. Interview with Walter B. Smith II.

48. Kissinger, White House Years, pp. 366-67.

49. Ibid., p. 367.

50. Ibid.

51. Ibid., pp. 368-69.

52. Ibid., p. 369.

53. Ibid., pp. 371-72.

54. Ibid., p. 372.

55. Interview with Walter B. Smith II.

56. Ibid.

57. Interview with a former defense official in the Nixon administration, Washington, D.C., July 7, 1977.

58. Interview with Charles Yost.

59. Interview with a former defense official in the Nixon administration, Washington, D.C., July 7, 1977.

60. U.S., Congress, House, Declaration for Peace in the Middle East, 91st Cong., 1st sess., April 22 to May 1969, Congressional Record 115: 10592; a study of related interest is Robert Trice's article "Congress and the Arab-Israeli Conflict: Support for Israel in the U.S. Senate, 1970-1973," Political Science Quarterly 92 (Fall 1977): 443-63.

61. Interview with a former defense official in the Nixon administration, Washington, D.C., July 7, 1977.

62. Interview with Charles Yost.

63. Interview with a former defense official in the Nixon administration, Washington, D.C., July 7, 1977.

64. Ibid.

65. U.S., President, Public Papers of the Presidents of the United States (Washington, D.C.: Government Printing Office, 1971), Richard Nixon, 1970, p. 558.

66. Bernard Reich, "New Directions in Middle East Policy," Research Analysis Corp., Strategic Studies Department Paper, RAC-P-47 (January 1969): 3.

67. Ibid., pp. 3-6.

68. U.S., President, U.S. Foreign Policy for the 1970's: A New Strategy for Peace: A Report to the Congress by Richard Nixon, (Washington, D.C.: Government Printing Office, February 18, 1970) p. 7.

69. Ibid., p. 8.

70. Fuad Jabber, Israel and Nuclear Weapons: Present Options and Future Strategies (London: Chatto and Windus, 1971), pp. 23-24; also see William B. Bader, The United States and the Spread of Nuclear Weapons (New York: Pagasus, 1968), p. 94.

71. Aubrey Hodes, "Implications of Israel's Nuclear Capability," The Wiener Library Bulletin 22 (Autumn 1969): 3-4; also see Bader, The United States and the Spread of Nuclear Weapons, p. 94.

72. Hodes, "Implications of Israel Nuclear Capability," p. 5.

73. Yair Evron, "A Nuclear Balance of Deterrence in the Middle East," New Outlook (Israel) 18 (July/August 1975): 16.

74. Ibid., pp. 17-18; also see Robert Pranger and Dale R. Tahtinen, Nuclear Threat in the Middle East (Washington, D.C.: American Enterprise Institute for Public Policy Research, 1975), pp. 3-5.

75. Fuad Jabber, "Israel's Nuclear Options," Journal of Palestine Studies 1 (Autumn 1971): 26-31.

76. Interview with Harold H. Saunders, NSC (Middle East) Washington, D.C., July 26, 1977.

77. Ibid.

78. Jabber, Israel and Nuclear Weapons, pp. 58-60.

79. Interview with Harold Saunders.

80. See, for instance, President Nixon's new conference of January 27, 1969, in U.S., President, Public Papers of the Presidents of the United States (Washington, D.C.: Government Printing Office, 1971), Richard Nixon, 1969, p. 18.

81. See Pierre Salinger's interview with Henry Kissinger, "Secretary Kissinger on Foreign Policy from 1969 to 1975," Department of State Newsletter, No. 168 (May 1975), p. 17.

82. U.S., President, U.S. Foreign Policy for the 1970's: A New Strategy for Peace, p. 80.

83. Ibid.

84. U.S., President, U.S. Foreign Policy for the 1970's: Building for Peace; A Report to the Congress by Richard Nixon (Washington, D.C.: Government Printing Office, 25 February 1971), pp. 122-23; also see Abba Eban's assessment of the future of the Middle East in the Jerusalem Post Week-End Magazine, May 30, 1969, p. 3.

85. See President Nixon's news conference of March 4, 1969, in U.S., President, Public Papers of the Presidents of the United States (Washington, D.C.: Government Printing Office, 1971), Richard Nixon, 1969, p. 191.

86. Interview with William B. Quandt, NSC (Middle East) Washington, D.C., July 25, 1977.

87. Joseph Sisco, "The United States and the Arab-Israeli Dispute," The Annals of the Academy of Political and Social Science 384 (July 1969): 67.

88. See the Congressional Quarterly Weekly Report, No. 48, November 29, 1968, p. 3218.

89. See the Gallup Opinion Index, Report 44, February 1969, p. 7.

90. Ibid.

91. Time, May 2, 1969, p. 17.

92. Ibid.

93. Ibid.

94. William B. Quandt, "Domestic Influences on United States Foreign Policy in the Middle East: The View From Washington," in The Middle East: Quest for American Policy, ed. William A. Belling (Albany: State University of New York Press, 1973), p. 269.

95. Ibid.

96. See Warren L. Young, "American Interests in the U.A.R.," New Outlook 13 (January 1976): 29-31.

97. Shlomo Slonim, United States-Israel Relations, 1967-1973: A Study in the Convergence and Divergence of Interests, Jerusalem Papers on Peace Problems, No. 8 (Jerusalem: Leonard Davis Institute for International Relations, Hebrew University, 1974), pp. 12-13.

98. Jerusalem Post, April 14, 1969, p. 8.

99. William B. Quandt, Fuad Jabber, and Ann Mosely Leach, The Politics of Palestinian Nationalism (Berkeley and Los Angeles: University of California Press, 1973), p. 50; also see Ibrahim Abu Lughod, "Altered Realities: The Palestinians since 1967," International Journal 28 (Autumn 1973): 648.

100. Hisham Sharabi, Palestine Guerillas: Their Credibility and Effectiveness, Supplementary Papers, February 1970 (Washington,

D. C.: Center for Strategic and International Studies, Georgetown University, 1970), p. 17.

101. Fuad Jabber, "The Arab regimes and the Palestinian Revolution, 1967-1971," Journal of Palestine Studies 2 (Winter 1973): 87.

102. Abu-Lughod, "Altered Realities: The Palestinians since 1967," p. 658.

103. Michael Hudson, "The Palestinian Arab Resistance Movement: Its Significance in the Middle East Crisis," The Middle East Journal 23 (Summer 1969): 299.

104. Jabber, "The Arab Regimes and the Palestinian Revolution," 1967-1971, p. 85.

105. Ibid., 87.

106. Interview with Harold Saunders.

107. See the comments by the U.S. ambassador to the United Nations, Charles Yost, cited in the Jerusalem Post, February 13, 1969, p. 1; also see Hudson, "The Palestinian Arab Resistance Movement: Its Significance in the Middle East Crisis," p. 302.

108. Abu-Lughod, "Altered Realities: The Palestinians since 1967," p. 65; also see Tareq Y. Ismael, "The Palestinian Emergence and U.S. Foreign Policy," Middle East Forum 46, nos. 2 & 3 (1970): 69.

109. Quandt, Jabber, and Lesch, The Politics of Palestinian Nationalism, p. 71.

110. Ibid., pp. 71-72.

111. Ibid., p. 96.

112. Ibid., pp. 96-99.

113. Ismael, "The Palestinian Emergence and U.S. Foreign Policy," p. 69.

114. Moshe Ma'oz, Soviet and Chinese Relations with the Palestinian Guerrilla Organization, Jerusalem Papers on Peace Problems, No. 4 (Jerusalem: Leonard Davis Institute for International Relations, Hebrew University, 1974), p. 10.

115. Ibid., p. 12.

116. Ibid., pp. 11-12.

117. See the statement by Ishwer Ojha in U.S., Congress, House, Committee on Foreign Affairs, A Sino-Soviet Perspective in the Middle East, Hearings before the Subcommittee on the Near East of the Committee on Foreign Relations, 92d Cong., 2nd sess., 1972, p. 6.

118. Ma'oz, Soviet and Chinese Relations with the Palestinian Guerrilla Organization, p. 17.

119. Hudson, "The Palestinian Arab Resistance Movement: Its Significance in the Middle East Crisis," pp. 302-3.

120. Ibid.

121. Ma'oz, Soviet and Chinese Relations with the Palestinian Guerrilla Organization, p. 20.

122. See Quandt's analysis in The Politics of Palestinian Nationalism, pp. 99-100.

123. See the statement by William Griffith in A Sino-Soviet Perspective in the Middle East, p. 13.

124. Edward R. F. Sheehan, "The United States, the Soviet Union, and Strategic Considerations in the Middle East," Naval War College Review 23 (June 1971): 27.

125. Heikal, The Road to Ramadan, p. 56.

126. See, for instance, Nasser's speech to the second meeting of the National Congress of the Arab Socialist Union, in Al-Ahram, March 28, 1969, p. 4; also see Al-Ahram, April 2, 1969, p. 1, for Nasser's decision to call the first meeting of the Egyptian National Defense Council in order to discuss the minister of defense's report, "Strategy of Confrontation with the Enemy."

127. Interview with a former defense official in the Nixon administration, Washington, D.C., July 7, 1977.

128. Ibid.

129. Ibid.

130. See, for instance, President Nasser's speech in Al-Ahram, May 2, 1969, p. 11.

131. Interview with a former defense official in the Nixon administration, Washington, D.C., July 7, 1977.

4

THE ROGERS PLAN
AND BEYOND

By the end of 1969, the Nixon administration's enthusiasm for its initial approaches to the Middle East conflict had faded. What had happened to reduce the initial expectations? At least three reasons could be cited: The two-power and four-power talks had clearly failed to produce a settlement; the antagonists in the Middle East were as uncompromising as ever; and the diplomatic and military situation in the region was steadily deteriorating. Against this background, the Rogers Plan sought to salvage the negotiating process from a complete breakdown.

THE ROGERS PLAN

On December 9, 1969, Secretary of State Rogers outlined to the American people the State Department's proposal for a settlement of the Arab-Israeli conflict. The speech contained most of the American proposals that were presented earlier to the Soviet Union, on October 28, 1969.[1] In brief, Rogers stressed three principal elements considered necessary for a peaceful settlement.[2] First, there should be a binding commitment, by Israel and Egypt, to peace and a mutual agreement to prevent hostile acts from originating from their respective territories. Second, the Rhodes formula would be used in the negotiating process, and the issues to be negotiated by Egypt and Israel would include the establishment of demilitarized zones, a final agreement on the Gaza Strip, and some safeguards regarding the area of Sharm al-Shaykh. Third, Israel would have to withdraw its forces from the Egyptian territory to the international border of 1949, in return for a peaceful settlement and an end to the state of belligerency between the local parties.

Rogers also emphasized, as part of his plan, an effort by the Nixon administration to achieve a comprehensive peace in the area—a peace including all the states accepting UN Resolution 242 of November 22, 1967. The plan was not an attempt to promote a separate peace between Israel and Egypt.[3] In fact, on December 18 the administration presented a parallel plan to the big four powers regarding a settlement on the Israeli-Jordanian front.[4] In sum, Rogers viewed his plan as a balanced one in which the minimum demands of both sides would be satisfied, i.e., Israeli withdrawal from the occupied territories, in exchange for a formal peace settlement between Israel and the Arab states.[5]

On the Arab side, the Egyptians (officially) neither accepted nor rejected the Rogers Plan, but, in fact, they did not consider it adequate for a settlement.[6] The rejection was made by the Arabs' patron, the Soviet Union. It came as no surprise since the plan was a modified version of the October 28 American proposal to the Soviet Union that the latter never approved. The Soviets were unwilling to support a plan that their local clients had not accepted, and, most importantly, they were against the idea of a peaceful settlement under American auspices.

On December 10, 1969, Israel, too, rejected the Rogers Plan. It considered the American plan a basic contradiction: On the one hand, the administration requested that parties to the Middle East conflict negotiate, while on the other hand, it was laying down the final guidelines for a peaceful settlement. As Israeli Foreign Minister Eban characterized it, ". . . it is unprecedented and very prejudicial and utterly unacceptable for our friends to lay down specific restrictive conditions on vital points in advance of a negotiation."[7] Thus, Israel viewed the Rogers Plan as a threat to its negotiating strategy— it being an appeasement to the Arabs—that would lead, not to a real settlement, but to an Israeli withdrawal similar to the one made from Sinai after 1956.[8] In all, the Israeli and Soviet rejections of the Rogers Plan represented a temporary halt in the Nixon administration's active strategy.

The failure of the Rogers Plan could be attributed also to other reasons. Neither Nixon nor Kissinger supported the plan, though publicly they did not oppose it. In fact, the White House told Secretary Rogers not to press Israel for concessions or to push the idea of "evenhandedness."[9] Nixon believed it was essential for his administration to support Israel, rather than work for compromises in the Arab-Israeli conflict—at least until after the 1972 elections.[10]

Nixon, furthermore, wanted to use the Rogers Plan to improve American relations with the moderate Arab states. He never considered it a final guideline for an overall resolution of the Arab-Israeli conflict. As he stated:

> I knew that the Rogers Plan could never be implemented,
> but I believed that it was important to let the Arab world

know that the United States did not automatically dismiss its case regarding the occupied territories or rule out a compromise settlement of the conflicting claims. With the Rogers Plan on record, I thought it would be easier for the Arab leaders to propose reopening relations with the United States without coming under attack from the hawks and pro-Soviet elements in their own countries. [11]

In addition, Kissinger had personal reservations about the tactics implied by the Rogers Plan. [12] The plan rested on UN Resolution 242 and therefore required Soviet help, but Kissinger was skeptical about the degree of Soviet cooperation and about their intentions in the Middle East. [13] Besides Soviet-American cooperation, the plan required negotiations between the local parties; and, given the American-Israeli differences that now existed, Kissinger feared the Arabs' position would grow inflexible as they became aware of these differences. [14]

Kissinger also felt the foreign-policy bureaucracy had underestimated Israel's will and ability to resist the administration's pressure due to congressional and public support. Kissinger knew it would be very difficult to pressure Israel for concessions in the circumstances where concessions from the Arabs and the Soviet Union were not forthcoming. [15]

Finally, the Rogers approach to the Middle East conflict failed because of the changed military situation in the area. The war of attrition at the Suez Canal, including some actual Soviet military operations, created opposition too great to be overcome by diplomatic negotiations. [16] By 1970, Nixon and Kissinger had viewed the conflict in the Middle East as an East-West conflict through proxies; therefore, diplomatic initiatives such as the four-power talks, the two-power talks, and the Rogers Plan gradually faded from the policy arena.

THE JARRING MISSION

The Jarring mission was established by UN Secretary General U Thant, through the authority provided in Articles III and IV of UN Resolution 242 (November 22, 1967). [17] Ambassador Gunnar V. Jarring of Sweden accepted the assignment as special representative of the UN secretary general and established the headquarters of the UN Middle East Mission in Cyprus. [18] Ambassador Jarring's efforts were primarily aimed at promoting a peaceful agreement between Israel and Arab states such as Egypt and Jordan. To a lesser degree, Lebanon was also involved in the talks. By contrast, Syria stayed out since it did not accept either Resolution 242 or the Jarring mission. [19]

In broad terms, the Jarring discussions with Israel and the
Arab governments involved two types of questions. The first dealt
with the fundamental issues of the Arab-Israeli conflict, as enumer-
ated in Resolution 242. The second encompassed specific concerns
such as the exchange of prisoners of war and other humanitarian
issues.[20]

The first phase of the Jarring mission, which lasted from December 1967 until November 1968, was marked by diametrically
opposed views held by Israel and by the Arab states regarding the
mechanics of the negotiations. Israel insisted that there would be no
withdrawal from the occupied territories until a peace treaty was
agreed upon through direct negotiations. In line with this view, it
presented to Jarring, on December 27, several proposals for peace
with Egypt. These proposals covered a number of issues related to
the economic, territorial, and political—especially security and
navigation—dimensions of the conflict.[21] Egypt and Jordan, on the
other hand, insisted these issues could not be discussed until Israel
had withdrawn its forces from the occupied territories to the border
lines of June 4, 1967.[22] As a maximum concession to the Jarring
mission, Egypt and Jordan agreed to accept negotiations if Israel
were ready to state in specific language that it would implement all
the provisions of Resolution 242. Israel responded by noting that its
original acceptance of the resolution implied acceptance of all its
provisions. Egypt and Jordan then affirmed their willingness to implement Resolution 242 as a "package deal" and insisted that Israel
should do the same. Jerusalem defined the Arab demands as requiring
exactly what it had always requested—sitting down and directly negotiating the package deal. The dialogue always seemed to circle back
to its point of origin. Neither side, the Arabs or the Israelis, was
willing to compromise its political positions. The first phase of the
Jarring mission, therefore, came to an abrupt end.

The second phase of the UN representative's mission, which
lasted from November 1968 until June 1970, involved a brief period
of shuttle diplomacy. Ambassador Jarring submitted a series of questions to the Arabs and the Israelis regarding their attitudes toward
Resolution 242.[23] But the replies were similar to each side's earlier
interpretations of the resolution; Jarring's reconciliation mission
proved a failure. On April 5, 1969, he returned to Moscow to resume
his duties as Sweden's ambassador to the Soviet Union.[24]

There was one more effort by Jarring. This time he sought to
hold the talks under his (personal) auspices. In June 1970, the Nixon
administration urged Israel, Egypt, and Jordan to participate in the
discussions under Jarring's renewed efforts. Specifically, the administration was worried about the area's deteriorating situation caused
by the war of attrition between Israel and Egypt (which included Israel's

deep-penetration bombing).[25] The administration felt the Jarring discussions had a good chance to achieve at least a temporary cease-fire. The administration hoped Jarring's mission would, in the long run, successfully mediate Israel's withdrawal from the occupied territories, in return for Arab commitments to peace.[26]

Eventually, the Nixon administration resorted to a two-stage policy. In the first stage, American negotiations with Israel concerning military weapons would be used "to encourage Israel's discussions with Jarring."[27] As a second stage, the administration decided to augment Jarring's efforts by conducting bilateral talks with both the Arab and Israeli governments.

These American bilateral talks eventually produced a cease-fire in the war of attrition (which had the potential to escalate into an East-West war). Both Egypt and Israel accepted the American proposals for a standstill cease-fire agreement effective August 7, 1970.[28] However, immediately after the cease-fire went into effect, Israel made several charges regarding Egyptian violations of the agreement. In fact, Egypt engaged in a large-scale violation of the standstill zone, but the Nixon administration, at first, refused to admit the violations because it was anxious to bring Israel back to the Jarring talks; it also wanted to extend the cease-fire beyond its expiration date of November 1970. Israel refused to return to the discussions until the cease-fire violations were rectified. The American initiative thus came to an abrupt halt as Egypt failed to rescind her violations of the cease-fire agreement.

At this point in time, a new explosion in the Middle East conflict occurred in the Jordanian civil war, which later became known as "Black September." As a result of the events, American policy abandoned the pressure on Israel and replaced it, at least temporarily, with a more partisan, pro-Israel alignment to curtail the Syrian threat of war (with Soviet aid) against King Hussein's government in Jordan.

On October 15, 1970, the administration approved $90 million worth of arms for Israel.[29] Kissinger, then, increased promises of financial aid and military weapons to Israel in order to bolster Israel's security and to entice it to return to the talks under Jarring.[30] On December 28, Israel announced that it would resume discussions.

The Jarring mission was reactivated in January 1971. In this round of discussions, Jarring sought parallel and simultaneous prior commitments from the regional parties on the major issues of the Middle East conflict. Jarring believed his approach would clarify, in greater detail, the attitudes of both sides and would contribute to an eventual peace settlement.[31] On February 8, 1971, Jarring handed Egypt and Israel identical aides-mémoire requesting them to make prior commitments to him. The replies were made later in February.

They were basically a repetition of earlier positions and included no breakthroughs for a peace agreement.[32] The Jarring mission had reached its final impasse. The Nixon administration now switched its efforts from the mission to the promotion of an interim agreement between Israel and Egypt for reopening the Suez Canal.

Jarring's multilateral mediation efforts failed for a number of reasons. To begin with, both the Arabs and the Israelis, as well as the two superpowers, recognized that Jarring and the United Nations did not possess sufficient power to succeed; clearly, the Jarring mission had inadequate leverage to move the parties toward a compromise peace settlement. For instance, Israel supported the Jarring mission at times because it was even less enthusiastic about the other approaches, namely, the two-power and the four-power talks and the Rogers Plan. The Soviets and the Arabs, in turn, went along with the mission mainly because the talks were conducted under UN auspices rather than directly with Israel. The Soviets, in particular, preferred the United Nations—despite their general, a priori preference for two-power talks—because they would be involved actively in the negotiating process. By contrast, the Soviets resisted the unilateral American approach, such as the Rogers Plan, because it intended to put the United States in control of the negotiating process, thus isolating the Soviet Union from opportunities to pursue its interests in the Middle East.[33]

Second, Jarring could not get the Arabs and the Israelis to compromise their interpretations of Resolution 242. Israel regarded the resolution as a statement of principles or as a framework for agreement within which the parties would negotiate a peace. The Arab states (Egypt and Jordan), on the other hand, considered Resolution 242 an actual settlement of the dispute; they insisted it was Jarring's mandate to carry out the agreed-upon settlement.[34]

Third, the changed military situation in the Middle East, in the light of the war of attrition between Israel and Egypt and the inter-Arab conflict stemming from Syria's threatened invasion during the Jordanian civil war, diverted the attention of the major powers and prevented them from giving full support to the Jarring mission. Henry Kissinger, in particular, was worried about the increased Soviet military activity in Egypt; he worried about its regional and global implications. Israel, on the other hand, was concerned about Soviet arms shipments to Egypt, especially the SAM-2 and SAM-3 missiles. Israel believed the balance of power might favor the Arabs in the next round of fighting.[35] These security concerns overshadowed Israel's (and America's) interests in the Jarring mission.

Finally, the mission collapsed because the Nixon administration stopped supporting it. Jarring initially received strong American support. Under the umbrella of the United Nations, the American government appeared to be neutral, or even pro-Arab since Egypt and Jordan reacted positively to the mission as they defined it. However, after Washington was forced to admit Egypt's large-scale violation of the American-sponsored standstill agreement (a violation which received Moscow's secret approval), and after the threat to Western interests from the Syrian invasion of Jordan (again, tacitly supported by the Soviet Union), the Jarring mission no longer embodied a viable purpose in American Middle East policy. [36]

Kissinger now became much more concerned about the Soviet factor inasmuch as the Soviets had failed to exercise the restraint and the responsibilities that were to serve as an essential trade-off in the policy of détente.

U.S. POLICY AND THE WAR OF ATTRITION: 1970

By 1970, American policy makers had realized the limitations to the various approaches to the Arab-Israeli conflict: the two-power talks, the four-power talks, the Rogers Plan, etc. There was little likelihood of a reconciliation of U.S.-USSR interests in the Middle East. The United States would find it difficult to check the growing Soviet influence in the Middle East or to reconcile the bitter relations among states in the area—the most intractable, of course, being those reflecting the Arab-Israeli dispute.

American relations with Israel, especially after the failure of the Rogers Plan, might have deteriorated further had it not been for two things. First, the Soviets rejected the Rogers Plan; this enabled the Israelis to claim Soviet and Arab opposition to a peace agreement. It also provided an opportunity for new Israeli requests for arms from the United States. Second, the Soviets increased the number of their military advisors and other personnel inside Egypt—a development which had a tremendous impact on the formulation of American foreign policy toward the Middle East. [37]

In effect, direct Soviet involvement in the Middle East conflict added a new dimension to the regional conflict between Israel and the Arab states. The Nixon administration now had to take into account the global implications of Soviet moves such as increased Soviet pressure along the oil-supply route to Western Europe, threats to the security of the southern flank of NATO, and the new antagonism to Israel. In view of these implications, President Nixon, in early April 1970, ordered a complete review of American Middle East policy. The review concentrated on the new Soviet role in Egypt, the growth of Soviet naval power in the Mediterranean, the possibility of another peace initiative to break the diplomatic deadlock between the local parties, and the ongoing war of attrition between Israel and Egypt. [38]

What really motivated this review was not necessarily the problem of finding another peace initiative, but Nixon's and Kissinger's concerns about the rapid expansion of Soviet power; Egypt was becoming a serious threat to the West. [39] In their view, the intensity of Soviet involvement in Egypt called for a new U.S. containment policy toward the Soviet Union, one similar to the American containment policy in Europe after World War II.

Unlike the earlier European situation, however, spheres of influence were not clearly drawn in the Middle East. In assessing its Middle East policy, the administration had to make sure the new containment policy fit within the given parameters of other American Middle East objectives, such as the security of Israel and Western access to oil. It would be important to integrate the resurrected containment efforts into the overall foreign-policy strategy.

On January 31, 1970, the Nixon administration received what Kissinger considered the first Soviet threat to the new administration—a letter from Soviet Premier Kosygin, stating:

> We would like to tell you in all frankness that if Israel
> continues its adventurism, to bomb the territory of the
> U.A.R. and of other states, the Soviet Union will be
> forced to see to it that the Arab states have the means
> at their disposal, with the help of which a due rebuff to
> the arrogant aggressor could be made. [40]

Washington's reply was delivered on February 4. It rejected the Soviet charges; the cease-fire was being violated by both sides; [41] Egypt had started the war of attrition in early 1969; and, finally, it urged a more positive Soviet response to the Rogers Plan and proposed talks on limiting arms shipments to the Middle East. [42] In short, the administration wanted to maintain the military balance of power there.

Kissinger was worried about the escalating military situation in the Middle East. These new developments, symbolized by the war of attrition, might get out of hand. There were rumors of new Soviet weapons being considered for Egypt—very sophisticated weapons that would require Soviet military personnel to operate them. Accordingly, on February 10, Kissinger met with Dobrynin and expressed the administration's opposition to any Soviet combat role in Egypt. [43] In reply (March 10), Dobrynin proposed a de facto cease-fire along the Suez Canal. Additionally, he outlined two other concessions: a settlement that would not only end the state of belligerency, but would also establish a state of peace; and a promise from the front-line Arab states to curb guerrilla (PLO) activity launched (against Israel) from their territories. [44] Kissinger, however, remained unimpressed by the Soviet reply since it avoided the question of Soviet combat forces in the area. The United States, nevertheless, transmitted the Soviet proposal to Israel. To entice the Israelis to agree to the proposed cease-fire, Nixon promised to replace their aircraft losses. Israel, in turn, accepted the proposal in principle—providing that the United States would deliver on the promised arms aid.

After Israel acquiesced to the cease-fire, the Soviets immediately shipped to Egypt their most advanced anti-aircraft system—the SAM-3 missiles.[45] Consequently, Kissinger told Dobrynin on March 20 that America had no choice but to end its efforts to promote the proposed cease-fire. Kissinger insisted the Soviets could not be allowed to gain advantages for their Arab clients at Israel's expense—at the expense of an American client state. U.S. interests in the area could only be protected if the local states realized Washington, not Moscow, controlled the rewards and penalties in the Middle East. Earlier, Kissinger had proposed to the Soviet Union a joint strategy for cooperation to keep the Middle East pacified; but Moscow rejected the offer—in fact, it overestimated the comparative advantage in not accepting Kissinger's offer and continuing instead to follow a policy of unilateralism with its own client states in the Middle East.

To Kissinger, the proper response to this Soviet action now was to counter it by increasing American military aid to Israel. By contrast, the prevailing view of others in the national security bureaucracy was that Israel—by its bombing deep inside Egypt—had provoked the Soviet action; Israel, therefore, should be more flexible in its negotiating position.[46] Instead of Nixon backing Kissinger, he seemed to lean toward the State Department's assessment. In fact, by the end of March, Nixon had decided to postpone the delivery of Phantom jets to Israel. The move was designed as a message to the Soviet Union, to show that the United States was willing to slow the arms race in the Middle East if the Soviets would restrain their own weapons delivery to their Arab clients. President Nixon also hoped to bolster American influence in the Arab world, particularly with Egypt and Syria.[47]

Israel viewed the Nixon decision as another setback in American-Israeli relations. The American president tried to appease both sides by reassuring Israel of American support, especially in crisis situations. Nonetheless, his decision was based on strategic considerations that transcended regional concerns. President Nixon defended his actions on the basis of a global perspective of American national interests: "What I was trying to do . . . was to construct a completely new set of power relationships in the Middle East—not only between Israel and the Arabs, but also among the United States, Western Europe, and the Soviet Union."[48]

President Nixon realized American national interests were not coterminous with the circle of Israeli national interests, but he could not publicly share it, for PR reasons. U.S. interests included backing off from unconditional support of Israel, if it would reduce the Middle East arms race; would strengthen the moderate Arab states in their rivalry with the Middle East's radical Arab leadership; and would help rebuild relations with Egypt and Syria. For public-relations purposes, Nixon found it necessary to color his policy rationale by conceptualizing it as also being in the true, long-run interests of Israel. In a confidential memorandum to Kissinger, Nixon emphasized that utopian, pro-Israeli liberals of both parties were unreliable in regard to Israel's continuing, long-run security needs. Responding to the liberals who charged Nixon with an anti-Israel policy because he postponed the Phantom shipments to Israel, Nixon retorted:

> What they must realize is that these people are very weak reeds. They will give Israel a lot of lip service, but they are peace-at-any price people. When the chips are down they will cut and run, not only as they are presently cutting and running in Vietnam, but also when any conflict in the Mideast stares them straight in the face.
>
> On the other hand, their real friends (to their great surprise) are people like Goldwater, Buckley, RN et al., who are considered to be hawks on Vietnam but who, in the broader aspects, are basically not cut-and-run people whether it is in Vietnam, the Mideast, Korea, or any place else in the world. . . .
>
> We are going to stand up in Vietnam and in NATO and in the Mideast, but it is a question of all or none. This is it cold turkey, and it is time that our friends in Israel understood this. [49]

Israel, in contrast to the United States and its national interests, could not take this risk when its own survival was at stake. It felt the only way to prevent Egypt from gaining a decisive military advantage was to retaliate by deep-penetration bombing in Egyptian territory.[50] Israel realized this strategic move might extend Soviet involvement in Egypt, but it would have to count on the Nixon administration to check Soviet advancements there.[51] Therefore, the war of attrition would not only expose the weakness of Nasser's regime to the whole world, but also divert the attention of the big powers from discussing a peace agreement. Nevertheless, the ultimate outcome of the Israeli decision for counterattrition was quite different from what the Israeli leaders had expected. Even though Israel had demonstrated its military superiority, the Nasser regime was not shaken. More importantly, Israel's strategy of retaliation did result in driving Egypt closer to the Soviet Union.[52] Consequently, the prospects of a superpower confrontation increased as a result of the expanded Soviet involvement in Egypt.

American policy makers were deeply troubled by the possibility of the Middle East conflict escalating into a global confrontation. In fact, the extended Soviet involvement in the Middle East prompted the Defense Department to play a more active role in Washington's decision making. From the beginning of 1970, every major decision on the Middle East was heavily influenced by the Defense Department.[53] The secretary of defense, for instance, forwarded position papers to President Nixon on all important aspects of the Middle East conflict, including the cease-fire initiative of July-August 1970, and the Israeli requests for more sophisticated weapons such as the F-4 Phantom jets.[54]

In summary, during the two-power and four-power talks, the Defense Department had only a secondary role. With the increased Soviet military involvement in Egypt, however, American military planners came to assume a primary role in the decision-making process regarding the Arab-Israeli conflict.

The increased Soviet military presence in Egypt also gave Kissinger the opportunity to transfer Middle East decision making from the national security bureaucracy to the White House. Kissinger clearly preferred to exclude the Defense Department from involvement in the diplomatic transactions with the Middle East.[55] As early as the spring of 1970, he was annoyed at the Department of Defense for "dragging its feet" and delaying arms transfers to Israel.[56] There were critics, however, who charged that Kissinger was already playing the game of duplicity (as he did later during the Yom Kippur War)— being angry publicly while secretly supporting the Defense Department's restraint in arms shipments to Israel.

By this time, the Israelis had started to contact Kissinger and complain about the Defense Department tactics regarding arms transfers. In addition, Israel supported the short-circuiting of U.S.-Middle East decision making by avoiding the State Department, which traditionally handled the Middle East conflict.[57] In general, the Israelis resented the idea of linking arms transfers to the progress of the talks. A case in point was the Nixon administration's linking of the second Israeli request for Phantom jets with Israel's acceptance of the cease-fire agreement, in July-August 1970.[58]

In addition to withholding the delivery of Phantom jets to Israel, the Nixon administration decided to send Assistant Secretary Sisco to the Middle East for exploratory talks with Nasser. Sisco informed the Egyptian president of the administration's flexibility toward the Arab-Israeli conflict; it was trying to pursue a "balanced policy."[59] Sisco presented a rather convincing position to Nasser: The United States, alone, had the ultimate power to pressure Israel's withdrawal from the occupied territories; the Rogers Plan was the appropriate framework for peace.[60] Nasser, in turn, emphasized that the United States continued to support Israel in the United Nations, regardless of its actions against Egypt. He also pointed out Israel's use of American warplanes to make deep-penetration bombing runs into Egyptian territory.[61] Although the meeting between Nasser and Sisco was unproductive, it had given the administration a better view of the Egyptian position regarding the Rogers Plan.

Despite the failure of Sisco's visit, the State Department decided—after the NSC meeting of June 10—to have Secretary of State Rogers take the initiative again in asking Israel and the Arab states "to stop shooting and start talking."[62] The State Department preferred to have its new initiative linked to the Jarring mission. In addition, it urged the local parties to agree to a standstill cease-fire of at least 90 days.

Kissinger was skeptical about the new State Department initiative. He presented his objections to various aspects of the plan to President Nixon. In the first place, he felt the plan was not viable. It embodied "a little arms and a little proposal" that gave the United States the worst probable outcome. The proposal to dole out a few aircraft to Israel, in return for its acceptance of this limited initiative, would simply be inadequate to resolve the confrontation. Secondly, Kissinger felt the initiative was too much a repetition of the American efforts that had failed in 1969. This plan would simply make the Arab and the Soviet positions more inflexible.[63] Thirdly, Kissinger insisted it was inadvisable to launch the initiative until the issue of Soviet combat forces in Egypt was resolved. Nasser needed to be convinced that only the United States—not the Soviet Union—had the key to a peace agreement. Accordingly, the withdrawal of Soviet forces from Egypt would have to be a part of any settlement.[64]

But rather than back Kissinger, President Nixon decided to approve the State Department's initiative. The reason was simple: President Nixon was clearly not prepared to confront the State Department by telling Rogers his proposal was bad policy. The easy way out was for Nixon not to "make waves" with his foreign policy bureaucracy; the plan would probably "be rejected anyway," and Nixon preferred to "deal with a deadlock," rather than become involved in "another hassle with his bureaucracy."[65]

From the Arab side, the Egyptians had earlier indicated to the Soviets, during Nasser's visit to Moscow in late June 1970, their desire to accept the Rogers initiative.[66] The rationale behind the Egyptian decision was twofold: Israel would only accept an American-sponsored cease-fire, and the Egyptians would gain the opportunity to transfer their missiles to the Suez Canal zone.[67] For these reasons, the Egyptians formally accepted the Rogers initiative on July

22, 1970. Israel, for its part, was under pressure from the Nixon administration to accept the Rogers proposal,[68] and, realizing its heavy military dependency on the United States, it reluctantly did so on July 31. A week later, the cease-fire agreement went into effect between Israel and Egypt. The Soviets now also decided to support the Rogers proposal, including the idea of a military standstill in the canal zone.[69]

Immediately, the Egyptians, with apparent Soviet support and under the cover of darkness, violated the agreement by moving SAM-2 and SAM-3 missile sites into the forbidden standstill zone.[70] Israel promptly pressed the United States for a reconciliation in terms of the agreement which Washington had pressured Israel into accepting. At first, the State Department tried a series of evasive statements and excuses. Eventually, the pressure became too great, and the American government felt compelled to publicly acknowledge (September 3) the Egyptian violation,[71] and the inability of the United States to do anything about it. Henry Kissinger was vindicated in his skepticism about the initiative.

Israel now announced its suspension from participation in the Jarring talks. Soviet aid continued, and the Egyptians went ahead with the building of an extensive missile network that could create major problems for Israeli national security on the Suez front.[72]

By now, Kissinger had convinced President Nixon that the growing Soviet influence posed a greater threat to the United States than the conflict between Israel and Egypt. Thus, the Nixon administration gradually became more concerned about the global implications of Soviet influence in the Middle East than it was with achieving a local peace settlement there. As Kissinger asserted (June 26):

> We are trying to get a [Mideast] settlement in such a way that the moderate regimes are strengthened, and not the radical regimes. . . . But we certainly have to keep in mind that the Russians will judge us by the general purposefulness of our performance everywhere. What they are doing in the Middle East, whatever their intention, poses the gravest threat in the long term for Western Europe and Japan and, therefore, for us.[73]

American commitments in the area were now being put to a severe test. Though the Egyptians eventually removed some of the missiles, Washington was still uncertain as to how far the military balance now favored Egypt.[74] Kissinger, in particular, was concerned about the political impact the Soviet missiles (especially SAM-3 missiles) would have on such an explosive area.[75]

The Soviets showed little restraint in their military aid to Egypt, despite the cease-fire agreement. The Bureau of Intelligence and Research (Department of State) finally concluded it would be appropriate for the administration to exert diplomatic pressure on the Soviets in order to correct the situation.[76] Kissinger and Rogers basically agreed with that conclusion.[77] On September 1, a group of advisors, including Kissinger, Rogers, and Sisco, met with President Nixon to discuss the Middle East. The meeting resulted in a new set of policy directions. Nixon directed a very strong protest to both Cairo and Moscow regarding the cease-fire violations. Israel was asked to resume talks with Ambassador Jarring of the United Nations.[78] Finally, a decision was made to resume the delivery of Phantom jets to Israel.[79] The administration wanted Nasser to consider the shipment of Phantom jets as an answer to Egyptian missile deployment rather than as a retreat from the Rogers peace initiative.

THE PLO-JORDANIAN CIVIL WAR OF 1970

The acceptance of the Rogers initiative by Egypt, Jordan, and Israel had a drastic impact on the events that followed. In Jordan, the major result was a civil war between the forces of King Hussein and the Palestine Liberation Organization. The PLO viewed the Rogers initiative as a threat to its own objectives. The PLO leadership saw Nasser's and Hussein's acceptance as a political setback that could undermine its resistance movement. The Palestinian National Council, convening in late August 1970, denounced the Rogers initiative; at the extreme, some factions also called for Hussein's destruction.[80] One of these factions, the Popular Front for the Liberation of Palestine, carried out a series of hijackings at the beginning of September. Its objectives seemed to be threefold: to force Israel (and some European countries) to release guerrilla prisoners, to gain a militant reputation, and to provide a confrontation with the Hussein regime.[81] These events ultimately resulted in open warfare between the Palestinians and Hussein's forces in September 1970.

To Kissinger and the president, the deteriorating situation in Jordan was more than just a civil war between a moderate Arab regime and Palestinian guerrilla extremists.[82] In their view, Soviet influence was paramount. At the beginning of the civil war, Kissinger observed, "It looks like the Soviets are pushing the Syrians and the Syrians are pushing the Palestinians. The Palestinians don't need much pushing."[83]

The Nixon administration insisted the United States could not allow pro-Soviet Arab governments to use force against King Hussein's government.[84] First, Kissinger believed a Soviet-inspired PLO toppling of King Hussein might trigger a wider war in the Middle East because Israel most likely would find a revolutionary regime in Jordan intolerable. Secondly, the administration believed an Israeli preventive strike against the PLO in Jordan might lead to interventions by Soviet clients such as Syria, Iraq, or Egypt, which would certainly increase the possibility of a Soviet-American confrontation in the Middle East. Thirdly, Kissinger moved to demonstrate a resolve, backed by force, to correct Soviet misperceptions about the Nixon Doctrine. The best way to eliminate any misperception was to use the threat of American military power to confront any Soviet client state threatening the integrity of Jordan, Saudi Arabia, or Iran.[85] It was important to dispel any Soviet illusions about the Nixon Doctrine being a cover for weakness.

In fact, the Nixon administration had been worried about the survival of the Jordanian and the Lebanese regimes for some time. For instance, on June 11, the Washington Special Action Group (WSAG), a subgroup of the NSC concerned with crisis management, met to explore the circumstances under which Americans would have to be evacuated from Jordan, and the kind of response that would be given to King Hussein if he asked for American aid.[86] In general, Kissinger insisted on strong American support for the Hussein regime. Other voices in the WSAG meetings were more hesitant. (The Cambodian operations were still in progress and the pickets were still stationed near the White House.) Some WSAG voices felt the very act of American military intervention in Jordan would discredit King Hussein in the Arab world.[87]

Again in July, there was some discussion within the national security bureaucracy about the possibility of active American intervention should the regimes of either Jordan or Lebanon be threatened; but all options had serious liabilities for American policy makers. The United States lacked sufficient ground forces in the area. There was a lack of effective staging areas in the eastern Mediterranean region if it became necessary to airlift troops to the Middle East.[88] Only Israel could supply the ground and air support if the situation required it, even though the two Arab regimes would be highly reluctant to ask for Israeli intervention. This option had two additional problems since it assumed American military aid to Israel. One problem was the budgetary aspect of replacing military materials that, on this short notice, would have to be taken from the existing supplies in the American arsenal.[89] The other problem was the difference of opinion between the Defense Department and the State Department/NSC staff over the supplying of arms to Israel. The State Department/NSC staff was inclined to send arms with no strings attached; the Defense Department favored obtaining some concessions from Israel regarding the negotiations over the occupied territories.[90] Why was the Defense Department so keen on negotiations? It wanted a peace agreement between Israel and the Arab states because it felt American strength vis-à-vis the Soviet Union was diminishing in the eastern Mediterranean area. Soviet power and influence in the area might undermine Western security, including the security of Israel, [91] in the context of America's continued support of Israel in the Arab-Israeli dispute.

By September, the Jordanian regime was facing threats from the extremist factions of the PLO and, to a lesser degree, from the troops stationed in eastern Jordan—these were still in Jordan from the 1967 war. Accordingly, on September 8, President Nixon met with Rogers, Kissinger, Sisco, and other advisors to discuss the Jordanian crisis. Rogers, for his part, did not favor any military resolution of the crisis. Nixon, in turn, made no decisions; he preferred, nonetheless, an American intervention rather than an Israeli one should such a situation develop in the future. President Nixon, in a personal aside to Kissinger, suggested the hijackings should be used as a pretext to defeat the PLO. [92]

On September 9, the WSAG met to devise a political and military strategy to deal with the crisis. Politically, the participants recommended American pressure on the European countries—West Germany, Britain, and France—affected by the hijackings so as to discourage them from making their own separate deals with the PLO. [93] Militarily, Kissinger preferred—for the sake of preserving American long-term interests in the Middle East—the use of American forces for evacuation purposes only; with American forces still in Vietnam, Kissinger felt there was too great a risk in becoming militarily involved in Jordan in a possible long-term military action against Syria and Iraq. The national security advisor therefore favored the use of Israeli forces to counter any intervention by either Syria or Iraq. This contrasted with Nixon's views, as mentioned above; the president opposed the use of Israeli forces to resolve the crisis. [94]

On September 10, the WSAG met again to discuss the situation in Jordan. The Defense Department opposed President Nixon's earlier proposal to use American military forces if Syria or Iraq moved militarily against King Hussein's government; the department especially opposed the involvement of American ground forces in the Middle East. [95] Kissinger, on the other hand, wanted no specific recommendations to be given to Nixon. The purpose should be to make a range of options available to the president—options including the use of ground forces. [96] The following day some State Department officials sounded out the Defense Department as to whether the United States could pose a "credible threat" to Soviet military intervention in the Middle East. The department's reply was "not really." [97] Given this assessment, the national security bureaucracy reached a general consensus: The NATO bases in Greece were indispensable to any American action in the Mediterranean area; accordingly, the United States should immediately proceed to improve its relations with that country. [98]

By September 16, the fighting between the PLO and the Jordanian army had escalated into a full-scale civil war. From the outset, the Nixon administration warned against outside intervention; the intent was to discourage the Soviets and their local clients from intervening in Jordan. In demonstrating its commitment to the Hussein regime, Washington kept augmenting American military forces in the area. President Nixon could afford the luxury of another aside to Henry Kissinger—this time an emotional outburst after the giving of orders for the rapid deployment of American military forces, triggered by the outbreak of the Jordanian civil war; said Nixon, "The main thing is there's nothing better than a little confrontation now and then, a little excitement."[99] In Nixon's view, if the United States appeared to be capable of carrying out highly unpredictable actions, the Soviets might have second thoughts about intervention in the war.[100] Nixon and Kissinger had already demonstrated unpredictability to the Soviets in the spring of 1970 when the United States invaded Cambodia. As a strategic thinker, Kissinger linked the impact of an action in one area upon another; he hoped the Soviets would get the appropriate message at the global and regional levels.

From the American standpoint, the civil war required close cooperation among Washington, Israel, and the Hussein regime. In fact, the Israelis kept advising the administration of their strategic planning for the area. Nixon and Kissinger did not object to this planning since they found Israel's position to be basically sound;[101] however, both Kissinger and Nixon wanted Israel to recognize Washington as the strategic command center that included decision making regarding an Israeli intervention in the war. Both believed American power and influence had to be used not only as a deterring factor against the possibility of Soviet adventurism, but also as a restraining factor against a premature Israeli action.[102] In the end, the Israelis agreed with the administration; both felt Hussein should solve the problem by himself if his military force was adequate to get the job done.

Two new developments (December 18 and 20) threatened the above strategy decision relegating the military task to Hussein: The Soviet Union was discovered constructing a nuclear-submarine base in Cienfuegos Bay, in Cuba; and Syrian tanks crossed the border into Jordan in support of the PLO against King Hussein's army.

The Nixon administration saw the Soviet activity in Cuba as a clear violation of the 1962 understanding, between Kennedy and Khrushchev, regarding Cuba in the aftermath of the October 1962 missile crisis. In 1962, the United States had agreed not to move against Castro's Cuba, in exchange for a Soviet promise to keep its nuclear weapons out of the island. Nixon and Kissinger now viewed Soviet actions in Cuba as a test of American global resiliency against Soviet advancements in several troubled areas, including the Middle East.

In the context of these somber Soviet-initiated developments, it was easy for the Nixon administration to assume Soviet encouragement in the Syrian invasion of Jordan. The administration based its assumption on several factors. There were the recent Soviet missile violations in the Suez Canal standstill zone. At the same time, the Soviet actions in Cuba were considered contrary to the spirit of détente. Kissinger and Nixon also suspected the Soviets might be testing American determination and staying power in a military commitment, in view of domestic anti-Vietnam protests. Finally, Kissinger was apprehensive about the Soviets becoming operationally involved within Syria, as they had in Egypt, with the result of releasing Syrian units to attack Jordan. [103]

The administration's response to the Syrian invasion was decisive: The Syrians were asked to halt the invasion forthwith. Kissinger promptly sent a hard-line communication to the Kremlin when news of the Syrian invasion broke. [104] Some American forces were put on alert and dispatched to the eastern Mediterranean to augment the Sixth Fleet. [105] Nixon at first issued an order approving Israeli air strikes and ground operations against the Syrian's invasion force. According to Kissinger's account of the events, the president was induced, by Kissinger, to modify the order to "an approval in principle," subject to further consultation. [106]

The administration's immediate strategy called for leaning on the Soviets to pressure the Syrians to withdraw to their borders. Nixon, in particular, was hardly encouraged by the Soviet note of September 18, which diverted attention from the real issue by asking for a mutual pledge against outside intervention in Jordan. [107] By contrast, Kissinger was encouraged by the Soviet note, but he was still angry about Soviet behavior. As he remarked to a Soviet diplomat during the crisis, "You and your client started it, and have to end it." [108] By September 22, Jordanian forces had gained the upper hand in the fighting. Shortly afterwards, the remnants of the Syrian forces started to withdraw back into Syria. The net outcome of the civil war was the biggest political and military defeat the PLO had suffered since its establishment in 1964.

The PLO's defeat could be attributed to several factors. First, the limited Syrian intervention in Jordan lacked air support, and there was no significant coordination between the Syrians and the PLO. Furthermore, the Iraqi troops, which were stationed in Jordan, remained aloof from the fighting and gave no military assistance to the PLO. And worse, Egypt, the PLO's main political backer, did not come to its aid either. Nasser opposed Hussein's move against the

PLO, but, at the same time, he recognized the tactical need for preserving the Hussein regime; after all, Jordan agreed with Egypt on
the principle of a peaceful settlement with Israel.[109]

Nixon and Kissinger were concerned lest the Soviet Union should
jeopardize détente at the global level by adventuristic policies at the
Middle East regional level. For instance, in terms of the Nixon Doctrine, the outcome of the crisis confirmed the Kissinger belief that
Israel and Jordan were vital anchors for a Middle East peace strategy.[110] The PLO's defeat had restored a degree of stability to the
region at a time when the United States was facing foreign-policy
challenges nearly everywhere—in Vietnam, Cambodia, and Cuba. In
truth, this relative stability was an illusion because the Soviet Union
was still in a position to threaten Western interests if it chose to do
so. Also, from the Palestinian viewpoint, the Jordanian episode was
not totally unproductive because it temporarily stymied American
peace efforts in the region.

Israel attributed the survival of the Hussein regime to the fighting capability of Hussein's forces, American power, and Israeli
threats to intervene in Jordan. In this context, the Israelis kept reminding the Nixon administration, in later years, of their important
role as an ally in saving an American friend, King Hussein. Yet, a
pro-Western regime in Jordan would be even more important to
Israeli security than to that of the United States.[111] Nonetheless,
the Jordanian civil war and its aftermath had forged a strategic unity
between Israel and the United States which lasted until the October
War of 1973.

NOTES

1. William B. Quandt, Decade of Decisions: American Policy
Toward the Arab-Israeli Conflict, 1967-1976 (Berkeley and Los
Angeles: University of California Press, 1977), pp. 89-91.

2. William Rogers, "A Lasting Peace in the Middle East: An
American View," Department of State Bulletin 62 (January 5, 1970):
10-11.

3. Ibid., p. 10.

4. Quandt, Decade of Decisions, pp. 91-92.

5. Richard Nixon, RN: The Memoirs of Richard Nixon (New
York: Grosset and Dunlap, 1978), p. 478.

6. Mohammed Heikal, The Road to Ramadan (New York:
Quadrangle, 1975), p. 91.

7. The Jerusalem Post Week-End Magazine, January 23, 1973,
p. 3.

8. Ibid.; also see Meir's statement to the Israeli Knesset in the
Jerusalem Post, December 30, 1969, p. 3.

9. Interview with Ray Cline, Department of State, Washington, D.C., March 16, 1977.

10. Ibid.

11. Nixon, RN: The Memoirs of Richard Nixon; 479; in fact, Nixon informed the American Jewish community, through his aide, Leonard Garnment, and Attorney General John Mitchell, that the Rogers Plan did not originate in the White House; see Henry Kissinger, White House Years (Boston: Little, Brown and Co., 1979), pp. 29-30.

12. Nixon, RN: The Memoirs of Richard Nixon, pp. 478-79.

13. Interview with Walter B. Smith II, Department of State, Washington, D.C., July 25, 1977.

14. Ibid.

15. Quandt, Decade of Decisions, p. 93.

16. Interview with Walter B. Smith.

17. United Nations, Security Council, Resolutions and Decisions of the Security Council, 1967, Security Council Official Records: Twenty-Second Year (New York, 1968), pp. 8-9.

18. United Nations, Security Council, Official Records, Supplement for January, February, and March 1971, Report of the Secretary-General on the activities of the Special Representative to the Middle East, Documents S/10070 and Add. 1 and 2 (New York, 1972), p. 18.

19. Ibid.

20. Bernard Reich, "The Jarring Mission and the Search for Peace in the Middle East," The Wiener Library Bulletin 26 (1972):13.

21. United Nations, Report of the Secretary-General, p. 19.

22. Ibid.

23. Ibid., p. 22.

24. Ibid.

25. Reich, "The Jarring Mission and the Search for Peace in the Middle East," p. 16.

26. Quandt, Decade of Decisions, p. 131.

27. Ibid.

28. Reich, "The Jarring Mission and the Search for Peace in the Middle East," p. 16.

29. Quandt, Decade of Decisions, p. 131.

30. Ibid., pp. 131-32.

31. Reich, "The Jarring Mission and the Search for Peace in the Middle East," p. 17.

32. Ibid., pp. 17-18.

33. Ibid., p. 20.

34. United Nations, Report of the Secretary-General, p. 21.

35. Robert J. Pranger, American Policy for Peace in the Middle East, 1969-1971: Problems of Principle, Manoeuvre and Time (Washington, D.C.: American Enterprise Institute for Public Policy Research, 1971), p. 38.

36. Interview with a former defense official in the Nixon administration, Washington, D.C., July 9, 1977.

37. Shlomo Slonim, United States-Israel Relations, 1967-1973: A Study in the Convergence and Divergence of Interests, Jerusalem Papers on Peace Problems, No. 8 (Jerusalem: Leonard Davis Institute for International Relations, 1974), pp. 21-22.

38. Marvin Kalb and Bernard Kalb, Kissinger (Boston: Little, Brown and Co., 1974), p. 190.

39. Interview with Walter B. Smith II, Department of State, Washington, D.C., July 25, 1977.

40. Nixon, RN: The Memoirs of Richard Nixon, p. 479.

41. Henry Kissinger, White House Years (Boston: Little, Brown and Co., 1979), p. 561.

42. Nixon, RN: The Memoirs of Richard Nixon, p. 479.

43. Kissinger, White House Years, p. 562.

44. Ibid., p. 567.

45. Ibid., p. 569.

46. Ibid., pp. 570-71.

47. Nixon, RN: The Memoirs of Richard Nixon; Kissinger asserted that the Pompidou affair triggered Nixon's action to delay the F-4s to Israel, p. 480; see Kissinger, White House Years, pp. 565-66.

48. Ibid., pp. 480-81.

49. Ibid., pp. 481-82.

50. Golda Meir, My Life (New York: G. P. Putnam's Sons, 1971), pp. 381-82.

51. Yair Evron, The Middle East: Nations, Super-Powers and Wars (London: Elek Books, 1973), pp. 111-12; also see Meir, My Life.

52. Evron, The Middle East: Nations, Super-Powers and Wars, pp. 111-12.

53. For instance, see Kissinger, White House Years, p. 563; also, interview with a former defense official in the Nixon administration, Washington, D.C., July 9, 1977.

54. Interview with a former defense official in the Nixon administration, Washington, D.C., July 9, 1977.

55. Ibid.

56. Ibid.

57. Ibid.

58. Ibid.; also see Kissinger, White House Years, p. 576.

59. Heikal, The Road to Ramadan, p. 91.

60. Ibid., p. 92.

61. Ibid.

62. Kissinger, White House Years, pp. 575-76; also see Heikal, The Road to Ramadan, p. 92.

63. Kissinger, White House Years, p. 577.

64. Ibid., p. 578.

65. Ibid., pp. 577-78.

66. Heikal, The Road to Ramadan, p. 95.

67. Ibid.

68. Michael Brecher, Decisions in Israel's Foreign Policy (New Haven: Yale University Press, 1975), p. 493.

69. U.S., Department of State, United States Foreign Policy, 1969-70: A Report of the Secretary of State to Congress, Department of State Publication No. 8575, March 1971 (Washington, D.C.: Government Printing Office, 1971), p. 76.

70. Ibid., p. 77.

71. Interview with Ray Cline, Department of State, Washington, D.C., July 12, 1977. (In fact, Cline accompanied Rogers to the CIA photo laboratory to check the missile violations.)

72. Ibid.

73. Cited in David Landau, Kissinger: The Uses of Power (Boston: Houghton Mifflin Co., 1972), p. 120, note 13; also see Kissinger, White House Years, pp. 579-80.

74. Interview with Ray Cline.

75. Interview with a former defense official in the Nixon administration, Washington, D.C., July 9, 1977; also see Kissinger, White House Years, p. 569.

76. Interview with Ray Cline; also see Kissinger, White House Years, p. 591.

77. Ibid.

78. Kissinger, White House Years, p. 591.

79. Quandt, Decade of Decisions, p. 109.

80. Ibid., pp. 110-111.

81. Ibid., p. 111.

82. Kissinger, White House Years, pp. 596-97.

83. Nixon, RN: The Memoirs of Richard Nixon, p. 483.

84. Ibid.

85. Interview with Ray Cline.

86. Kissinger, White House Years, p. 596.

87. Ibid.

88. Quandt, Decade of Decisions, p. 111.

89. Elmo R. Zumwalt, Jr. On Watch: A Memoir (New York: Quadrangle, 1976), p. 278.

90. Ibid., pp. 278-79.

91. Ibid., p. 279.

92. Kissinger, White House Years, p. 602.

93. Ibid., p. 604.

94. Ibid., p. 606.

95. Zumwalt, On Watch: A Memoir, p. 295.

96. Ibid.

97. Ibid., p. 296.

98. Ibid., p. 297.

99. Kissinger, White House Years, p. 614.

100. Henry Brandon, "Jordan: The Forgotten Crisis (I) Were We Masterful," Foreign Policy, No. 10 (Spring 1973): 167; also see Kissinger, White House Years, pp. 614-15.

101. Interview with Ray Cline.

102. Nixon, RN: The Memoirs of Richard Nixon, p. 484.

103. Interview with Walter B. Smith II.

104. Kissinger, White House Years, p. 619.

105. Nixon, RN: The Memoirs of Richard Nixon, p. 485.

106. Kissinger, White House Years, pp. 625-26.

107. Ibid., p. 617; Nixon, RN: The Memoirs of Richard Nixon, pp. 483-84.

108. Kalb and Kalb, Kissinger, p. 207.

109. Fuad Jabber, "The Arab Regimes and the Palestinian Revolution 1967-71," Journal of Palestine Studies 2 (Winter 1972): 93.

110. Quandt, Decade of Decisions, p. 113.

111. Interview with Walter B. Smith II.

5

U.S. FOREIGN POLICY FROM 1971 TO THE OIL EMBARGO

The Jordanian crisis and its aftermath had a noticeable impact on Kissinger's conceptualization of Middle East politics. The increased Soviet penetration of the area, he now felt, was a threat to Israel. America had to anticipate serious developments because we were, as Kissinger emphasized, committed to the survival of Israel (although not to the occupied territories). America's future assessment of the Arab-Israeli conflict would have to consider the increased Soviet influence in the Middle East. Would the Kremlin be predisposed to gamble with another bold stroke against U.S. interests in the region? The war of attrition and the debacle of the standstill-zone cease-fire escalated problems for American foreign policy in the Middle East. The United States was forced into a greater anti-Soviet focus as well as a greater military orientation toward the problem—this became especially noticeable when the Jordanian civil war exploded on the scene.

The changed American perception of the Middle East situation was not shared by the European allies. Even though most NATO members agreed with the American assessment of Soviet behavior and realized the importance of the Arab-Israeli conflict to American (and other Western) global interests, the major European powers, especially France, refused to share the U.S. perspective. To these Western European states, Israel was not containing Soviet advancements in the Middle East, nor serving as the main bulwark against Soviet dominance. A resolution of the Arab-Israeli conflict would depend not only on the local states, but also on the superpowers.[1] U.S. pressure should be applied to Israel to withdraw from the occupied territories.

In simple terms, the administration now felt a resolution of the Arab-Israeli conflict was primarily the responsibility of the local parties rather than the superpowers. Essentially, this meant the Washington administration was opposed to any resolution imposed by the big powers. After the American experience with the Soviets in the war of attrition and the Syrian threat in the Jordanian civil war, Kissinger opposed efforts to pressure Israel to make concessions.

A group of foreign-policy experts from the Common Market countries met in Munich in November 1970, and agreed to coordinate their foreign policies on such topics as the Middle East and the European security conference. [2] The European Economic Community (EEC) countries then met in Paris and agreed on proposals for a solution to the Middle East problem. [3] Even though the outcome of the Paris meeting was confined only to a working paper, it was a clear indication of an independent European stand. [4] Hitherto, the State Department had always welcomed European support for UN Resolution 242; now it was disturbed by the pro-Palestinian position taken by the European states. Nonetheless, the State Department was not altogether displeased with the EEC's statement on the Middle East because it indicated at least that the European community could act coherently. [5] The European initiative also suggested it would share the American responsibilities in the Middle East and, by implication, help combat the Soviet threat there—outcomes that harmonized with the Nixon Doctrine.

From the Soviet perspective, the European position on the Middle East was a clear sign of political turmoil in NATO. But if this made the Soviets happy, they were less satisfied to see European influence augment American influence in the Middle East. [6]

THE INTERIM AGREEMENT: A U.S. INITIATIVE

The Nixon administration's abandonment of Jarring's mission at the beginning of 1971 had opened the door for other ideas on the Arab-Israeli conflict. An interim agreement was one such idea. First stated publicly in November 1970, by Israeli Defense Minister Moshe Dayan, it would require the Egyptians and the Israelis to reduce their forces along the Suez Canal as a preliminary action to reopening the canal. [7] But Dayan's idea was not popular with American policy makers—despite Kissinger's hint to Golda Meir that it was a good idea—because it would probably require U.S. participation in the form of observers that would supervise the agreement. In their view, any American military involvement would only legitimize parallel Soviet activity on the Egyptian side of the canal, with no assurances of a future withdrawal. [8]

On February 4, 1971, President Sadat of Egypt publicly announced his own interim initiative. Egypt would reopen the canal in return for a partial Israeli withdrawal, provided that such activities would be linked to a final settlement. [9] The Nixon administration urged the Israelis to take Sadat's initiative seriously, and the Israelis reluctantly agreed to explore the initiative further, though they noted that the Nixon administration would do better to concentrate on Soviet advancements.[10] Having obtained this concession from Israel, the White House instructed the State Department to start work on drawing up a concrete interim canal agreement.

President Nixon, for his part, authorized Kissinger to explore this interim-agreement initiative with the concerned governments—the Soviets, the Arabs, and the Israelis—but not to negotiate it. Though Kissinger viewed the idea of an interim agreement as a first step toward a final settlement, he preferred to break the impasse between the antagonists without making prior commitments on ultimate goals. But as he quickly found out, the Soviets would not discuss an interim agreement—only a comprehensive one; similarly, neither the Arabs nor the Israelis were willing to accept an interim agreement at this time.[11]

The American efforts continued, despite Kissinger's reservations. Secretary of State Rogers and Assistant Secretary Sisco visited the Middle East, in May 1971, for exploratory talks on Sadat's diplomatic proposal of February 4. In Egypt, Rogers discussed the possible elements of a "partial solution," i.e., an indefinite cease-fire, the reopening of the Suez Canal, and a limited Israeli withdrawal. He emphasized, however, that the extent of the Israeli withdrawal would depend upon the type of guarantees that Egypt was willing to give.[12] From the Egyptian standpoint, the Rogers proposals were unacceptable because they were not linked to a final settlement. The Egyptians wanted a positive Israeli answer to the Jarring questionnaire and a full withdrawal in two stages.[13] In Israel, Rogers found the leaders even less flexible than the Egyptians. Israel wanted no linkage between an interim agreement and a final one. However, the Israelis did not totally reject Sadat's initiative and, in turn, even offered their own version of a limited withdrawal.[14]

Given these considerations, the Nixon administration began soft-pedalling Sadat's initiative. But with the Soviet activity on the upswing in the region, Nixon and Kissinger realized that a new American initiative was called for, and, after Kissinger's historic trip to Peking in July, President Nixon met with him and other foreign-policy advisors to discuss American options. It was decided to carry out one option—to send Sisco to Israel in order to find out whether it would drop its objection to a limited Egyptian military presence on the east bank of the canal. But Sisco—Nixon personally insisted—should avoid applying any direct pressure on Israel, especially in the light of the upcoming presidential election of 1972. Sisco went to Israel in late July but failed to obtain Israeli acceptance.[15] Clearly, as long as Nixon and Kissinger were unwilling to pressure Israel into changing its negotiating posture, Sadat's initiative would be still-born; in fact, Sadat publicly abandoned it soon afterward. Later, on September 16, he blasted the American stand on the Middle East and called for a joint strategy between Egypt and the Soviet Union to advance their common interests.[16]

Even though Kissinger supported the idea of an interim agreement, he saw it as faulty on several grounds. To begin with, he felt the administration was becoming too quickly involved in the core of the negotiations. The American substantive recommendations on the core issues should have been held up until after the regional parties themselves were nearing an agreement.[17] Kissinger believed that the mediation efforts of Rogers and Sisco had raised false hopes and expectations in their zeal to present each side's negotiating position favorably to the other. In his view, successful negotiations had to be conducted in secret; publicly stated positions in Cairo and Jerusalem created insurmountable barriers to a necessary compromise.[18] By August 1971, the Sadat initiative of February 4 was dead.

Events outside the negotiating arena had also contributed to the failure. Vietnam was increasingly demanding the attention of the highest levels of decision making in Washington. Early in May, Sadat's domestic situation deteriorated when he ousted his rival, Ali Sabry, from power in the Arab Socialist Union. On May 27 the signing of the 15-year Egyptian-Soviet Treaty of Friendship and Cooperation was not reassuring to Washington in terms of future projections of Egyptian foreign policy. After the United States reestablished informal relations with mainland China in July, the Far East absorbed increasing attention and diverted concentrated efforts from the Middle East at the highest policy levels in Washington. Finally, by late 1971, Richard Nixon had become sensitive to the approaching 1972 elections. Nothing must be done to alienate the Zionists, given the important role that domestic group was expected to play in his bid for a second term.

To Kissinger, the idea of an interim agreement was acceptable only if it were not linked to a final settlement;[19] his reasoning was threefold. First, an interim agreement would bring some kind of stability to the area, and, in terms of the Nixon Doctrine, stability was a desired goal at all regional levels. Second, any agreement that would ensure a Soviet military withdrawal from Egypt should be encouraged.[20] Third, since both parties were not ready to negotiate, Israel should not be pressured as long as Soviet military presence threatened its security. Israel would be amenable to a compromise from a position of security, not of insecurity.

Sadat's abandonment of his February initiative did not discourage the State Department from continued efforts to promote an Israeli-Egyptian agreement. On October 4, 1971, Secretary Rogers proposed the idea of "proximity talks," an arrangement in which Israel and Egypt would negotiate under American auspices.[21] Though Sadat accepted the American proposal, Israel was not anxious to engage in such talks until it cleared two important issues with the Nixon administration. First, it wanted an understanding with the administration on arms supply; second, it wanted to know what the American and Soviet roles would be in future negotiations. On November 1, Israel and the United States signed a memorandum of understanding regarding the question of military aid. Israel feared the loss of a source of military supplies.[22] Nixon and Kissinger felt, especially after the new Soviet arms supply to the Arabs, that Israel should negotiate from a position of strength.

Prime Minister Golda Meir, still disturbed by the Soviet military presence in Egypt, went to Washington, in early December 1971, to discuss a new arms agreement. The Soviets were not showing restraint in arms deliveries to their regional clients. Only a long-term agreement would convince the Soviets and their Arab clients that they could not drive a wedge between the United States and Israel, and that any attempted military solution was futile.[23] The administration also felt it was advisable to reach an agreement with Israel before the elections. Besides the obvious purpose, it seemed important to solidify the U.S.-Israeli agreement immediately, because to wait until serious negotiations resumed after the elections would be a direct affront to Egypt at a time when special efforts for Egyptian cooperation would be sought.

The outcome of the Israeli-American discussions was another memorandum of understanding between the two countries (signed on February 2, 1972). The Nixon administration agreed to sell more aircraft to Israel; and, more importantly, it assured Israel the Soviets would play no substantive role in the proposed talks. Washington also promised Israel it would take no initiative in the talks without prior consultations.[24] After signing the February memorandum, Israel agreed to participate in the talks. It was now the Egyptians' turn to cause trouble; they refused to join the talks. The Egyptians clearly realized President Nixon would not allow pressure on Israel in a presidential-election year. By now, Egypt had also realized it was Kissinger and his White House back channel, not Rogers's State Department, that handled the important foreign-policy problems, e.g., détente with the Soviet Union and the establishment of informal relations with China.[25]

As a result of the diplomatic impasse, the White House instructed the State Department not to push any new initiative until after the 1972 presidential election.[26] A case in point was the Hussein initiative, of March 1972, announcing a plan to link a quasi-autonomous Palestinian state of the West Bank, with Jordan to form a United Arab Kingdom. One would have expected the State Department to seize this opportunity. In view of Nixon's directive, however, the Hussein plan was not taken seriously in Washington, especially in the light of Israeli and Egyptian opposition to it.[27]

In summary, Nixon's critics have charged that the administration compartmentalized the Middle East problem—that it failed to view the Arab-Israeli conflict in the total perspective.[28] Perhaps it is more accurate to emphasize the energies devoted to other demanding issues such as the Vietnam war, a new policy toward mainland China, new security arrangements in central Europe, etc; the administration's belief that the confronting parties in the Middle East were not yet amenable to a compromise settlement; and a freeze, until after the 1972 elections, on diplomatic efforts attempting to reconcile controversial issues. Ambassadors and emissaries to the Middle East became "active in a holding pattern." They were encouraged to give the appearance of exploring new avenues to an Arab-Israeli peace; but in fact, the administration wanted no serious innovations until after the elections.[29]

THE UNITED STATES AND THE USSR
IN THE MIDDLE EAST

The pattern of traditional Soviet foreign policy can be described in terms of a triad: expand-consolidate-hold. After the easing of the cold war, however, global and regional events, the process of détente, and domestic constraints superimposed a new pattern on Soviet policy: one of holding and exploring.[30] In this pattern the Soviet Union emphasized maintaining and stabilizing its relations with the Western world in order to gain more flexibility in dealing with China and in exploring new opportunities for expanding its influence in the Middle East, North Africa, and the Indian Ocean.[31]

The Soviets pursued a strategy of controlled tension, i.e., a no-war, no-peace situation in the Middle East. In part, Moscow's strategy was designed to insure Arab dependency on the Soviet Union, but it was also aimed at maximizing Soviet interests in the area while avoiding a confrontation with the United States. Specifically, to enhance their overall position, the Soviets embarked on a two-track military program. In the Mediterranean, the Soviets expanded their naval squadron so as to pose a threat to NATO's southern flank. In Egypt, the Soviets increased their military mission to the point where it could threaten Israeli security, even though the original purpose of the Soviet military mission was to deter Israeli deep-penetration bombing inside Egypt. In all, the heavy military commitment to Egypt in 1970-71 marked a significant departure from Moscow's previous cautious behavior toward the Arab-Israeli conflict.

The new Soviet military expansion in the Middle East could be explained on several grounds: American involvement in Vietnam had distracted the Nixon administration's attention from the Middle East;

the final British withdrawal from the Persian Gulf area by 1971 had made it attractive for the Soviets to fill the military vacuum of the region; and the growing strategic parity between the Soviet Union and the United States provided the Soviets with an opportunity to test Western resolve in the Middle East. Closely linked to these Soviet incentives was the domestic political instability of most states in the area. It provided the Soviets the opportunity to pose as an alternative to the United States for shaky regimes needing outside support. In addition, available evidence suggests that the Soviet military pushed Moscow's leadership into Middle East military expansion because of strategic concerns.[32] Finally, the success of Ostpolitik in Europe enabled the Soviets to devote more time to the eastern Mediterranean area.[33]

To augment their military effort in Egypt, the Soviets consummated, in May 1971, the Soviet-Egyptian Treaty of Friendship and Cooperation. Similar treaties were signed with India in August 1971 and with Iraq in April 1972. The Soviet Union pushed for the treaty with Egypt to discourage any attempt by Washington to wean Egypt from its pro-Moscow position.[34] Equally important, the Soviets wanted to insure their long-term position in the Middle East in case the United States was successful in producing an interim agreement between Israel and Egypt. The Kremlin also hoped the new treaty would restrain Egyptian behavior toward Israel. Sadat had indicated his impatience with a no-war, no-peace status quo; he implied a willingness to risk a general war in the area.

The Soviet treaty with Iraq was designed to serve two aims: The Soviets regarded it as a backup option in the Arab world in case Sadat reversed some of Nasser's policies; also, it would give the Soviets a strong foothold in the Persian Gulf, with its abundant oil resources, especially now, after the British withdrawal from the Persian Gulf area in December 1971.[35]

President Nixon had realized, by the fall of 1971, that a settlement acceptable to Israel was unobtainable. As mentioned above, he decided—despite Rogers's proposal for proximity talks—to have Kissinger's efforts directed toward keeping things quiet until after the 1972 election; i.e., he wanted negotiations behind the scenes to buy time. Accordingly, Kissinger wanted to explore whether the Soviets were prepared to moderate their position; otherwise, he intended to drag the negotiations out until they or their Arab clients changed their position.[36]

Given these considerations, on September 30, 1971, Kissinger met with Gromyko to discuss the Middle East. In Kissinger's opinion, the discussions should be kept at the exploratory level before moving to concrete discussions. Gromyko, on the other hand, rejected Kissinger's approach. He wanted an interim agreement linked to a comprehensive one. He also stressed the need for a full Israeli withdrawal from the occupied territories. In effect, he was advocating the maximum Arab position on a settlement.[37] Kissinger, quite obviously, was unwilling to accept these terms.

The discussions between Kissinger and the Soviets, nonetheless, were resumed in January and February. As usual, the Soviets were unprepared to explore a limited disengagement without a linkage to a final settlement. In a memorandum to Nixon, Kissinger explained the Soviet dilemma:

> Their client cannot win a war with the Israelis. Therefore a continuation of the present simmering crisis can only lead to one of two situations: either a conviction on the part of the Arabs that their alliance with the Soviet Union is inadequate to produce a settlement, or a war by the Egyptians which would face the Soviets with a decision on military support and a risk out of all proportion to anything that could be achieved.[38]

Kissinger suggested a formula to break the diplomatic deadlock. The proposal called for the separation of the issue of security from that of sovereignty; Egypt would regain sovereignty over all of Sinai, but Israel would be allowed to retain several military posts there for security reasons. The Soviets, however, were unenthusiastic about Kissinger's formula. Indeed, this time (March 1972) the Soviets put the burden on Kissinger; he was to come up with an American position regarding a comprehensive settlement; after all, it would be easier for them, they argued, to consider an American position than to deviate from the position of their Arab clients.[39]

Kissinger was reluctant to push for such a settlement. In his view, a comprehensive American settlement approved by Israel would be rejected by the Arabs; he also believed the Soviets would use the American position to demonstrate to their Arab clients the futility of dealing with the United States. At the same time, he feared that an independent (from Israel) American position would be exploited by the Soviets as a showcase (to the Arabs) of what could be achieved via Moscow. In short, Kissinger stuck to his strategy of dragging the discussions out without making an explicit American proposal. The Arabs should realize it was Washington, and not Moscow, that held the key for a settlement.[40] Again, the issue of a settlement was raised by the Soviets when Kissinger visited Moscow on April 20-24, to prepare for the proposed summit. The Soviets presented their own version of a comprehensive settlement under which a limited disengagement on the Egyptian-Israeli front was possible, providing it was linked to what they described as the "global" issues. In truth, what they ultimately wanted was a comprehensive settlement (on their own terms) to be accompanied by the withdrawal of American forces from Iran.[41] Kissinger obviously turned down the Soviets' proposals.

Against this background, Nixon and Kissinger and the Soviet leadership devoted one meeting at the summit conference in Moscow (May 1972) to the Middle East. During the meeting, the Soviets expressed concern over that region's explosive nature.[42] As it turned out, Kissinger and Gromyko reached a tentative working agreement on seven principles that would serve as a framework for an Arab-Israeli settlement. In brief, it covered the problems of an Israeli withdrawal from the occupied territories, and such other issues as security arrangements, freedom of navigation, and peace between Israel and the Arab states.[43] Nixon and Kissinger intended, by this agreement, to buy time—a delaying tactic until they could see a real change in either the Soviet or the Arab position, or in both;[44] at the same time, they considered it a holding action until after the upcoming election in November.

Even though this agreement remained a secret, the May summit ended with a joint statement of Basic Principles, which was issued on May 29, 1972. This statement dealt with a number of major international problems including the Middle East. Regarding the Arab-Israeli conflict, the Soviet-American Basic Principles Agreement stated, in part:

> The two Sides set out their positions on this question.
> They reaffirm their support for a peaceful settlement
> in the Middle East in accordance with Security Council
> Resolution 242. . . . In the view of the U.S. and the
> U.S.S.R., the achievement of such a settlement would
> open prospects for the normalization of the Middle East
> situation and would permit, in particular, consideration
> of further steps to bring about a military relaxation in
> that area.[45]

The Egyptians viewed the outcome of the summit meeting with apprehension; the two superpowers seemed to assign a lower priority to the Middle East as compared to SALT and other outstanding issues of mutual interest. If the Egyptians were right, then the two superpowers were more interested in stabilizing détente than in solving regional problems that might undermine that process.[46] The Egyptians were worried because superpower perpetuation of the status quo in the Middle East would favor Israel.[47]

In April 1972 the new secret channel of communication between Cairo and Kissinger's desk in the White House was opened. It was designed to bypass the regular State Department channel—a channel which Sadat felt had involved an element of deception and incredibility, since it lacked White House support in the February-August negotiations concerning an interim Egyptian-Israeli agreement on the Sinai front. Sadat felt he had been misled in the State Department's diplomatic initiative by Rogers, Sisco, and Ambassador Donald Bergus in Cairo.

Now, after the May 1972 superpower summit memorandum was announced, Egypt came to realize it would have to do something dramatic to thaw the diplomatic front. Sadat felt that now was the appropriate time to use his ace in the hole, the Soviet military presence in Egypt. He had been aware for some time that Kissinger and Nixon considered the Soviet presence the immediate obstacle to peace, and that the administration would never pressure Israel to make concessions as long as the Soviet forces remained; therefore, the logic of the situation dictated the speedy withdrawal of Soviet military personnel from Egypt. On July 18, 1972, Sadat announced the decision to have the Soviet military forces leave Egypt.

To the Egyptians, the Soviet military presence had become a liability because the Soviets opposed any military resolution of the Arab-Israeli stalemate. In fact, Soviet weapons supplied to the Arabs after the 1967 war were intended mainly for Arab defensive purposes.[48] The Soviet Union considered the Egyptian decision a major political and military setback, but not a collapse of its position in the Arab world. Politically, Sadat's move indicated, to both the United States and China, the vulnerability of the Soviet position, especially in a strategic area in which the Soviet Union had invested heavily in political influence and military aid since 1955. Strategically, the threat to Israeli security and to the southern flank of NATO diminished drastically with the Soviet loss of Egyptian air facilities for protecting the Soviet naval squadron in the Mediterranean.

The United States was surprised by Sadat's move. Kissinger welcomed it; a reduction of the Soviet military presence was, a priori, very important to American interests in the Middle East.[50] It would take some time to reorient American policy and develop a more pro-Sadat momentum.[51] One reason was the necessity for tact and restraint in view of the domestic sensitivity during a presidential-election year.[52] The foreign-policy staff also expressed concern that Sadat might come to expect too much too soon.[53] For both reasons, the Nixon administration continued to adopt a cautious position on the Middle East throughout 1972.

On January 13, 1973, diplomatic negotiations succeeded in ending the Vietnam War. The Nixon administration could now turn its attention to Europe and the Middle East. Although 1973 was designated as the Year of Europe, to highlight the importance of Western Europe in American global policy, it was also decided to handle the Middle East problem at the highest levels; President Nixon wanted Kissinger to become more active in finding a settlement. Intensive NSC preparations now took place to present a solid background for Kissinger's meetings with Middle East leaders. The NSC strategic papers dealt not only with the normal background matters, but with developing realistic positions which could lead to an eventual settlement.[54]

To Nixon, the chief problem was to find the appropriate approach to the Arabs because, at this juncture, Israel would only accept an interim agreement, especially in the light of the upcoming Israeli elections in October. In his view, the Arab states would have to be content with an interim agreement, on the assumption that the administration would strive to obtain a comprehensive settlement in the future.[55]

Given these considerations, Nixon and Kissinger had to be careful not to approach the Arabs too soon after the Soviet forces were withdrawn from Egypt. To do so would make Israel suspect that the administration was only trying to improve its relations with the Arab world. Of even greater concern in Washington was the Soviet sensitivity to American initiatives. Without careful U.S. tact and timing, the Soviets would view the United States as seeking to replace the Soviet Union in the region. Under these circumstances, Moscow was unlikely to cooperate in the necessary future negotiations. Kissinger was convinced that a final settlement needed Soviet support. If alienated, the Soviets might even urge the Arabs to use the oil weapon against the United States and Europe.[56]

In view of these issues, Kissinger insisted the Middle East negotiations should follow the "China model": All negotiations would be conducted secretly and the results would then be announced as faits accomplis.[57] This strategy represented a switch from the American peace efforts of 1969-70 in which the administration had channeled its primary diplomatic efforts through the United Nations. One hitch remained: This new strategy would not necessarily guarantee Israeli acquiescence.

The new strategy got its initial airing at a meeting between Kissinger and Sadat's national security advisor, Hafez Ismail, in February 1973. Kissinger, according to Heikal, laid down three principles as guides for discussions: mutual confidence, no cheating, and complete secrecy.[58] The Kissinger-Ismail talks were basically a substantive discussion of the outstanding issues; but they were also exploratory in the sense that Kissinger wanted to learn about Egyptian concerns.[59] As one American diplomat put it, the first half of 1973 was the "review and exploration" phase of the negotiations.[60]

From the Egyptian perspective, the Kissinger-Ismail meeting was a test of Washington's ability to find a diplomatic solution to the Arab-Israeli problem, after the Sadat initiative vis-à-vis the Soviets.[61] In essence, Sadat wanted to find out whether the Nixon administration was willing to pressure Israel to withdraw from the occupied territories.[62] According to Heikal, Kissinger presented to Ismail a general summary of the American position. The Nixon administration was always prepared to discuss the Arab-Israeli dispute with the Russians, but the greatest opportunity for some kind of negotiated settlement of the dispute lay in dealing directly with the regional parties on the specifics of the disagreement.[63] Moreover, Kissinger frankly cautioned Egypt against playing off the Soviet Union against the United States to get better terms.[64] It was necessary, said Kissinger, to gain a balance in the sovereignty-security formula between the Arab states and Israel. Arab verbal assurances would be insufficient in exchange for concrete Israeli concessions.[65] In spite of Kissinger's frank discussions with members of Sadat's government, the Egyptians were at least encouraged by the Nixon administration's serious initiative regarding the Arab-Israeli conflict.[66]

Kissinger and Ismail met again in Paris during May 1973, but the conversations failed to yield concrete results. Overall, the Egyptians made a pessimistic assessment of the meeting; they felt there was no sense of urgency in Washington concerning the Egyptian frustration with Israel at the Suez Canal. As long as Israel enjoyed strategic superiority, Washington felt no deadline for changing the status quo.[67] Sadat's government now felt Kissinger's earlier diplomatic initiative was fading.[68]

The Middle East was again an important agenda item at the June 1973 meeting between Nixon (along with Kissinger) and Brezhnev. The Soviet leader expressed his concern to the American president about the Middle East; the situation was very explosive and might threaten a superpower confrontation in the area.[69] Nixon and Kissinger shared Brezhnev's concern, but no mutually acceptable formula was found to solve the problem.[70] The United States and the Soviet Union, Brezhnev suggested, should agree on a statement of principles that could be used as a guide to a peace settlement.[71] Brezhnev's position called for the withdrawal of Israeli troops from the occupied territories, the recognition of national boundaries, and international guarantees for the settlement.[72] With some modifications, Brezhnev advanced the main principles of the Kissinger-Gromyko secret agreement (on general working principles) concluded at the 1972 summit. To Nixon, the Brezhnev principles were tantamount to an imposed settlement favorable to the Arabs; and he suggested, alternatively, superpower encouragement for the regional powers to enter into negotiations without prior conditions. Brezhnev disagreed. He hinted at dire consequences— even the possibility of war—if the United States and the Soviet Union failed to reach agreement on a common approach to the Middle East.[73] Despite this vague warning, Nixon and Kissinger still objected to his formula for a solution. Nixon assumed the Soviets were only trying to use scare tactics. By pushing for a cooperative working arrangement with the United States, they were trying to salvage their diminishing influence in the Middle East.[74]

Even though there was no agreement on the Middle East, a brief joint Soviet-American communiqué was issued, outlining the Middle East problem. The communiqué stated, in part:

Both parties agreed to continue to exert their efforts to promote the quickest possible settlement in the Middle East. This settlement should be in accordance with the interests of all states in the area, be consistent with their independence and sovereignty and should take into due account the legitimate interests of the Palestinian people.[75]

The June 1973 summit meeting could be summarized as giving détente a priority ranking in the interests of the two superpowers; Middle East regional concerns now had to defer to détente considerations. From the Egyptian standpoint, the outcome of this summit was even more disappointing than that of the 1972 summit. Sadat anticipated greater American efforts to push for an Arab-Israeli settlement. He expected greater backing after having expelled Soviet military personnel in 1972. By June 1973, the added factor of the Watergate revelations was pushing against Richard Nixon's presidential stature; the White House was no longer in a position to promote American interests in the Middle East—especially when the results had an unpopular domestic impact.[76]

After the June summit, Kissinger became increasingly concerned about two issues: Soviet involvement in the region and American-Israeli relations. On the first issue, he was suspicious of Soviet intentions in the strategic area of the Middle East. Between the summer of 1973 and the October War, there was at least one NSC meeting devoted to the issue, as well as one special study dealing with Soviet behavior. Although there was some concern shown in the NSC about the possibility of war, its research did not analyze that possibility in depth; the study was still underway when the October War started.[77] On the second issue, Kissinger realized the very limited leverage the United States had in the Middle East as compared to the situation in Vietnamese negotiations; thus he preferred that Israel should not be pressured as long as the Arab position remained unchanged. In any case, Kissinger did not expect any movement on the diplomatic front until after the Israeli elections in the fall of 1973.[78] In all, he considered the solid American-Israeli relationship an effective deterrent to Soviet advancements and to the possibility of the Arabs' resorting to the military option.

CRISIS MANAGEMENT: THE OCTOBER WAR OF 1973

From the Egyptian perspective, the Kissinger Middle East policy lacked the momentum and the sense of urgency necessary for movement toward a resolution of the Arab-Israeli dispute. Sadat's earlier optimism about a new American effort tended to fade. American policy seemed to parallel Israeli objectives—i.e., a policy of delay based on the assumption that, sooner or later, the Arabs would have to negotiate because they would realize the futility of a military solution.

Kissinger, as a strategic thinker, utilized a conceptual approach to the Arab-Israeli conflict, before going into concrete policies and operational planning; however, the NSC strategic papers dealing with the Middle East became more specific as the negotiations progressed. With the passing of time, the Nixon administration felt pressed by other, more urgent political issues like threats to the fragile Vietnam agreement, European affairs, and domestic problems including Watergate and the American economy; inevitably, these concerns diverted the administration's attention from the Arab-Israeli dispute.

Despite Kissinger's assurances to the Arabs (shortly after he became secretary of state in September 1973) that the administration was committing itself to an active peace policy, Sadat was not convinced. He decided to go ahead with the planned military action—an action which he felt had become necessary to break the diplomatic deadlock.[79] Thus, on October 6, 1973, Egypt and Syria launched carefully coordinated military operations against Israel on two fronts.

The war was, for Sadat, a calculated means to gain his political objectives. Sadat's "limited war" was designed to break the diplomatic deadlock resulting from the American-Israeli perception of the post-1967 war situation. In brief, the war was a message to Nixon and Kissinger: The Middle East must not be ignored any longer. Equally important, Sadat's action forced a Soviet reaction by triggering a threat to Soviet Middle East interests in the case of Moscow's priority on détente with the United States—a priority at the expense of Arab interests vis-à-vis Israel. Sadat had no particular a priori opposition to détente; he only objected to superpower collusion at the expense of the Arab Middle East.[80] President Sadat, above all, sought to destroy Israel's security strategy, which assumed its security against an Arab attack could be maintained by extended borders.[81]

In a variety of ways, the Arab attack on Israel was a surprise to the United States. First, Kissinger apparently ignored Brezhnev's earlier warnings about the potential for war in the Middle East. A balance of power in the region, he assumed, would deter any Arab military attack. Second, Kissinger assumed the Arabs would not attack without Soviet encouragement; furthermore, the administration insisted the Soviets would not tolerate Arab adventurism in the light of the bitter lessons of the 1967 war.[82] Third, Kissinger also assumed the Soviets would restrain the Arabs from launching an attack because it would destroy détente—a serious move in view of the growing Chinese threat (created by Peking's new rapprochement with Washington). Finally, with the exception of the State Department, which consistently warned about the possibility of war if Sadat did not get major political gains, the national security bureaucracy did not expect such a drastic action by the Arabs.

American intelligence failed to detect the war threat. On the day before the massive preemptive attack occurred, the CIA reported that a war was unlikely in the immediate sense.[83] Ray S. Cline, director of intelligence and research (INR) at the State Department, has claimed credit for predicting the hostilities 24 hours in advance.[84] The public record does not, however, back up Cline's claim. After the war was over, Cline recorded, in a memo addressed to Secretary of State Kissinger, that his intelligence organization had accumulated evidence, by October 5, that "convinced . . . [Cline] the chances of an attack at that time had become at least better than even."[85] Obviously, a "better-than-even" chance is not adequate for taking drastic policy steps which would involve serious liabilities if the event did not occur. In these situations, what is also important is whether the same prediction was previously made without the event taking place.[86]

In the end, Cline decided not to inform Kissinger of even this limited, "better-than-even" prediction because the latter was in New York at the time. Cline did orally share his intelligence estimate with Kissinger's personal staff and the Near East Bureau of the State Department.[87] In fact, the input had no significant influence on decision making in Washington.

Early Saturday morning (October 6), Israel flashed the news to Washington: The Arabs would launch a surprise attack in a matter of hours.[88] Kissinger immediately contacted Moscow, Cairo, and Jerusalem, asking each to exercise restraint. The effort was too late. Egypt and Syria were on course to implement a carefully organized plan of action and could not afford to abort a deliberately adopted war policy.[89]

From the outset of the conflict, the Nixon administration had three principal concerns: It wanted to avoid a direct confrontation with the Soviet Union; it wanted to preserve Israeli security; and it sought to keep American wartime support for Israel from causing irreparable damage to American-Arab relations.[90]

With these concerns in mind, Nixon and Kissinger decided to move cautiously. An effort was made to utilize the Security Council to stop the fighting; however, the Soviets were against an early ceasefire in the light of the initial Arab military success. Not surprisingly, the British and the French decided to maintain a neutral position in the United Nations because of their heavy dependence on Arab oil.[91] In this situation, President Nixon decided against trying to impose a cease-fire through the United Nations—a cease-fire which neither side would be expected to observe.[92] The Nixon administration felt the situation would be conducive to a cease-fire only after the mutual exhaustion from a military stalemate.[93]

Kissinger now assumed a controversial role; some have charged him with deliberate deception in the context of Machiavellianism at the tactical level. What happened was the infamous three-cornered game in which Kissinger played the role of "the good guy" promising Israel the prompt weapons it so desperately needed, while Secretary James Schlesinger, of the Defense Department, had the role of "the bad guy" always finding excuses as to why the military equipment could not be delivered.[94] In all fairness to the secretary of state (Kissinger became secretary of state only a month before the October War), the evidence indicates a consistent role in terms of his overall strategic values. Ultimately, every political decision maker faces trade-offs in values. Frequently—but not always—the political decision maker is able to escape deception or duplicity in the relevant range of choices demanded in the political encounter. But American policy decisions could not escape the duplicity option in this case. Unfortunately, from an idealistic perspective, Kissinger's essential policy options were limited to constant-sum payoff alternatives that included deception. In this sense, however, deception is immoral only if a better net trade-off in total results is possible.

The war created the need for urgent and crucial decisions in Washington. Kissinger did not want the tide of the battle to turn against Israel, because American intervention might then be needed. At the same time, Israel would have to be amenable to certain American demands in its war objectives; the American demands were made and justified on the basis of the American commitment to insure the national survival of Israel—although not to the "survival" of all Israeli objectives. Furthermore, Kissinger wanted to avoid another Arab defeat. The 1967 war involved an Arab humiliation that only added to the difficulty of resolving the Arab-Israeli dispute. Another Arab humiliation might well lead to Soviet intervention to preserve the Arab regimes—a result which would only serve to magnify Soviet influence in the area.[95] On the other hand, Kissinger also wanted to avoid a direct confrontation with the Arabs. Such a confrontation might not only undermine the supply of oil to the West; it could be expected to solidify the Soviet position in the Middle East as well as reduce the process of détente with Moscow.

When the Arabs launched their attack on October 6, Nixon and Kissinger shared the Israeli view of the Arabs' fighting capability; Israel would win a quick victory and the Arabs would then ask for a cease-fire. On the basis of this assumption, the war created no major crisis for Washington since a quick Israeli victory would not imperil détente. Yet the scenario did not develop as assumed; Israel was unable to turn the tide of battle as the Nixon administration had projected.

Despite his domestic troubles (i.e., Watergate and the resignation of Vice President Agnew in the middle of the crisis), [96] Nixon met with bipartisan congressional leaders to reassure them concerning the administration's efforts to halt the hostilities and to start negotiations; the meeting took place on the fourth day of the war, October 10. The congressional leaders were apprehensive about the possibility of American involvement if the Arabs succeeded in driving Israel toward defeat. In brief, the congressional leaders wanted to avoid another quagmire similar to the Vietnam War. [97] The Defense Department opposed sending large-scale arms to Israel. The United States might then be held responsible for the war's turning against the Arabs; it would alienate the Arab states and cause an oil embargo. [98] At stake for the United States was its image of credibility—credibility as a deterrent to the Soviet Union and as a power capable of making its influence felt in the Middle East.

The Washington Special Action Group met on October 6, 7, and 8 to review the situation in the Middle East. At the latter meeting, Kissinger seemed puzzled by the Arab refusal to agree to a cease-fire; after all, the Arabs had already made their point by breaking the diplomatic deadlock. In fact, the Soviets appeared to be more conciliatory than the Arabs in the early days of the war. [99] To the Soviets, there was no point in engaging in overkill after the Arabs had demonstrated their initial military success; it would have been more prudent for the Arabs to consolidate their gains rather than to continue the hostilities. To Kissinger, the key to resolving the crisis was Soviet cooperation. On October 8, he delivered a speech at the Pacem in Terris III Conference, in which he stressed the need for Soviet restraint and the importance of détente:

> Coexistence to us continues to have a very precise meaning: we will oppose the attempt by any country to achieve a position of predominance either globally or regionally. We will resist any attempt to exploit a policy of détente to weaken our alliance. We will react if relaxation of tensions is used as a cover to exacerbate conflicts in international trouble spots. The Soviet Union cannot disregard these principles in any area of the world without imperiling its entire relationship with the United States. [100]

Despite Kissinger's moderate warning, the Soviet supply of arms to the Arabs continued unabated. By October 10, the Soviet airlift to

Egypt and Syria had reached substantial proportions. [101] Two days later, Kissinger again called on the Soviets to exercise restraint:

> And I can only emphasize again the great importance of restraint by all of those countries who have it in their capacity to bring about an escalation and an expansion of hostilities, and the expectation of the United States that all countries which have a capacity to influence events, influence them on the side of restraints and moderation, as we are attempting to do. [102]

Events on the battlefront, however, were discouraging to Israel. The Arabs' surprise attack had prevented Israel from repeating its 1967 strategy for swiftly defeating the Arabs. Furthermore, in contrast to their willingness in 1967 to allow their client Arab states to go down to defeat, the Soviets were now determined that the Arabs would not suffer a second military debacle.

During the first week, the war went badly for Israel. Preemption gave Egypt and Syria a decided advantage. Kissinger was not the only one who misjudged the events leading to the war, but it was his decisions that bore the major responsibility for insisting that Israel allow the Arabs to strike first. [103] The Israeli ambassador in Washington, Simcha Dinitz, now engaged Kissinger in a futile dialogue, pleading for large-scale arms in view of America's responsibility for Israel's predicament in the war.

The charges of deliberate deception by Kissinger focus on the ensuing dialogue involving Kissinger and Ambassador Dinitz's request, while, at the same time, accusing Secretary of Defense Schlesinger of being the culprit by opposing the aid so as to maintain favor with the Arabs and to avoid an Arab oil boycott against the West. In fact, there is considerable evidence to indicate the scenario was deliberately orchestrated by Kissinger in the situation where American national interests crucially diverged from Israel's interests. William Quandt supports this interpretation of the Kissinger scenario by noting that "when Dinitz complained about the slow American response, Kissinger blamed it on the Defense Department, a ploy he used repeatedly with the Israeli ambassador over the next several days." [104] As the situation was conceptualized by Edward Sheehan, Kissinger "recognized instinctively that . . . if he allowed neither side to win decisively, then he might manipulate the result to launch negotiations, and—ultimately—to compose the Arab-Israeli quarrel. All of Kissinger's ensuing moves must be understood in this perspective." [105]

After about a week of this Kissinger-Dinitz-Schlesinger drama, and after the major acceleration of the Soviet arms airlift to Egypt and Syria, the Nixon administration finally decided on a massive American airlift of military equipment to Israel. It was a clear warning to the Soviets against a miscalculation on their part regarding the actual military situation. To Kissinger, a prolonged war of attrition would increase the probability of Soviet expansion in the Middle East and increase the risk of a superpower military confrontation there.

The Arab states now organized their own response. The airlift to Israel and the Nixon request for $2.2 billion in emergency aid for Israel led the Organization of Arab Petroleum Exporting Countries (OAPEC), on October 17, to adopt a decision to cut oil production and eventually to impose a total embargo against the United States.[106]

The Soviets were determined to avoid the total defeat of their client Arab states (to avoid the disaster the Arabs suffered in 1967); they preferred to stop the fighting before the tide of battle would turn decisively against Egypt and Syria. Regarding the cease-fire, the Soviets tried to approach Sadat through President Tito of Yugoslavia, but their attempt was unproductive.[107] On October 16, Soviet Premier Kosygin himself went to Cairo "for consultations" to convince Sadat of the advisability of a cease-fire. Yet Sadat refused any cease-fire that would not consolidate Egyptian gains.[108] The Soviets now turned to the United States as the most logical alternative, since it was Washington that had leverage over both sides and was in a position to push for a cease-fire that would prevent an Arab debacle. In this way, Soviet influence in the area might be preserved.

Accordingly, on October 18, the Soviets asked the United States to jointly sponsor a Security Council Middle East resolution based on three principles: a cease-fire in place, an immediate withdrawal of Israeli forces to the pre-1967 borders, and the beginning of peace talks.[109] Nixon rejected the Soviet proposal, yet his reply emphasized the importance of keeping the diplomatic channels open between the two superpowers.[110] The following day, the Soviets invited Kissinger to Moscow for direct talks. Not only did Nixon agree, but he also indicated the administration would not consider Soviet airlifts to the Arabs as setbacks in détente.[111] For Kissinger, the trip to Moscow would yield another 24 to 48 hours of battlefield time for improving the conditions for American influence in working out an Arab-Israeli settlement at the expense of the Soviet presence in the Middle East.

To summarize the Kissinger-Nixon strategy during the October War, Washington originally assumed Israel would rapidly recover from the preemptive shock in the first few days and drive the Syrians and the Egyptians back to the prewar boundaries. The American government's initial policy pronouncements requested a cease-fire and a return to the antebellum status quo. The Arab states refused as long as they were winning; their minimum demands for a halt in operations required Israel to return to the pre-1967 boundaries. Because he believed the tide of battle would inevitably turn against them, Kissinger felt the Arabs would sooner or later realize the desirability of his cease-fire proposals. After all, the Egyptian and Syrian armies had made their point in the opening military successes. They had avenged the military humiliation of 1967. Wisdom would dictate that they ought to settle for a cease-fire before another military defeat.

American expectations and assumptions about the course of the war were shattered when the Israeli military forces failed to stop the Arab armies in the early days of the onslaught. The days of October 9 to 12 were crucial inasmuch as Israel was still taking heavy casualties and suffering extensive losses in heavy military equipment without having success in decisively changing the course of the war—particularly on the Egyptian front.

Israel, also running out of ammunition, needed to replace its heavy equipment lost in the fighting. Kissinger began to see the possibility of exploiting Israel's increasingly desperate situation to further U.S. national interests; Israel might not be able to defeat Egypt without extensive U.S. aid in the replacement of planes and tanks consumed by the war. In line with this new American opportunity, Kissinger now pressed the Jerusalem government for a "cease-fire in place." In Washington, Israeli Ambassador Dinitz's desperate pleas for speedy military aid received evasive responses from the White House, and especially from Defense Secretary Schlesinger. Quandt notes: "In one of the most controversial decisions of the war, the president used the supply of arms to Israel to obtain Israeli acceptance of the principle of a cease-fire in place. By late evening, October 12, this had been successfully accomplished."112

Surprisingly, this pro-Arab push by the United States (based largely on a concern for access to Arab oil), was rejected by President Sadat, who still insisted on forcing Israel to agree to the pre-1967 boundary lines as a precondition for a cease-fire.

Kissinger saw an opportunity not only to promote Israeli dependence on the United States (and thereby expand America's ability to bring Israel to a satisfactory postwar settlement of the Arab-Israeli dispute), but also to gain convincing influence among Arab states—the side receiving American support must be seen by the Arabs as winning the war. Therefore, with the large-scale Soviet military aid flowing to Egypt and Syria, Washington now felt its national interests would best be served by giving massive aid to Israel to demonstrate the value of siding with the United States as compared to a client relationship with the Soviet Union.

The strategy worked. Once large-scale American military deliveries to Israel occurred, Sadat complained bitterly of the hopelessness of Egypt having now to fight "the United States." "Suddenly I found myself confronting the United States. . . . I wasn't prepared to fight the U.S.A."113 On October 19 Egypt made the decision to accept a cease-fire.

On October 21, Kissinger and Brezhnev agreed in Moscow on the draft of a proposed cease-fire agreement. Both superpowers were to inform their regional clients of the results. During the discussions, it became clear that the Soviets wanted not only a cease-fire, but also a joint role with the United States in the postwar diplomacy.114 Kissinger was willing to consider a cease-fire, but he insisted that negotiations for a settlement had to begin after the termination of the hostilities.115 Kissinger did not want to discuss the essentials of a peace agreement during the crisis itself. Nixon and Kissinger, however, were willing to accept the idea of a Soviet cochairmanship of a peace conference after the war; it would give the Soviet Union a formal role in approving what, hopefully, would be negotiated under U.S. auspices. In any case, Kissinger and Brezhnev reached an agreement that called for a cease-fire in place, the implementation of UN Resolution 242 once hostilities ceased, and negotiations for a durable and lasting peace in the Middle East.116 In all, the Moscow meeting was the basis for Security Council Resolution 338 of October 22, 1973, and for the Geneva Conference of December 1973.117

To the United States, the agreement was significant because the Soviets had agreed to a resolution that called for direct negotiations without prior commitments from belligerents. Furthermore, it marked the first time the Soviets had agreed to a call for implementing Resolution 242 without prior Israeli commitments to withdraw from the occupied territories.118 After the Moscow meeting, Kissinger briefly visited Israel to gain the government's acceptance of the new Soviet-American agreement. Not surprisingly, the Israelis were disturbed by the American fait accompli. Israel was now on the offensive, they told Kissinger, and their military forces needed only a few more days to achieve Israel's military objectives. But Kissinger argued that a few more days of fighting were not in the interests of either side; a decisive Israeli victory would only hamper the long-term objective of peace, making the Arabs psychologically unwilling to negotiate, as had happened after the 1967 war. In brief, Kissinger was trying to convince Israel to exchange the short-run focus for the more important long-term benefits.

Eventually, the Arabs and the Israelis reluctantly accepted the provisions of the Moscow meeting. In turn, this led to the cease-fire of October 22 via UN Security Council Resolution 338. The resolution called on the parties to terminate all military activity immediately, to start the implementation of Resolution 242 of 1967, and to negotiate a just and durable peace in the Middle East.119 Shortly after the cease-fire went into effect, both sides charged each other with violating the terms of the cease-fire. On October 23, Kissinger received a message from Moscow charging Israel with violating the cease-fire. Sadat now asked for a joint Soviet-American action to separate the Egyptian and Israeli forces.120 On the same day, the Soviets sent another message via the hot line to Nixon, repeating the charge of Israeli cease-fire violations. They urged the United States to take decisive steps to stop Israel. The Nixon administration decided on a counterdiplomatic thrust; the Egyptians were the first party to violate the cease-fire terms, and the Soviets should restrain them.121 Brezhnev then sent another message, indicating the Egyptians were ready for another cease-fire if Israel agreed. Jerusalem affirmed a second cease-fire via UN Security Council Resolution 339 of October 23, 1973. Essentially, Resolution 339 urged the parties to pull back their forces to the cease-fire lines of October 22. In addition, the Security Council resolution requested the secretary general to send UN observers to the scene to supervise the cease-fire.122

Despite the second cease-fire, Sadat asked for a joint American-Soviet peacekeeping force to guard the cease-fire lines. Nixon and Kissinger opposed Sadat's request: Not only was it unprecedented; it might inject the Soviet-American global rivalry into the regional conflict; joint Soviet-American forces in Egypt had the potential for endless friction and intrigue. It would also give the Soviets an opportunity to reestablish their military presence in Egypt.123 To Kissinger, the situation called for a determination of the facts—a demarcation of the cease-fire lines, and a determination of who was continuing the fighting so that the Security Council could take the appropriate measure.124 Under no circumstances would he allow a Soviet-American military condominium to be imposed on the regional belligerents.

On October 24, Brezhnev sent another message to the White House; despite the second cease-fire, the Soviets again charged Israel with cease-fire violations. Then came the bombshell: If the United States would not agree to a joint action, the Soviet Union would consider a unilateral action to stop the Israeli advance into Arab territory.125 Nixon and Kissinger were suspicious of Soviet motives. In Kissinger's view, the Soviet Union had already violated the spirit of the 1972 and 1973 summit understandings by its large-scale arming of Egypt and Syria.126 Furthermore, Kissinger knew Moscow was urging the Arabs to use the "oil weapon" against the West.

To counter Brezhnev's threat, Nixon ordered Kissinger and General Haig to formulate plans for thwarting any Soviet intervention. The Nixon administration also sent Sadat a message outlining American objections to the proposed Soviet intervention; such a course would destroy superpower cooperation in future peace talks.127 Meanwhile, Kissinger, Haig, Secretary of Defense Schlesinger, and other top American policy makers met to discuss the Soviet threat. A consensus reached by the group recommended a worldwide military alert of all

American conventional and nuclear forces;[128] accordingly, on October 24, the White House ordered a worldwide alert of U.S. military forces. It was another means of communicating with Moscow.

To enhance American credibility, Nixon also sent a message to Brezhnev stressing American opposition to either the proposed joint Soviet-American force or the Soviet unilateral force.[129] Though Nixon was prepared to agree in principle to the idea of sending some noncombat Soviet and American personnel to act as cease-fire observers—perhaps under UN auspices—he soft-pedalled that idea.[130] In turn, Brezhnev sent another message; the Soviet Union proposed sending 70 "observers" to the combat zone. To the Nixon administration, this represented a change from the earlier Soviet position on intervention; nevertheless, the United States responded by opposing even "independent observers" from the superpowers.[131]

Against this background, a third cease-fire agreement was reached via UN Security Council Resolution 340 of October 25, 1973. It reaffirmed Resolutions 338 and 339 and empowered the Security Council to send a UN Emergency Force to the area to guard the cease-fire.[132] More specifically, the UN force would not include military personnel from either the United States or the USSR (it would be composed of forces among the nonpermanent members of the Security Council only).

On balance, the American military alert was designed to preserve American credibility at both levels, the global and the regional. Militarily, it was the Nixon-Kissinger-Schlesinger answer to the Soviets' military alert of their airborne forces. Kissinger saw this as a threat of intervention.[133] On the regional level, it helped to preserve the Sadat regime by thwarting Soviet intervention in Egypt—an intervention thwarted also by Kissinger's restraint of Israeli expansion into Egyptian territory.[134] Still, the American military alert was not as serious as the confrontation during the Cuban missile crisis. President Nixon did not order any comprehensive intelligence evaluation of the situation.[135] Moreover, there was no serious effort to coordinate the alert with, or to send a prior notice to, the NATO allies.[136] Nixon and Kissinger felt a slight violation of "deference procedures," in the case of European NATO members, was in order inasmuch as most NATO members had refused to permit American use of their bases during the airlift to Israel.

Politically, despite the chance of endangering détente, Kissinger considered the alert a success because it stabilized the situation vis-à-vis the Soviet Union.[137] At a minimum, the alert provided the president with more options than he would have otherwise had, for American forces would have been placed on alert in any case, if Soviet troops had been sent to Egypt.[138] In brief, the alert was intended not only as a restraint on Soviet behavior, but also as a precautionary measure against Soviet unpredictability in a crisis situation that involved the clients of the superpowers, but not the superpowers directly. In these circumstances, it was designed to provide the United States with a high degree of flexibility.

The October War of 1973 also had an impact on the regional politics of the Middle East. From the Arab perspective, the military stalemate in the Middle East was now broken. Even though Egypt and Syria lost more territory, they gained certain political advantages. Israel was forced to make its negotiating posture more flexible, or it would face isolation from the international community. Militarily, the Arab surprise attack had put an end to the fiction of Israeli invincibility. The Arab attack was successful in casting doubts on Israel's security strategy as defined in territorial terms. The Arab attack had forced Israel to fight the kind of war it had hoped to avoid. The Arabs had succeeded in forcing greater superpower involvement in the Arab-Israeli dispute—the stalemate was broken.[139] In addition, the oil weapon was effectively transformed into considerable political leverage against the Western countries that traditionally supported Israel, especially the United States.

From the Israeli perspective, the war demonstrated Israel's vulnerability and its virtual dependency on the United States for military, economic, and political support.[140] It also created an awareness of how a cleavage between American and Israeli national interests could develop in a crisis—a situation of potential disaster for Israel in terms of how the latter defined its own interests.

The European countries that had previously supported Israel were in no position to help, because of their heavy dependency on Arab oil. In addition, they were already unhappy with Israel's negotiating posture in the aftermath of the 1967 war. The 1973 war added to Europe's disenchantment with Israel's policy toward the Arabs. Domestically, the impact on Israel's psychological and political mood was considerable—Israeli leaders were confronted with a somber reassessment of Israel's security doctrine vis-à-vis the Arabs. The 1973 war destroyed the optimistic perspective of Israel's international situation created by the 1967 war. It forced Israel to modify its negotiating position in the diplomatic efforts to defuse the long-term Arab-Israeli dispute.

From the Soviet perspective, there were both gains and losses. On the negative side, its client states suffered a second consecutive military defeat. The Soviet Union was not popular in Egypt and Syria after again having failed to deliver a victory against American-supported Israel. However, the 1973 war had also registered Soviet strategic gains. The unity of the NATO alliance was badly shaken by the war. More importantly, the Soviets were pleased with the Arab oil embargo. It was no longer possible to conceal Western dependence on Middle East oil. The dependency itself was a catalyst for further divisiveness in NATO and with Japan.[141] Furthermore, the Soviets demonstrated an impressive ability to monitor events accurately on the battlefield and to make decisions based on the changing regional situation. To maintain credibility as a superpower with influence in Middle East regional politics, the Soviets, backed by well-developed airlift and sealift capabilities, exhibited a high degree of flexibility in managing the crisis.[142]

From the American perspective, the October War transformed the Arab-Israeli dispute from a secondary to a primary issue in foreign policy.[143] Until October of 1973, the Middle East conflict was regarded as being relatively stabilized, but the war demonstrated how inadequate that assumption was. The war also escalated various issues into major concerns—issues which had previously been largely ignored in American foreign policy; these included the energy crisis and America's relations with its European and Japanese allies.

THE ENERGY CRISIS AND AMERICAN FOREIGN POLICY

An oil embargo in the Arab-Israeli conflict was not unprecedented. Before 1973, the Arabs had used the oil weapon against the Western countries on three occasions. But it was only with the 1973 oil embargo that the Arabs were able to achieve some of their major objectives. The bargaining power of supply had finally exceeded the bargaining power of demand—the economic bargaining power of oil-consuming states.

The first Arab oil boycott against the European countries took place during the 1948 Arab-Israeli conflict, but it proved ineffective because the Western Europeans were not then heavily dependent on oil.[144] Furthermore, the Arab action had no definite political objectives, and therefore, the measure was doomed to failure.

The second oil boycott against the Western countries came in the aftermath of the 1956 Suez crisis. The oil supply was interrupted from December 1956 until April 1957. Ironically, even though the United States had opposed the Anglo-French-Israeli attack on Egypt, the oil shortage of Western Europe was alleviated by close cooperation between Washington and the Organization for European Economic Cooperation (OEEC).[145] As a result, the embargo failed to produce political gains for the Arabs.

The third boycott arrived during the 1967 June war. The Arab states imposed an oil embargo against the United States, Britain, and West Germany, following the Israeli attack on Egypt, Syria, and Jordan. This marked the first Arab boycott against the United States. The 1948 and 1956 embargoes had been directed only against those West

European countries considered pro-Israel.[146] In 1967 the rupture in supply was more serious, and involved not only the transportation, but the production, of oil. Furthermore, the European demand for oil had sharply increased since the first Arab boycott. However, the American oil reserves were still sufficient to supply Europe, and the Arabs failed once more to make oil serve as a formidable political weapon.[147]

After their total military defeat by Israel in June 1967, the Arab states' finance and oil ministers met in Baghdad in August and agreed to utilize oil to develop their collective power as a political instrument in the service of Arab foreign policy. Unlike the Organization of Petroleum Exporting Countries (OPEC), which was formed, in 1960, by Arab and non-Arab states primarily for economic reasons, the Organization of Arab Petroleum Exporting Countries was formally established (in January 1968) to advance Arab—both economic and political—objectives.[148]

After the formation of OAPEC, Washington's foreign-policy experts expressed apprehension about the possibility of future Arab oil boycotts and the whole question of increasing international dependency on energy. In the fall of 1969 the United States raised the question of a common approach to energy problems among the Common Market countries.[149] The energy issue was again raised by the United States in May of 1970 at the Organization for Economic Cooperation and Development (OECD) meeting in Paris. It urged the Europeans to consider a multilateral approach to the problem. The Europeans, however, failed to respond to the American concern.[150] Nonetheless, Washington continued its efforts to convince its allies concerning the seriousness of the problem. For several months, the United States attempted to interest Europe in a joint approach on energy, but each time it encountered the same apathy. Finally, in October 1972, Washington again asked its European allies for joint planning to meet a future potential energy crisis; this time they responded favorably to the proposal.[151] Nevertheless, there was a failure of Western resolves to develop a common oil strategy. Nothing was done to secure Western access to Arab oil when future threats might arise.

Even though the Europeans procrastinated, Washington moved forward unilaterally. Several agencies were instructed to undertake studies. One State Department study (May 1973) concluded that Sadat would go to war in several months if no progress were made on the diplomatic front. In September, however, a new projection reversed that conclusion; now Sadat was not expected to use the military option; rather, he was said to be planning a long-term strategy in which the oil weapon would play a crucial role.[152] American planners were thus unprepared when war erupted soon afterward. They had underestimated the extent of Arab solidarity. Sadat had demonstrated unexpected skill

in building Arab support for the war. After all, Saudi Arabia and
Egypt were traditional rivals in Middle East politics. American
planners considered the new Cairo-Riyadh axis as incapable of bear-
ing the strains of an oil embargo. Saudi Arabia's oil cutoff came as
an unpleasant surprise to Washington's policy planners.

Unlike earlier Arab boycotts, the 1973 embargo succeeded due
to several factors. The embargo had a specific and limited objective,
i.e., the implementation of the Arab interpretation of Resolution 242,
which included justice for the Palestinians. Such a drastic action by
OAPEC caught the Western world unprepared. The oil embargo coincided with a world economy facing a host of other problems, e.g.,
inflation, balance-of-payments difficulties, and the devaluation of
leading currencies.[153] The embargo was a catalyst that magnified
these other international economic difficulties. In the past, these
economic issues had been overshadowed, at the top policy-making
level, by security issues; henceforth, they began to replace direct
security issues as the main concern among the United States and its
allies.[154] The oil embargo was also accompanied by OPEC's sharp
increase in oil prices; this compounded the problem because OPEC
included the major non-Arab oil-exporting states. Washington seemed,
however, to be more concerned about the oil supply than with its
price.[155] Some analysts even maintained the United States had encouraged oil-price increases since World War II to improve its economic position in relation to its allies.[156] Nonetheless, in 1973 the
United States found itself relatively powerless to counter the international oil cartel, whose actions could threaten future Western security
interests. In truth there were really two cartels, OPEC and OAPEC;
the latter created the threat to the West after the October War in
1973.[157]

In summary, the Arab oil embargo and the massive increase in
oil prices produced a major reevaluation of America's global strategy
and, more specifically, a reappraisal of its Middle East policy. In
broad terms, the success of the oil weapon, even though limited, had
ended the fiction that Middle East oil and politics did not mix. It made
American policy makers aware of a new dimension in the Arab-Israeli
conflict, although Kissinger made a valiant attempt to maintain the
separation of the two issues as much as possible.[158]

The oil dimension had its impact on several aspects of American
foreign policy dealing with the Middle East. First, the energy crisis
was not expected to change the basic American commitments to Israel,
yet it could magnify public attention to traditional differences between
the United States and Israel in relation to the Arab-Israeli dispute.
For instance, it might make Israel more suspicious of American policy
in the light of recent changes in attitudes among America's allies in
Western Europe and Japan. A case in point was the November 6, 1973,

European-community declaration on the Middle East that, inter alia, called for the restoration of Palestinian rights.[159]

Secondly, American policy makers had to worry about the oil-rich Arab states' financial backing of the Arab front-line states against Israel. This development might accelerate the Arab-Israel arms race and undermine mutual deterrence in the region by encouraging one of the disputants to launch a preemptive war.[160]

Thirdly, though the energy crisis, in part, now replaced the Soviet Union as the overriding American concern regarding the Arab-Israeli conflict, the Soviet concern, ironically, shifted from the Arab-Israeli scene to the oil-rich Persian Gulf area.[161] Thus, the American-British cooperation in the Indian Ocean area and the development of the Diego Garcia military facility in the early 1970s were designed to insure the stability of the oil-rich gulf region and the containment of anticipated Soviet expansion there.[162]

Finally, the energy crisis had a multiple impact on America's relations with its allies. Japan proved especially vulnerable to foreign sources of supply.[163] Not surprisingly, it was led to change its neutralist position to a pro-Arab stand—much to the disappointment of American policy makers.[164] In the European case, the oil crisis not only resulted in the modification of the Common Market's attitudes toward the Arab-Israeli conflict; it also threatened to erode the social and political foundation of NATO.[165] In conclusion, the energy crisis, with its potential for economic disruption, spilled over into other areas of interest among the allies—détente, issues of interdependence, and the Middle East.[166] The European community was motivated to become more independent from American policy. It would henceforth take a more active, European role in Middle East affairs. To discourage this, Kissinger pushed for the Washington Energy Conference in early 1974, not only to reinforce American Middle Eastern policy, but also to reassert American leadership over the allies.[167]

In spite of Washington's efforts, the European community soon began an effort to initiate talks with the Arab states. The Arabs, in turn, insisted the Euro-Arab dialogue cover both realms, the economic and the political. Kissinger was apprehensive about the wisdom of the Euro-Arab dialogue; he opposed bilateral technical contacts between the Europeans and the Arabs, and he saw danger in the Europeans' acting as a unit in the negotiations. He feared the radical Arab regimes would benefit disproportionately from these contacts.[168] To Kissinger, the proper strategy for the United States and its allies would be cooperation—first, on a joint comprehensive program of energy conservation in order to reduce dependence on Arab oil. The next step would be to organize what, in effect, would be a consumer cartel for bargaining with the Arabs across a potentially broad economic spectrum of goods and services.[169]

NOTES

1. See the full text of John C. Campbell's statement in U.S., Congress, House, Committee on Foreign Affairs, Soviet Involvement in the Middle East and the Western Response; Joint Hearings before the Subcommittee on Europe and the Subcommittee on the Near East of the Committee on Foreign Affairs, 92d Cong., 1st sess., 1971, pp. 177-80.

2. New York Times, November 20, 1970, p. 2; also see John C. Campbell and Helen Caruso, The West and the Middle East (New York: Council on Foreign Relations, 1972), p. 36.

3. New York Times, May 15, 1971, p. 3; also see Campbell and Caruso, The West and the Middle East, p. 36.

4. Campbell and Caruso, The West and the Middle East, pp. 36-37. This independent European effort was also recommended by Campbell in testimony presented to the House Foreign Affairs Committee, November 3, 1971; see pp. 180-81 in Soviet Involvement.

5. Interview with George S. Springsteen, Department of State, Washington, D.C., July 18, 1977.

6. Robert O. Freedman, Soviet Policy Toward the Middle East Since 1970 (New York: Praeger 1975), p. 5.

7. William B. Quandt, Decade of Decisions: American Policy Toward the Arab-Israeli Conflict, 1967-76 (Berkeley and Los Angeles: University of California Press, 1977), p. 136.

8. Lawrence L. Whetten, The Canal War: Four-Power Conflict in the Middle East (Cambridge: Massachusetts Institute of Technology Press, 1974), p. 168.

9. Quandt, Decade of Decisions, p. 136; also see Mohammed Heikal The Road to Ramadan (New York: Quadrangle, 1975), p. 116.

10. Quandt, Decade of Decisions, pp. 138-39.

11. Henry Kissinger, White House Years (Boston: Little, Brown and Co., 1979), pp. 1281-82.

12. Heikal, The Road to Ramadan, p. 132.

13. Ibid.

14. Quandt, Decade of Decisions, p. 139.

15. Ibid., p. 143.

16. Whetten, The Canal War, p. 199.

17. Quandt, Decade of Decisions, p. 144.

18. Ibid.

19. Kissinger, White House Years, p. 1281.

20. Quandt, Decade of Decisions, pp. 144-145.

21. Ibid., p. 146.

22. Ibid.

23. Ibid.

24. Ibid., p. 147.

25. Heikal, The Road to Ramadan, p. 199.

26. Quandt, Decade of Decisions, p. 147.

27. Whetten, The Canal War, pp. 219-21.

28. See the full text of Alvin J. Cotrell's statement in U.S., Congress, House, Committee on Foreign Affairs, The Middle East 1971: The Need to Strengthen the Peace, Hearings before the Subcommittee on the Near East of the Committee on Foreign Affairs, 92d Cong., 1st sess., 1971, p. 28.

29. See Malcolm H. Kerr, ed., The Elusive Peace in the Middle East (Albany: State University of New York Press, 1975), p. 12.

30. Roman Kolkowicz, "The Soviet Policy in the Middle East," in The U.S.S.R. and the Middle East, ed. Michael Confino and Shimon Shamir (New York: John Wiley & Sons, 1973), pp. 77-80.

31. Ibid.

32. See Roman Kolkowicz's statement in U.S., Congress, House, Committee on Foreign Relations, Soviet Involvement in the Middle East and the Western Response, Joint Hearings before the Subcommittee on Europe and the Subcommittee on the Near East of the Committee on Foreign Affairs, 92d Cong., 1st sess., 1971, p. 92.

33. Whetten, The Canal War, p. 166.

34. Freedman, Soviet Policy Toward the Middle East Since 1970, p. 51.

35. Ibid., pp. 70-71.

36. Kissinger, White House Years, pp. 1285-87.

37. Ibid., pp. 1287-88.

38. Ibid., p. 1290.

39. Ibid., pp. 1290-91.

40. Ibid., p. 1291.

41. Ibid., pp. 1291-92 and p. 1288.

42. Interview with a top Kissinger aide, Washington, D.C., July 13, 1977.

43. Kissinger, White House Years, p. 1494.

44. Ibid., pp. 1246-48.

45. See the text of the Basic Principles of May 29, 1972, in the Department of State Bulletin 66 (June 26, 1972): 902.

46. Quandt, Decade of Decisions, p. 151.

47. Anwar el-Sadat, In Search of Identity: An Autobiography (New York: Harper and Row, 1978), p. 274.

48. For instance, see Robert E. Hunter, "In the Middle East," Foreign Policy (Winter 1971-72): 138-39; also see Sadat, In Search of Identity, pp. 264-65; and Oleg M. Smolansky "Strategic Implications of the Soviet Withdrawal from Egypt: I," Bulletin of the American Academic Association for Peace in the East 62 (January 1973): 66.

49. Freedman, Soviet Policy Toward the Middle East Since 1970, p. 79; also see Smolansky, "Strategic Implications of the Soviet

Withdrawal From Egypt I," p. 5; and William Kinter, "Political Implications of the Soviet Withdrawal from Egypt: II," Bulletin of the American Academic Association for Peace in the Middle East 2 (January 1973): 7.

50. Interview with Ray Cline, Department of State, Washington, D.C., March 16, 1977; also see Kissinger, White House Years, pp. 1295-97.

51. Interview with Ray Cline.

52. For instance, see Quandt, Decade of Decisions, p. 152.

53. Interview with Ray Cline.

54. Interview with William B. Quandt, NSC (Middle East), Washington, D.C., July 25, 1977.

55. Richard Nixon, RN: The Memoirs of Richard Nixon (New York: Grosset and Dunlap, 1978), pp. 786-87.

56. Edward R. F. Sheehan, "The United States, the Soviet Union, and Strategic Considerations in the Middle East," Naval War College Review 23 (June 1971): 27.

57. See Leslie Gelb, "The Coming New/Old Faces in the Middle East," Bulletin of the American Academic Association for Peace in the Middle East 2 (January 1973): 2; also see Heikal, Road to Ramadan, pp. 201-02.

58. Heikal, Road to Ramadan, 202.

59. Interview with a top Kissinger aide, Washington, D.C., July 13, 1977.

60. Alfred LeRoy Atherton, Jr., "The Nixon Administration and the Arab-Israeli Conflict," in The New World Balance and Peace in the Middle East: Reality or Mirage?, ed. Seymour Maxwell Finger (London: Associated University Press, 1975), p. 204.

61. Interview with William B. Quandt.

62. Marvin Kalb and Bernard Kalb, Kissinger (Boston: Little, Brown and Co., 1974), p. 451.

63. Heikal, The Road to Ramadan, pp. 202-03.

64. Mohammed Heikal, The Sphinx and the Commissar: The Rise and Fall of Soviet Influence in the Arab World (London: Collins, 1978), p. 225.

65. Heikal, The Road to Ramadan, p. 203.

66. Interview with William B. Quandt.

67. Sadat, In Search of Identity, pp. 285, 342-43.

68. Interview with William B. Quandt.

69. Interview with a top Kissinger aide, Washington, D.C., July 13, 1977.

70. Ibid.

71. Nixon, RN: The Memoirs of Richard Nixon, p. 885.

72. Ibid.

73. Ibid.

74. Ibid.

75. See the text of the joint U.S.-USSR communiqué of June 25, 1973, in the Department of State Bulletin 62 (July 23, 1973): 132.

76. Interview with William B. Quandt.

77. Ibid. Quandt had completed most of the research, but it was, technically, not finished.

78. Quandt, Decade of Decisions, pp. 160-62.

79. Sadat, In Search of Identity, p. 285; also see Nadav Safran, "Arab Politics, Peace and War," Orbis 2 (Summer 1974): 378.

80. Walter Laqueur, Confrontation: The Middle East and World Politics (New York: Quadrangle, 1974), pp. 47-48.

81. Sadat, In Search of Identity, pp. 303-05.

82. See William B. Quandt, "Soviet Policy in the October 1973 War," Rand Memorandum R-1864-ISA, May 1976, pp. 3-12; also see Nixon, RN: The Memoirs of Richard Nixon, p. 921.

83. Nixon, RN: The Memoirs of Richard Nixon, p. 920.

84. Interview with Ray Cline.

85. Ray Cline, "Policy Without Intelligence," Foreign Policy 17 (Winter 1974-75): 132.

86. Sadat, In Search of Identity, pp. 241-42. Egypt deliberately organized military procedures to deceive Israeli intelligence into predicting an Egyptian preemptive attack. In fact, Egypt did deceive Israeli intelligence into reporting to the government an expected attack. Both times Israel falsely mobilized at an unnecessary "cost of ten million dollars." Also see Moshe Dayan, Story of My Life (New York: William Morrow and Co., 1976), p. 459.

The United States had also warned Israel not to preempt, nor to mobilize reserves. Washington felt Israeli initiatives were the greatest dangers to political destabilization in the Middle East.

Further, William Quandt explains the failure of Israeli intelligence by the fact that "well placed Israeli intelligence agents in Egypt had been captured early in 1973" (Quandt, Decade of Decisions, p. 169).

87. Interview with Ray Cline.

88. Quandt, Decade of Decisions, p. 166.

89. Nixon, RN: The Memoirs of Richard Nixon, p. 921.

90. Ibid., pp. 921-22; also see Quandt, Decade of Decisions, p. 170.

91. Nixon, RN: The Memoirs of Richard Nixon, p. 921.

92. Ibid.

93. Ibid.

94. See Matti Golan, The Secret Conversations of Henry Kissinger (New York: Quadrangle, 1976); Gil Carl AlRoy, The Kissinger Experience: American Policy in the Middle East (New York: Horizon Press), 1975; New York Times Magazine, July 1974; William Quandt, Decade of Decisions, pp. 175-76; Seyom Brown, The Crises of Power (New

York: Columbia University Press, 1979), pp. 95, 162; Tad Szulc, Illusion of Peace: Foreign Policy in the Nixon Years (New York: Viking Press, 1978),pp. 735-39; Edward N. Luttwok and Walter Laqueur, "Kissinger and the Yom Kippur War," Commentary 58, no. 3 (September 1974): 36.

95. Quandt, Decade of Decisions, p. 171. Also see Nixon, RN: The Memoirs of Richard Nixon, p. 921.

96. Nixon, RN: The Memoirs of Richard Nixon, p. 922.

97. Ibid., p. 924.

98. Ibid., pp. 924-27.

99. Quandt, Decade of Decisions, p. 175.

100. Henry Kissinger, American Foreign Policy, 3rd ed. (New York: W. W. Norton & Co., 1977), pp. 123-24. The conference was organized by the Center for the Study of Democratic Institutions and convened October 12, 1973, in Washington, D.C.

101. See Kissinger's press conference of October 12, 1973, in the Department of State Bulletin 69 (November 29, 1973): 537.

102. Ibid., pp. 538-39.

103. John Stoessinger, Henry Kissinger: The Anguish of Power (New York: W. W. Norton Co., 1976), pp. 179-80.

104. Quandt, Decade of Decisions, p. 175.

105. Edward R. F. Sheehan, The Arabs, Israelis, and Kissinger: A Secret History of American Diplomacy in the Middle East (New York: Readers Digest Press, 1976), p. 32.

106. Nixon, RN: The Memoirs of Richard Nixon, p. 931.

107. Sadat, In Search of Identity, p. 304; also see Galia Golan, Yom Kippur and After: The Soviet Union and the Middle East Crisis (London: Cambridge University Press, 1977), p. 107.

108. Ibid., pp. 308-10; and Ibid., pp. 106-10.

109. Nixon, RN: The Memoirs of Richard Nixon, pp. 930-31.

110. Ibid.

111. Ibid., p. 933.

112. Quandt, Decade of Decisions, p. 176.

113. Sadat, In Search of Identity, p. 290.

114. Interview with a top Kissinger aide; also, interview with Helmut Sonnenfeldt, NSC and State Department, Washington, D.C., August 13, 1977; also see Quandt, Decade of Decisions, p. 192.

115. Interview with a top Kissinger aide.

116. Nixon, RN: The Memoirs of Richard Nixon, p. 936.

117. Interview with a top Kissinger aide.

118. Nixon, RN: The Memoirs of Richard Nixon, p. 936.

119. United Nations, Security Council, Resolutions and Decisions of the Security Council, 1973, Official Records, (New York, 1974), p. 10.

120. Nixon, RN: The Memoirs of Richard Nixon, p. 936.

121. Ibid., pp. 936-37.

122. United Nations, Security Council, Resolutions and Decisions of the Security Council, 1973, p. 11.

123. Nixon, RN: The Memoirs of Richard Nixon, p. 938; also see Kissinger's press conference of October 25, 1973, in the Department of State Bulletin 69 (November 12, 1973): 587.

124. See Kissinger press conference of October 25 in the Department of State Bulletin 69 (November 12, 1973): 587.

125. Nixon, RN: The Memoirs of Richard Nixon, p. 938.

126. See Quandt, "Soviet Policy in the October 1973 War," p. 2, fn. 2.

127. Nixon, RN: The Memoirs of Richard Nixon, pp. 938-39.

128. Ibid., p. 939.

129. Ibid., pp. 939-40.

130. Ibid.

131. Ibid., pp. 940-41.

132. United Nations, Security Council, Resolutions and Decisions of the Security Council, 1973, p. 11.

133. See Secretary Schlesinger's news conference of October 26, 1973, in the Department of State Bulletin 69 (November 19, 1973): 617-19.

134. Shlomo Slonim, "American-Egyptian Rapprochement," The World Today 31 (February 1975): 55; also see Quandt, Decade of Decisions, pp. 197-98.

135. Interview with Ray Cline.

136. Ray Cline, "Policy Without Intelligence," Foreign Policy 17 (Winter 1974-75): 128.

137. Interview with Ray Cline.

138. Interview with Helmut Sonnenfeldt.

139. Nadav Safran, "The War and the Future of the Arab-Israeli Conflict," Foreign Affairs 52 (January 1974): 215-19; also see Bernard Reich, Quest for Peace: United States-Israel Relations and the Arab-Israeli Conflict (New Brunswick, N.J.: Transaction Books, 1977), pp. 244-45.

140. Reich, Quest for Peace, pp. 246-48.

141. For instance, see Quandt, "Soviet Policy in the October War," p. 27, fn. 28.

142. Ibid., pp. 35-38.

143. Interview with William B. Quandt.

144. Farouk A. Sankari, "The Character and Impact of Arab Oil Embargoes," in Arab Oil: Impact on the Arab Countries and Global Implications, ed. N. A. Sherbiney and Mark A. Tessler (New York: Praeger, 1976), p. 226.

145. Ibid.

146. Ibid.; also see Fuad Itayim, "Strengths and Weaknesses of the Oil Weapon," in The Middle East and the International System: II,

Security and the Energy Crisis, Adelphi Papers, No. 115 (Spring 1975), p. 1.

147. Sankari, "The Character and Impact," p. 267; and Itayim, "Strengths and Weaknesses," p. 1.

148. Don Peretz, "Energy: Israelis, Arabs, and Iranians," in The Energy Crisis and U.S. Foreign Policy, ed. Joseph S. Szyliowicz and Brad E. O'Neil (New York: Praeger, 1975), pp. 91-92.

149. James E. Aikens, "The Oil Crisis: This Time the Wolf is Here," Foreign Affairs 51 (April 1973): 485-86.

150. Ibid.

151. Ibid., pp. 486-87.

152. See William B. Quandt, "U.S. Energy Policy and the Arab-Israeli Conflict," in Sherbiney and Tessler, Arab Oil: Impact on the Arab Countries and Global Implications, p. 284.

153. Yusif A. Sayigh, "Arab Oil Policies: Self-Interest versus International Responsibility," Journal of Palestine Studies 4 (Spring 1975): 60-61.

154. C. Fred Bergsten, Toward a New International Economic Order: Selected Papers of C. Fred Bergsten, 1972-74 (Lexington, Mass.: D. C. Heath and Co., 1975), pp. 3-6.

155. Quandt, "U.S. Energy Policy and the Arab-Israeli Conflict," pp. 285-88.

156. For instance, see V. H. Oppenheim, "Why Oil Prices Go Up: I, The Past: We Pushed Them," Foreign Policy 25 (Winter 1976-77): 24-25; also see Edith Penrose, "Origins and Development of the International Oil Crisis," Journal of International Studies 3 (Spring 1974): 38-39.

157. Walter J. Levy, "An Atlantic-Japanese Energy Policy," Foreign Policy 11 (Summer 1973): 184-85.

158. Quandt, "U.S. Energy Policy and the Arab-Israeli Conflict," p. 288.

159. For instance, see Ibrahim Sus, "Western Europe and the October War," Journal of Palestine Studies 3 (Winter 1974): 75-76.

160. Paul Jabber, "Petrodollars, Arms Trade, and the Pattern of Major Conflicts," in Oil, the Arab-Israeli Conflict and the Industrial World, ed. J. C. Hurewitz (Boulder: Westview Press, 1976), p. 155; also see Peretz, "Energy: Israelis, Arabs, and Iranians."

161. Robert Hunter, The Energy Crisis and U.S. Foreign Policy, Headline Series, No. 216 (New York: Foreign Policy Association, 1973), pp. 39-46; also see Alvin Cottrell, "The Politico-Military Balance in the Persian Gulf Region," in Szyliowicz and O'Neil, The Energy Crisis and U.S. Foreign Policy, pp. 126-28.

162. Cottrell, "The Politico-Military Balance in the Persian Gulf Region," pp. 126-28.

163. Makoto Momoi, "The Energy Problem and Alliance System: Japan," in The Middle East and the International System: II, Security and the Energy Crisis, pp. 25-26.

164. Ibid.

165. Karl Kaiser, "The Energy Problem and Alliance System: Europe," in ibid., p. 18.

166. Ibid., pp. 18-21.

167. Robert Gilpin, "Three Models of the Future," in World Politics and International Economics, eds. C. Fred Bergsten and Lawrence Krause (Washington, D.C.: Brookings Institution, 1975), pp. 55-56.

168. Interview with Helmut Sonnenfeldt.

169. Ibid.

6

U.S. POLICY FROM THE EMBARGO
TO SHUTTLE DIPLOMACY

The Arab oil embargo was not only a partial success for the Arabs; it was also a measure of success for the Soviet Union, the first non-Arab country to advocate the use of oil as a weapon against the West. Nonetheless, the Soviets remained apprehensive about conditions in the combat zone, given the deep penetration of Israeli forces through Arab defense lines. At the end of October 1973, Brezhnev used the hot line, for the second time during the crisis, to express Soviet concern about what he regarded as belligerent Israeli behavior with regard to the supply problems of the encircled Egyptian Third Army. He also expressed concern about the spirit of détente which had been threatened by the American military alert. [1]

In reply, Nixon reassured Brezhnev that survival supplies would reach the trapped Egyptian Third Army. As for the American military alert, he characterized it as a response to the unilateral threat of Soviet intervention in the Middle East. The Soviet threat of unilateral intervention in the Middle East indeed violated the 1973 Soviet-American agreement on the prevention of nuclear war. [2] Later, Brezhnev was to repeat the claim of sincere Soviet efforts to restrain the Arabs when they launched the 1973 war—the upheaval responsible for all the new challenges in Soviet-American relations that Brezhnev complained about in his hot-line messages. [3]

On the whole, the firm but nonbelligerent American stand toward Moscow during the crisis was motivated by two overriding concerns: the need to avoid a direct confrontation in the region, and the necessity for Soviet cooperation in the postwar diplomacy. Kissinger realized how essential such cooperation would be in achieving a final peace settlement; the Soviets could hamper negotiations at any stage. [4] Yet during the process of step-by-step negotiations, Kissinger preferred to exclude the Russians, although keeping them informed on developments. Kissinger supported the Geneva-conference arrangement because it would confine Soviet participation in the negotiations to a minimum. Furthermore, it would satisfy the Kissinger–Brezhnev Moscow agreement of October 21, 1973, giving the Soviets a role in the postwar diplomacy.

U.S. POLICY AND STEP-BY-STEP DIPLOMACY

Ironically, the step-by-step approach, which seemed to be the hallmark of Kissinger's Middle Eastern diplomacy, was not his invention. The idea of a staged approach to the Arab-Israeli conflict had been floating about within the national security bureaucracy since 1970-71. The Defense Department, in particular, found this approach more realistic than efforts aimed at a comprehensive settlement, but, at that time, both the White House and the State Department had been unconvinced of its practicality.[5]

The conceptual basis of the new American policy rested on several considerations. To begin with, unlike previous American initiatives, such as the Rogers Plan, which had called for a comprehensive settlement, Kissinger's current diplomacy would not aim for an American resolution of the Arab-Israeli conflict.[6] Instead, the Nixon administration would confine itself to advancing ideas at some critical junctures during the negotiating process.

Next, the step-by-step approach would not commit the United States to a specific final result; rather, the U.S. commitment was to a process involving only initial diplomatic transactions.[7] The American approach, therefore, sidestepped the central issues of the Middle East conflict—issues such as the fate of the Palestinians, final borders, and the status of Jerusalem. Unlike the negotiations involving Vietnam and China, in which the United States had been committed to specific policies, Kissinger would act only as a mediator between the Arabs and the Israelis. Such mediation would be directed toward psychologically preparing both parties, especially the Israelis, for a final settlement. As a trusted mediator, Kissinger would be able to explain the domestic and foreign constraints that each party had to consider if it wanted the negotiations to progress.[8] Both Nixon and Kissinger hoped this approach would increase American leverage over both sides and maintain American control of the negotiations.

There were other opportunities. Negotiations under American auspices would give the United States a good opportunity to reduce Soviet influence in the Middle East. It followed that President Sadat, who shared the American apprehensions about Soviet intentions in the region, would become the focus of Kissinger's initiatives.[9] Simultaneously, these initiatives would permit the United States to associate itself more closely with the moderates in the Arab world. The moderates had grown in influence after the October War and had dampened the traditional Arab cold war and inter-Arab rivalry, especially the earlier Egyptian-Saudi antagonism.

One element never far removed from Kissinger's diplomacy was the oil embargo. Ending it through diplomatic means now became a front-line priority on the Kissinger agenda.[10] As he saw it, diplomatic progress in the Arab-Israeli conflict would invariably ease the embargo's severity. The United States, however, could not afford to appear publicly as being pressured in its diplomacy.

Washington wasted no time in conveying to both sides the image of a new Middle East policy. It was explained to both Ismail Fahmy (Egypt's foreign minister) and Israeli Prime Minister Golda Meir when they arrived in Washington for exploratory talks—Fahmy in late October, and Meir in early November (1973).

The talks with Fahmy covered Kissinger's forthcoming trip to the Middle East, the return of Israeli forces to the October 22 lines, and the latest Egyptian, 11-point, proposal for a military disengagement with Israel. Kissinger tactfully responded to the Egyptian position by affirming its constructive qualities; nevertheless, Kissinger told Fahmy it was premature to insist on Israel's withdrawal. Furthermore, the October 22 lines were not that significant inasmuch as the inevitable later disengagement would have the Israelis withdraw beyond the October 22 lines.[11]

Meir's talks with Nixon and Kissinger raised the issues of Israeli prisoners in Egypt, nonmilitary supplies to the Egyptian Third Army, and a disengagement of forces.[12] Primarily, however, Kissinger used the occasion to present the new American proposals for ending the Arab-Israeli dispute. As outlined to Meir, it would use a step-by-step procedure; the United States would continue to stand up to the Soviets as it had in the past, and the United States would insist on secure borders for Israel.[13] There were also requests to be made of Israel. Kissinger affirmed the need for a new Israeli policy based on restraint and flexibility, rather than the territorially oriented and excessively hard-line security policy, vis-à-vis the Arabs.[14] Israel was urged to adopt a policy reflecting the new realities created by both the October War and the energy crisis.

These initial talks set the stage for Kissinger's subsequent shuttle diplomacy. On November 5, he went to the Middle East for exploratory talks with both sides. While in Cairo, he was informed of the Israeli government's approval of a number of issues that could serve as a starting point for negotiations. These included mutual respect for the temporary cease-fire, the nonmilitary supply of the Egyptian Third Army and Suez City, the exchange of prisoners, the lifting of the Arab naval blockade at Bab al-Mandab, and the discussion of the October 22 lines within the framework of a disengagement of forces.[15]

Sadat, in turn, was ready to accept most of these points, but, as mentioned above, he was determined to have Israel pull back to the October 22 front lines as a prerequisite of negotiations. Kissinger said he understood Sadat's position, but he argued that a wider disengagement of forces would soon bypass the issue.[16] Surprisingly, Sadat agreed. He and Kissinger also agreed, in principle, on the resumption of diplomatic relations between the two countries; these had never been resumed since being severed during the June 1967 war. In general, Kissinger's initial breakthrough with Sadat could be traced both to the former's success in portraying himself as a detached mediator between the disputants and—even more—to his persuasive assessments of the situation, both regional and global. Equally important, Sadat realized the Soviet Union could provide arms for waging war but could not deliver a peaceful settlement in which Israel would return Arab territories. Only the United States had leverage over both sides; only the United States could deliver what the Arab states needed from Israel.[17]

With a successful conclusion of the Cairo talks, Kissinger sent his top aides, Joseph Sisco and Harold Saunders, to Jerusalem to work out the details of an initial agreement between Israel and Egypt. The Israeli government, though pleased with Sadat's flexibility, objected to some of the Cairo provisions. Israel insisted on its authority to control the supply route to the Third Army and insisted on the termination of the naval blockade against Israel. After several rounds of talks, the first issue was finally settled. The latter issue, however, was settled only after the United States assured Israel that the blockade would eventually be lifted.[18] On November 11, Israel and Egypt signed a six-point cease-fire agreement—the Kilometer 101 Accord, as it was called. It provided for the observance of the cease-fire, the nonmilitary supplies to the Third Army and Suez City, the exchange of prisoners of war, and discussions on the return to the October 22 lines.[19] To ensure the credibility of the accord, the United States pledged to Egypt, according to Sadat, a return to the October 22 lines, within the framework of a disengagement of forces.[20]

Before leaving the area, Kissinger made two important stops, in Jordan and in Saudi Arabia. In Jordan, he met with King Hussein to encourage him to join in the negotiations.[21] Kissinger was trying to rally support for Sadat's moves in the Arab world; he was also trying to demonstrate American support for the Hussein regime and for Hussein's attitude toward the PLO. In Saudi Arabia, Kissinger met with King Faisal, explaining to him the difficulty of continuing the peace process unless the oil embargo were rescinded. He shared with King Faisal the basic peace strategy, a gradual process involving step-by-step diplomacy.[22] Faisal responded favorably, indicating to Kissinger that the oil embargo would be lifted once Kissinger had achieved sufficient progress in the peace negotiations.[23] The Arab linkage between oil and Kissinger's diplomacy was thus a crucial factor in the scenario for the forthcoming peace negotiations.

Shortly after the Kilometer 101 Accord was signed, Egyptian and Israeli military leaders began to work out the details for its implementation. Israel wanted both sides to retreat to the pre-October War lines and the evacuated territories to be placed under UN supervision. Egypt insisted that its forces should stay in place while Israeli forces retreated to the strategic Mitla and Gidi passes.[24]

The negotiations at Kilometer 101 continued. Israel's offers centered on its willingness to pull back from the western bank of the Suez Canal in exchange for an Egyptian reduction of forces on the eastern side of the canal. In contrast, the Egyptians pressed Israel to withdraw to the Mitla and Gidi passes but insisted on their own strong military presence east of the canal.

General Gamasy, representing Egypt at the November Egyptian-Israeli negotiations at Kilometer 101, then offered a concession by proposing an Israeli withdrawal to the Mitla and Gidi passes, accompanied by a trizonal disengagement of forces. The three zones would include, from east to west, a lightly armed Egyptian zone. Israel was responsive to the Egyptian proposal. In the last week of November, General Yariv, negotiating for Israel, offered to withdraw Israeli forces to the east of the passes if Egypt would agree to withdraw almost all of its armor (except for a few pieces important for public-relations purposes) to the west bank of the canal. It appeared that a disengagement agreement might be reached at Kilometer 101 without the services of third-party mediation.

At this point the ageless subtleties of diplomacy—subtleties which have received the condemnation of moralists throughout history—came into play. A deception was in order. Kissinger confidentially suggested to Israel that it assume a harder line toward Egypt; it was important to maintain the image of a deadlock so as to give the anticipated Geneva peace conference more prestige in the public's image of international politics.[25] Also, Syria would demand similar prior concessions before attending the conference, and at this time Kissinger was making a major effort to get Syria to the proposed Geneva peace conference.[26] Furthermore, Golan suggests, with considerable plausibility, that a Yariv-Gamasy agreement at Kilometer 101 would have stolen the glory the American secretary of state was anticipating for his own role.[27] These expectations were fulfilled: Secretary of State Kissinger was later catapulted to diplomatic stardom for the accomplishment of disengagement resulting from his shuttle diplomacy.

At Kilometer 101, therefore, Israel withdrew its relatively generous proposal of November 26, which offered a military withdrawal to the eastern end of the passes under the stated conditions. Moshe Dayan in very generous public-relations rhetoric designed to protect

Kissinger from moral opprobrium, pointed out the essential role of the United States in any disengagement agreement; Dayan noted the vital initiative and responsibility the United States would have to assume in stabilizing any Egyptian-Israeli agreement. A U.S. role was essential not only in bringing the parties together in an agreement, but also in providing the means to implement that agreement—namely, the continuing trust, integrity, and influence in the relationship with each side.[28]

Later, Moshe Dayan met with Kissinger in Washington (December 7, 1973). He pressed hard for more arms from the United States. He suggested directly to Kissinger the possibility of a disengagement whereby Israel might withdraw to the west side of the Sinai passes if Egypt agreed to demilitarize its proposed Sinai territory and to open the Suez Canal. Furthermore, Dayan said this might be arranged even before the Israeli elections (scheduled for later in December). Once again, Kissinger's response, if it had become public knowledge, would have suffered the moralist's charge of deliberate deception. Kissinger cautioned Dayan about being too generous with concessions too soon; Israel would appear weak to the Arabs. According to Quandt's description of the conversation, Kissinger told Dayan "it was important for the Arabs to see that it was difficult for the United States to influence Israel [regarding concessions], otherwise their expectations would soar."[29]

As mentioned previously, in this sense Kissinger was Machiavellian, although in fairness to him, it was Machiavellian only in the means he used to achieve his own ultimate moral values, such as international and national political stability and avoidance of total nuclear war—goals to which he felt morally dedicated.

Kissinger now felt it was wise to emphasize the Geneva peace conference with the United States and the Soviet Union formally serving as cohosts. It would provide a broader forum for further negotiations on a larger disengagement of forces. He preferred the Geneva tactic for several reasons. It would give the Soviets a sense of participating in the negotiations, while, in reality, keeping them out of their substantive areas. It would still maintain American control of the negotiating process and provide continuity for the step-by-step approach. The talks could later be widened to include new participants and to alleviate Kissinger's fear that the Israeli-Egyptian talks were too narrow in scope and moving too fast; in this case the United States might lose control of the negotiating process.[30] Finally, it would please the Saudis to have the United States working so hard to achieve a settlement between Israel and the front-line Arab states—a contribution to resolving the oil embargo.

To implement this tactic, on November 18, Kissinger informed Egypt of his willingness to assign the disengagement of forces the top priority on the agenda of the proposed Geneva conference; however, the disengagement of forces could not be the precondition for convening the conference. He also explained the need for patience on the Palestinian issue. It could not be dealt with at this stage of preliminary maneuvering.[31] On December 8, the Egyptians agreed to attend the conference. Jordan was also expected to attend. It was Israel that threatened to torpedo Kissinger's project if the PLO attended; the Arab states (Jordan excepted) had recognized the PLO as the sole representative of the Palestinian people.[32] This recognition had been extended at the Arab summit conference held in Algiers on November 26-28, 1973.

To soften Israeli reluctance, Kissinger met with Dayan in Washington on December 7. In the course of the meeting, Kissinger used a trump card; he suggested that the Nixon administration would give the new Israeli request for arms a favorable review. As mentioned earlier, it was at this meeting that Dayan suggested a disengagement agreement which might be concluded even before the upcoming Israeli elections—a suggestion to which Kissinger responded with concern and caution lest Israel move too quickly and destroy the projected image of the United States appearing as the decisive force in a successfully negotiated outcome.[33]

On December 12, Kissinger journeyed to the Middle East to discuss the upcoming Geneva conference. In Egypt, he won Sadat's approval for a short delay in the conference, until after the upcoming Israeli elections later in December.[34] In Saudi Arabia, Kissinger's efforts were equally rewarding. The Saudis gave their approval to Sadat's policy and promised to end the oil embargo once an agreement could be reached on the disengagement of forces.[35]

But Kissinger did not record an equivalent success in securing either Syria's or Israel's promise to attend the conference. Despite his persistent efforts, the Syrians refused to go to Geneva, though they reserved the option, for the time being, to participate at a later date.[36] For their part, the Israelis made their participation conditional on a host of issues. Because of the dominating Arab and Third World powers in the United Nations, especially in the General Assembly, they opposed any major role for the General Assembly.[37] Beyond that, they categorically rejected any participation by the Palestinians, or any negotiations with the Syrians until Syria provided a list of Israeli prisoners.[38]

Nixon and Kissinger believed Israel would refuse to participate in the Geneva conference in the prevailing situation. For this reason, Nixon's personal intervention was deemed essential to convince Israel to fall in line with the administration's desire for a conference. To this end, Nixon sent Golda Meir a letter in which he explained the minimum and largely ceremonial role the UN secretary general would have. The conference would be the responsibility of the cochairmen. As for the Palestinians, their participation—or, for that matter, the participation of any other parties—would depend on the unanimous consent of all the original participants. To drive home his point, Nixon indicated that future American support for Israel could not be justified unless Israel attended.[39] Despite these assurances and warnings, Israel remained reluctant to attend the Geneva conference. Nixon felt called upon to send another message urging the Israelis to attend. In it he reminded them of their longstanding efforts to negotiate directly with the Arabs.[40]

In Israel itself, meanwhile, Kissinger reinforced the American pressure by warning the Jewish nation of the risks of international isolation.[41] More importantly, he said, without some cooperation from Israel, Sadat's moderate attitude might collapse. Together, Nixon's tough stand and Kissinger's personal diplomacy managed, in the end, to convince Israel to attend the conference.

On December 21, 1973, the long-anticipated Geneva conference was finally convened "under UN auspices." The participants were the United States, the Soviet Union, Israel, Egypt, and Jordan. As expected, the Syrians and the Palestinians were not represented. At the conference, Kissinger delivered a passionate speech in which he stated that the American objective in the Middle East was to achieve a peaceful settlement based on Resolution 242. More than that, the settlement should be achieved through a step-by-step approach in which the disengagement of military forces would be the essential first step.[42]

In reality, Kissinger probably did not know what to expect when he arrived in Geneva; he simply assumed the conference might be able to stay in continuous session and stumble toward some kind of "final settlement." He quickly found out that neither side was ready for final negotiations.[43] After one day, the conference was indefinitely recessed, but its framework was kept alive for two reasons: to provide a structure to which the recommendations of the various working groups could be submitted if and when agreements were reached; and to promote Kissinger's desire to keep the Soviets happy in their role as cochairmen of that framework.

THE EGYPTIAN-ISRAELI DISENGAGEMENT

The issue of disengaging Israeli and Arab forces had been discussed with both sides during Kissinger's mid-December 1973 trip to the Middle East. Kissinger and Sadat acknowledged the necessity of waiting until after the late-December Israeli elections before meaningful negotiations on disengagement could take place.

In Israel, Kissinger's efforts were directed not only toward convincing Israel to attend Geneva, but also to probing into the Israeli position on the question of disengagement. Kissinger shared with Golda Meir his concern about the importance of disengagement as a means of delaying the question of a comprehensive settlement.[44] The disengagement was also important to Kissinger as the means to end the oil embargo. A rescinding of the oil embargo, Kissinger reminded the Israelis, would help Israel because it would ease "oil-dependent" Europe's pressure against the Jewish state to make concessions to the Arabs. The disengagement would reverse the process of Israel's growing isolation in international relations. There was also the question of whether Sadat would lose patience and resort to a suicidal renewal of the war, with its extremely dangerous consequences in terms of both Middle East and global political destabilization. In this way he sought to link the global situation to the regional conflict. It would require more Israeli flexibility, yet the concessions must avoid undermining Israel's negotiating position.[45] Golda Meir countered Kissinger's argument by noting that it was tantamount to calling for a one-sided Israeli retreat rather than a mutual withdrawal of forces. In her view, an early withdrawal from the Canal zone would only give away Israeli bargaining chips vital for future negotiations.[46] What was more, the Arabs could resort to an oil embargo again in the future; an Israeli withdrawal would not make any significant difference on that score. Kissinger, in turn, explained that a disengagement would at least buy time for Israel until the Western countries would be in a better bargaining position with OAPEC. Israeli flexibility at this time was indeed extremely important. In Kissinger's view, OAPEC would be more hesitant in the future about an embargo if it knew the West would be better prepared to deal with the international oil cartel. When the Israelis then raised the question of asking the Soviet Union to put pressure on Egypt, Kissinger opposed the idea; any agreement should reflect the weight of the United States in the process, and the image of moderation on the part of Sadat.[47] It was very important to keep the Soviets from reaping credit in the matter at hand.

Overall, these Kissinger-Meir discussions laid the basis for the negotiations on disengagement expected after the upcoming Israeli elections. Once they were over, Israel sent its defense minister, Dayan, for talks with Kissinger on January 4 and 5, 1974. Dayan opposed the Geneva connection Kissinger felt was necessary. As far as Dayan was concerned, the Geneva forum could not produce a peace agreement. Dayan also had his own "private ideas," which included an Israeli military pullback to the vicinity of the strategic Mitla and Gidi passes—in return, of course, for equally important concessions from Sadat.[48] He presented Kissinger with a plan which involved a five-zone concept for disengagement in which each party would have two limited-force zones, separated by a buffer zone under UN auspices. Dayan's ideas also included the specific limits on the forces that would remain in these zones.[49] Equally important, he urged Kissinger to return to the Middle East to promote a prompt disengagement agreement. Kissinger checked with Sadat, who was equally anxious for him to return to the Middle East. In all, Dayan's plan became the conceptual foundation for the eventual disengagement agreement.

On January 10, Kissinger left for the Middle East. It was originally intended only as a two-step exploratory trip, with the negotiations then shifting to Geneva. Yet while Kissinger was in Egypt on his first stop, Sadat casually shocked him by suggesting the abandonment of the Geneva negotiations; rather, Kissinger should exclusively command the negotiations and run the shuttle diplomacy via his personal dynamics. Kissinger had preferred to mediate the main principle for an agreement and leave the details to the Israeli and Egyptian military working groups at Geneva. To entice the American secretary of state to stay, Sadat promised to help the United States get the oil embargo lifted once an agreement had been reached.[50]

Kissinger met again with Sadat on January 14, after returning from Israel. He presented the latest disengagement proposals to the Egyptian president. The proposals included the lifting of the naval blockade at Bab a-Mandeb; Israeli passage through the Suez Canal; the deemphasis of the military in commercial development of the canal zone; and the reduction of Egyptian forces on the eastern side of the canal.[51] Though Sadat was reluctant to publicly accept the Israeli proposals, he was ready to give the Israelis private assurances concerning many of the requests. Sadat strongly opposed, however, the limitation on Egyptian forces east of the canal. Kissinger sympathized with Sadat's reluctance; he knew how difficult it would be for the Egyptian president, politically and psychologically, to negotiate on the basis of the Israeli proposals.[52] To break the deadlock, Kissinger suggested they present the proposals as American ideas on force limitations, and in this way Sadat could appear to be accepting American proposals, not Israel's. Specifically, Kissinger proposed that the disengagement agreement should involve two documents: One would enshrine the American proposal combining elements of agreement for both parties, and the other would take the form of a "memorandum of understanding" between Sadat and the United States. In the end, Sadat accepted this suggestion.[53]

In Israel, Kissinger's efforts were also successful. He had long considered it premature for the Israelis to demand, at this point in the negotiations, that a disengagement agreement be conditioned on a peace treaty. He persuaded the Israeli premier to drop that demand.

Kissinger returned to Egypt to share with Sadat, on January 14, 1974, the Israeli map showing the proposed force-disengagement lines in Sinai, east of the Suez Canal. Sadat was open to Israel's insistence on having some military forces west of the passes. Sadat, however, demanded larger Egyptian military forces than Israel was willing to accept on the east side of the canal.

On January 17, President Nixon announced acceptance of the first disengagement of forces (the Sinai I agreement). It included a considerable reduction, of Egyptian military forces (east of the canal), from what Sadat had originally demanded.[54] President Sadat found the reduced force acceptable only after another brilliant Kissinger maneuver; he publicly presented the proposal as an American plan in which the formal documents were exchanges between Presidents Sadat and Nixon, including a secret memo of understanding that allowed Israeli cargo (but not Israeli ships) to transit the canal.

Furthermore, as an integral part of the disengagement agreement, Israel and the United States signed a ten-point memorandum of understanding, which included an American promise to play down the Geneva forum; a stipulation that UN forces could not be withdrawn without the consent of both parties; and a favorable review of Israel's defense needs on a long-term basis.[55] On the whole, the Sinai I agree-vindicated Kissinger's faith in the step-by-step approach; it succeeded where the previous (1969-71) approaches had failed. The fact that it made the United States the prime mover in Egyptian-Israeli negotiations signified a major diplomatic triumph for Washington. Sinai I symbolized the genius of Henry Kissinger. To some degree, he created the facts that made the agreement possible. The American secretary of state had achieved, for the United States, an enviable Middle East position vis-à-vis the Soviet Union; the United States had unilaterally succeeded in a first step of the peace process.

THE SYRIAN-ISRAELI DISENGAGEMENT

With the conclusion of the Sinai I agreement, Kissinger's diplomatic efforts were shifted toward the next most urgent issues: lifting the oil embargo and achieving a disengagement on the Syrian front and—if possible—on the Jordanian front as well. Kissinger pressed hard to have the oil embargo lifted immediately, but the Arabs wanted to ensure a prior disengagement on the Syrian front. The White House counted on Sadat to help persuade Saudi Arabia to lift the oil embargo. In a memorandum to President Nixon in December, Kissinger mentioned Sadat's promise to help end the embargo. Domestic pressures were mounting in the United States for Nixon to take drastic action, in view of the impending gasoline crisis. On December 28, Nixon responded to the memorandum, asking Sadat to use his influence in the Arab world to have the oil embargo removed (as previously promised).[56] In the request, Nixon stressed the importance of lifting the embargo without waiting for the outcome of the disengagement talks.[57] The effort failed.

In early 1974, Nixon again sought Sadat's help to remove the embargo. In February, President Sadat made a conscientious effort to convince his oil-producing Arab colleagues to rescind the policy. His efforts proved futile. OAPEC, as a minimum, insisted on a prior disengagement on the Syrian front—similar to the Egyptian-Israeli disengagement—before it would end the boycott.[58] The embargo thus remained in effect.

While this diplomatic effort was in progress, Kissinger decided to go to Jordan for talks with King Hussein. The trip was primarily designed to gain support for Sadat's disengagement diplomacy with Israel, and to encourage Hussein to initiate his own talks with that country. At this point in the negotiations, Kissinger encouraged the Jordanian monarch to keep his expectations modest: Israel, as he told Hussein, was adamantly opposed to the idea of a withdrawal on the Jordanian front; the most that could be attained at this time would be the gradual extension of Jordanian administrative authority over the West Bank.[59] But for Hussein, such an "administrative disengagement" would not be enough, since the other front-line states could count on achieving some territorial gains in the talks with Israel. Despite these differences, Kissinger and Hussein at this time shared the common objective of keeping the PLO out of the negotiations.[60] The objective was consistent with Kissinger's attitude toward the PLO since 1969. Before the October War, Kissinger had never considered the PLO as having a role in negotiating an Arab-Israeli settlement. After the war, he seemed to recognize the Palestinians as an essential parameter of the conflict. Did this mean making contacts with the PLO itself? Apparently not, though several Arab states were urging Kissinger to do so. Kissinger ignored these requests; if Israel refused to deal with the PLO, the United States would have to wait until either Israel's policy should change, or a new situation should arise.[61] In essence, Kissinger left his position unclear in order to maintain American flexibility for the future.

After the talks with Hussein, Kissinger went to Syria for discussions with President Assad concerning the Syrian front. In December, Syria insisted on a total evacuation of the Golan Heights as a precondition for a disengagement agreement. Now, the Syrian position was less rigid and included demands for only half of the territory occupied by Israel in 1967 (the Golan Heights) and all the territory that was occupied during the 1973 war.[62] But Assad maintained a tough stand on the issue of the Israeli prisoners in Syria. Kissinger, for his part, left Syria with the impression that Assad wanted a disengagement agreement but was unwilling to compromise over details.

To budge Damascus and Jerusalem, the Nixon administration, on

February 5, proposed a five-point plan for a disengagement on the Syrian front: Syria would submit the list of Israeli prisoners to the United States; the United States, in turn, would transmit it to Israel in exchange for a concrete proposal on disengagement. Both sides would then participate in further discussions in Washington, after which the negotiations would move to Geneva and follow the pattern of the Egyptian-Israeli military working groups there. On February 9, Assad agreed with this procedural plan. [63]

Shortly after Assad accepted the plan, a new diplomatic crisis arose. Several Arab states decided against ending the oil embargo until further progress had been made on the Syrian front. Clearly, the Arab decision was designed to put extra pressure on the Nixon administration to speed up the negotiations and, by implication, to increase the pressure on Israel for concessions. The Nixon administration responded in anger, but decided to continue the diplomatic process while dropping the embargo issue for the time being. Though the embargo and the energy crisis that followed had become inextricably linked to the Arab-Israeli conflict, Kissinger preferred, for domestic and other reasons, to avoid the appearance of directly linking the negotiations to requiring the Arabs to rescind the embargo.

On February 25, Kissinger left Washington to resume his shuttle diplomacy. In Syria, he found Assad flexible on procedural matters but tough on substantive issues. Assad insisted on an Israeli pullback beyond the cease-fire lines of the 1967 war; otherwise, there could be no agreement. On his way to Egypt, Kissinger found Sadat's attitude very cooperative;[64] Sadat even offered to use his good offices to help Kissinger arrange the disengagement between Israel and Syria.

After consultations with Sadat, Kissinger flew back to Israel, where the government presented its version of a disengagement accord with Syria. Specifically, the Israeli proposal followed the Egyptian-Israeli pattern; there would be a Syrian zone, an Israeli zone, and a UN buffer—all within territory occupied by Israel in 1973. [65] Returning to Damascus, Kissinger did not reveal to Assad the Israeli proposal because he felt it would be rejected outright. To keep the dialogue alive, Kissinger emphasized the concept of limited-force zones and a UN buffer zone. Even though he did not secure any concrete proposal from the Syrians, he obtained their consent for further talks in Washington on the issue. [66]

Before leaving the Middle East, Kissinger made two other stops, in Saudi Arabia and in Jordan. As expected, Kissinger urged the Saudis to end the embargo and support the efforts to arrange a disengagement on the Syrian front. He also raised some issues of mutual interest such as bilateral economic and security agreements. [67] Essentially, these talks laid down the foundation for future cooperation, e.g., the establishment of a joint economic commission later in 1974. In Jordan, he

met with King Hussein to discuss the Jordanian front and the role of
the PLO in the negotiations. Kissinger assured the Jordanian monarch
of American opposition to a Palestinian government-in-exile headed
by the PLO. Furthermore, he urged Hussein to be more patient with
Israel's "administrative-disengagement" proposal, on the assumption
that Israel might be more flexible in the future.68 Despite his efforts
to enlist the help of Egypt and Saudi Arabia in the matter, Kissinger
made little progress on either the Jordanian or the Syrian front. On
March 4 he returned to Washington.

It was now clear to the Nixon administration that a disengagement would be much harder to achieve on the Syrian than on the Egyptian front. Unlike the situation in the Sinai, Syria and Israel were too
far apart in their negotiating positions, both politically and militarily.
The domestic political environment in each country was not conducive
to compromises; the weakness of both governments limited each in
the compromises necessary to achieve a disengagement.69 In particular, it would be hard psychologically for Israel to make concessions
on the Golan Heights, given the increased Israeli settlements there.
The Soviet role at this stage also complicated the negotiating process.
Smarting because they had been left out in the Sinai I agreement, the
Soviets were showing signs of demanding a larger role in the Syrian
negotiations.

Back in Washington, President Nixon was under great pressure
to continue the diplomatic initiative. First, he was struggling with the
Watergate problem, and he hoped that dramatic diplomatic successes
might salvage his political career. Second, any progress on the Syrian
front might lead the Arabs to lift the oil boycott. Third, the possibility
of a renewed full-scale war on the Syrian front was much higher than
on the Egyptian front; such hostilities would undermine the intensive
American peace efforts made since the October War.70 Finally, the
specter of Soviet advancements in the region was an additional concern
that reinforced Nixon's resolve to keep Kissinger's Middle Eastern
mission alive.

To underscore American determination, Nixon warned the Arabs
on several occasions; American behavior in the Middle East must not
be linked to the oil embargo. The United States would not submit to
pressure; the longer the boycott continued, the harder it would be for
his administration to press ahead with its efforts for peace.71 The
OAPEC states, equally interested in the continuation of these efforts,
agreed on March 18 to lift the embargo against the United States,
though only on a quasitemporary basis, subject to review in June.

Even though Syria objected to lifting the embargo, Nixon and
Kissinger considered OAPEC's action a sign of Arab good faith. In
this situation, Kissinger's immediate task was to isolate the Syrian
regime from other Arab states such as Egypt, Saudi Arabia, and

Algeria. To that end, he stressed the need for Israel to be more forthcoming in its negotiating position. The encouragement of Syrian moderation would be crucial to the peace talks. Kissinger felt Israel would have to pull back to the boundary line of October 6, 1973, if not beyond, and to evacuate the Syrian town of Quneitra.[72] He did not expect Israel, however, to give up settlements on the Golan Heights at this stage of the negotiations.

On March 24, 1974, Kissinger left for the Soviet Union for talks on the Middle Eastern situation. The Soviets wanted the talks to be moved to Geneva, presumably to gain more leverage over the substance of the negotiations. The Soviets were very unhappy with Kissinger's activities in the Middle East; he was under sharp criticism. Kissinger defended his shuttle diplomacy by insisting it was requested by all the regional parties. Furthermore, the United States saw its role as achieving the necessary preliminary agreement that would then make a final settlement at Geneva possible.[73]

The Soviets insisted the Syrians wanted their participation at this stage of the negotiations. Kissinger quickly checked with Assad about this; to some degree, Kissinger did find Syrian support against the Soviet claim. Assad agreed to send representatives to Washington for talks, without requesting Soviet participation. After that, Kissinger was expected to travel to the Middle East for completion of the background negotiations; the military working groups would finalize the details in the context of the Soviet-American-organized conference at Geneva.[74]

After his return from Moscow, Kissinger met with Dayan on March 29 to review both the latest Israeli proposal for disengagement and the Israeli request for arms. Israel proposed a disengagement line that would run east of the October 6, 1973, line and retain Quneitra under Israeli control. Kissinger was unhappy with the proposal and warned the Israelis that the Syrians would reject it; however, he again said Israel need not, at this stage, abandon any settlements in the Golan Heights.[75]

On April 13, 1974, Kissinger met in Washington with Gen. Hikmat Shihabi, the Syrian representative at the negotiations. Shihabi presented Kissinger with a modified proposal in which the disengagement line would run west of Quneitra. Kissinger then showed Shihabi the Israeli map; as expected, the Syrian general refused the Israeli proposal, but did not reject the three-zone concept for disengagement. The Syrians were encouraged when Kissinger indicated he would try again to persuade the Israelis to go back to the October 6 lines and to evacuate Quneitra.[76]

Having built a negotiating foundation in March and early April, Kissinger began another round of shuttle diplomacy on April 28. On his way to the Middle East, he stopped in Geneva for consultations with Soviet Foreign Minister Gromyko. Kissinger's aim was to keep the Soviets informed about the progress of the talks. As always, these contacts with the Soviets were directed at preventing them from obstructing the negotiating process.

Middle East stops included Algeria and Egypt. The goodwill of the Algerians was thought necessary because they had friendly relations with the Syrians and the Palestinians; Kissinger felt they might be persuaded to act as a stabilizing influence. In Egypt, Kissinger received Sadat's solid backing for his ensuing mission on the issue of the Syrian front. Kissinger was seeking to build a pan-Arab consensus which could be used to influence Syria toward moderation in the disengagement negotiations.

On May 2, Kissinger went to Israel. The turmoil in Israeli politics had been relatively settled by the resignation of Golda Meir on April 10, 1974. But the interim government—still headed by Meir—continued to maintain an inflexible position on the details of a disengagement, even though Israel badly needed a respite from defense burdens, especially in the light of the miniwar of attrition on the Syrian front. To soften Israel's position, President Nixon sent a letter (on May 4) to the outgoing premier in which he warned the Israelis not to hamper the peace process; otherwise, the administration might reassess its whole range of relations with Israel. [77]

In addition to Nixon's pressure, Kissinger urged the Israelis to be realistic; they would have to make territorial concessions for the sake of peace. To Kissinger, the intricate details should not be allowed to destroy the overall objectives; disengagement was the essential objective. In particular, Assad had to be offered a deal similar to the Israeli-Egyptian one; since Egypt retained, under the Sinai I agreement, some territory that it had not held before the war, Assad would demand a similar offer for Syria. [78]

In Syria, Kissinger explained to Assad the domestic constraints on Israeli foreign policy and urged Syrian flexibility; Assad was not impressed. He was determined to have the disengagement line run west of the October 6 demarcation line. Thwarted at Damascus, Kissinger once more sought the help of the Egyptians, the Saudis, and the Algerians in an effort to moderate Assad's attitude. In the meantime, Israel itself began to modify its negotiating position on the disengagement line. Israel was now willing to return part of the town of Quneitra; but Kissinger indicated this was not enough. On May 7, he flew to Cyprus to meet with Gromyko "to maintain the U.S.-Soviet diplomatic front"—to succor the Soviet apprehensions about what was going on; the Soviet Union needed to be briefed on the developments in the talks. The Soviets were willing to stay neutral; at the same time, they were hoping that Kissinger would stumble. This would give them an opportunity to play a larger role in the talks. [79]

On May 8, there was a slight change in the Syrian position: Assad was now prepared to modify his position on the disengagement line. With this concession at hand, Kissinger urged the Israelis to be more forthcoming in the talks, but they were still intransigent. On May 9, Kissinger reported to Nixon about his upcoming and important meeting with Assad on May 11. To express his apprehensions about the situation, Nixon sent another letter to Israel on May 10, in which he expressed his concern about concluding a disengagement agreement. [80]

Despite these preparations, the Kissinger-Assad meeting on May 11 resulted in a deadlock. Both sides, the Israelis and Syrians, were adamant about their negotiating postures. Kissinger decided he would return to Washington after his upcoming round of talks with Assad on May 14. President Nixon now added support for Kissinger; he asked Kissinger to stay on and try harder for an agreement, promising more presidential intervention if necessary. [81] At this juncture, Kissinger decided to inject his own ideas into the talks. The same tactic had worked before, during the Egyptian-Israeli disengagement in January, when the Egyptians found the American ideas to be more acceptable than those originating in Jerusalem. By May 20, Kissinger had succeeded in obtaining an agreement from both sides regarding the disengagement lines. The problems of force limitations and of the size of the disengagement zones, however, remained unsolved. [82] After further deliberations with both sides, and with little progress in hand, Kissinger decided again to leave the region.

Once again, on May 22, President Nixon sent a letter to Golda Meir, in which he urged her to strive for a compromise for the sake of peace. Equally important, by May 23, Assad had modified his position regarding the force limitations and the size of the limited zones. He was now ready to accept a larger UN force in the buffer zone and limited-force zones of 15 kilometers. Assad's tactic was mostly designed to entice Kissinger to stay and finish the job. To Kissinger, nonetheless, this Syrian concession was a good sign and an incentive to resume his mission. He warned Israel that a failure now— after an agreement had been reached on the disengagement lines—would turn world public opinion against the Jewish state. [83] In short, Israel would have to give global political implications a higher priority than temporary military advantages.

Israel was not easily convinced; it, alone, would have to define its vital interests. Israel now responded with the following conditions: Syria should make a commitment to prohibit the PLO from launching guerrilla activities against Israel from its territory; the UN forces in the buffer zone could not be withdrawn without the consent of both sides; and Israel needed a long-term military-assistance commitment from the United States. [84] Back in Damascus, Kissinger faced two problems that threatened to undermine his entire mission: Assad now reopened the issues that Kissinger had assumed had already been settled; he also refused to commit himself publicly to prohibiting guerrilla activities from his territory. The first issue was settled when Assad backed down and sought compromises on the controversial points. The latter issue, however, was settled only after Assad had promised orally not to permit guerrilla activities from Syrian territory. The Nixon administration augmented this promise by a promise of its own to Israel; the United States would not consider it a violation of the disengagement agreement if Israel retaliated against guerrilla activities from the Syrian front. [85] With these issues out of the way, Israel and Syria reached an agreement on the separation of forces on May 29.

The Israeli-Syrian disengagement agreement was modeled after the Egyptian-Israeli treaty of January. Essentially, the agreement embodied the creation of five zones; two zones would be allotted to each country, and be separated by a UN buffer zone. The town of Quneitra, which was placed in the buffer zone, was given back to Syrian civilian authorities. In addition, there was an exchange of prisoners between the parties. Both sides also agreed to consider the agreement only a first step toward a durable peace based on UN Resolution 338 of October 22, 1973. Finally, Israel insisted on an American-Israeli memorandum of understanding dealing with contingencies such as the disintegration of the agreement. [86]

The Israeli-Syrian agreement seemed to be a triumph for American Middle East diplomacy; it represented the pinnacle of American influence and prestige in the region since the early 1960s. At the same time, Kissinger's step-by-step approach isolated the Soviets from participation in the post-October War settlement. On June 1, OAPEC decided not to reimpose the oil embargo on the United States. With these favorable conditions prevailing, President Nixon decided to make a June visit to the Middle East.

Even though Nixon's trip was motivated in part by Watergate, it had other purposes. The trip would reaffirm, symbolically, the agreements and the dramatic events that had taken place since the October War; it would help to solidify the bilateral relationships between the United States and the countries of the region; and it would give American policy makers an opportunity to discuss the general direction of American diplomacy in reference to future negotiations. [87]

Between June 10 and June 19, Nixon visited several Arab countries and Israel. In Egypt, Nixon promised Sadat economic assistance. This was aimed at encouraging Egyptian moderation in the Arab world and toward Israel. [88] Egypt would be permitted to buy an American nuclear reactor for nonmilitary purposes. The Nixon-Sadat talks involved some political issues as well. For instance, Nixon promised to work for the restoration of Egypt's international border (of 1949) in a final settlement and agreed that the Palestinians should be represented in the negotiations at an early date.[89] Sadat, in turn, urged Nixon to establish secret contacts with the PLO. Nixon seemed interested but remained noncommittal on this sensitive issue. The talks ended with the issuing of a joint statement of principles by the two countries.

In Saudi Arabia, the Nixon-Faisal talks touched on many issues, including the recent oil embargo and the Saudi role in the Arab world.[90] Nixon wanted to strengthen American bilateral economic ties with the Saudis; he also wanted to encourage them to continue supporting the peace process.

In Syria, the Nixon-Assad discussions reflected the Syrian concern about the next moves in the diplomatic process. Nixon felt the Geneva conference should be reconvened in September.[91] He encouraged Assad to support the diplomatic route rather than the threat of force. American-Syrian relations were improved with the resumption on June 16 of diplomatic relations between the two countries.

In Israel, the new Israeli premier, Yitzhak Rabin, inquired about the amount of economic and military aid Israel would receive in the future. Nixon assured Rabin of total support for Israel's security; he then noted that Kissinger's shuttle diplomacy was only the beginning of a long road toward a permanent peace in the area. In this endeavor, Israel would have to cooperate seriously with the United States so as to keep the momentum for peace going.[92] The Nixon administration also concluded a nuclear agreement with Israel, similar to the one with Egypt.

Israel had some reservations about American policy. It was unhappy with the American promise to supply Egypt with a nuclear reactor; Israel feared it would ultimately be used for military purposes. To ease the concern, the administration argued it was much better to have the United States supply Egypt within the framework of established safeguards, rather than have Egypt receive nuclear reactors from states which might be Israel's enemies or that might fail to require adequate safeguards.[93]

Before leaving the area, Nixon stopped in Jordan for talks with King Hussein. He pointed out the unique role the Jordanian monarch could play in a settlement of the Arab-Israeli conflict.[94] He also invited Hussein to Washington for talks in July on a disengagement on the Israeli-Jordanian front. Hussein, in turn, promised to continue a policy of restraint and moderation in the peace process.

On the whole, Nixon's trip to the Middle East could be viewed as a complement to Kissinger's shuttle diplomacy. At a minimum, it helped to strengthen American economic relations with the various states in the region. Nixon and Kissinger considered these economic relations to be an essential part of their political strategy.[95] During his shuttle diplomacy, Kissinger encouraged the idea of setting up joint economic commissions involving the United States and the Middle East countries. Later, in 1974, the United States did establish several joint economic commissions with states such as Saudi Arabia, Egypt, and Israel.[96]

SINAI II

Sinai II was achieved only after a turbulent interlude of other political developments and diplomatic efforts. The second Sinai disengagement should properly be seen in this context.

The May 31, 1974, Syrian-Israeli disengagement treaty, as discussed previously, provided the opportunity for a new assessment of possibilities for continuing the peace process. The Golan disengagement had truly been a major achievement, given the antagonism prevailing on each side. For Henry Kissinger it represented an accomplishment that was in doubt until the very end. The negotiation process developed into almost epic proportions. Kissinger met with Syrian President Assad only two days after signing Sinai I. In the end, the diplomatic challenge proved even more difficult. The American secretary of state left Washington for preliminary soundings of Syrian and Israeli demands on February 25; he returned on March 4, and then left for the Middle East to initiate the grueling shuttle negotiations on April 28, remaining in the Middle East until success was realized at the end of May. Several times the negotiations had been on the brink of failure. When it finally came, success seemed even a surprise to Kissinger himself. Mohammed Hassanein Heikal, the famous Egyptian political commentator and confidant of Egyptian presidents, exemplified a characteristic dimension of Middle East political culture in the Syrian disengagement. Syria's reluctance to accept a disengagement agreement with Israel was due, in part, he wrote, to the radical government of Iraq that exhorted Syria to avoid even a cease-fire with Israel. To induce Syria to become more open to an agreement during Kissinger's Damascus-Jerusalem shuttle, Heikal affirmed, Kissinger convinced the Shah of Iran to encourage Iraqi Kurds into a renewed war against the government in Baghdad. This eased Iraq's pressure against Syria in terms of a hard line against Kissinger's Syrian-Israeli disengagement efforts. The Kurdish insurrection broke out and by May, Syria had found itself capable of accepting the Kissinger negotiated agreement.[97]

The Syrian disengagement, however, was recognized as an achievement only in the sense of being a stepping-stone to further progress toward an ultimate reconciliation of the Arab-Israeli dispute. An American monopoly in superpower diplomatic initiatives would pay off only if, in fact, the United States could deliver a long-run resolution—or at least a permanent improvement—in the Arab Israeli conflict. Progress was urgently needed to realize American national interests in the Middle East.

Logically, Kissinger felt the next effort should concentrate on the Jordanian front. The long road to an overall settlement now needed the transferring of some West Bank territory to Jordanian control, in order to raise King Hussein's prestige in the face of competition with the expanding momentum of the more radical PLO.

The logic failed to prevail. The Turkish invasion of Cyprus occurred in July. Watergate's distractions added to the problem. President Nixon found out he could not escape his Watergate tormentors by escaping to the cheering masses in the Middle East. Furthermore, the president no longer had the power for necessary, but unpopular, acts such as pressuring Rabin's government in Israel for greater flexibility in yielding West Bank control. The "Jordanian option" also disintegrated in the face of domestic weakness within the Amman government and weaknesses in the inter-Arab coalition in general. Jordan had failed to achieve Arab respect in the October War. The Palestinians still had memories of "Black September" (1970). Jordan was increasingly becoming financially dependent on outside largesse—eroding further its status as being capable of following an independent foreign policy.

Shortly after Gerald Ford assumed the presidency, King Hussein went to Washington to discuss a disengagement on the Jordanian front. Not long after, Kissinger visited Amman to emphasize the importance of keeping the peace momentum going. Hussein proposed an Israeli pullback from the Jordan River in the context of a disengagement. Israel, however, strongly opposed any such move at this time.

In the course of the contacts with Jordan, Kissinger later perceived some ominous developments. King Hussein mentioned the upcoming October Arab summit at Rabat. The Arab heads of state might decide to designate the PLO as the exclusive authority to speak for the West Bank—as they had already done in principle at the November 1973 meeting in Algiers. Only at Rabat, they might well demand Jordan's public acquiescence in the matter. If this happened, the king said he would be compelled to withdraw entirely from the role Kissinger had proposed to him—a role extremely important to any further progress in the latter's conceptualization of the road to a settlement in the Middle East.

At the same time (between the Golan Heights disengagement and Sinai II), Syria continued to make pro-Palestinian public statements, but, when Kissinger approached Assad concerning Syria's support for the PLO's aspirations in Palestine, he equivocated. A Palestinian state would infringe upon Syria's nostalgic vision of Palestine as encompassed in the aspirations for Greater Syria. [98] The nature of this reality was demonstrated in 1976 when Syria joined with the (hated) Maronite Christians in common military operations against the PLO in Lebanon.

The Israeli government, at this time, was also too weak to accommodate the Jordanian option. [99] In June 1974, the Rabin government had a one-vote majority in the Knesset. The National Religious Party would not, for instance, have been willing to accept a significant concession to Jordan in "Judea and Samaria." Rabin found it politically expedient to reaffirm his predecessor's promise to make no concessions on the West Bank unless they were preceded by new elections. Having just become prime minister via the resignation of Golda Meir, Rabin sought to consolidate his position. He was certainly not interested in facing new elections at this time. When Kissinger impressed upon Israel the urgency of the Jordanian front as the next step in the peace process, Rabin diverted the thrust by encouraging another round of negotiations with Egypt.

The United States realized the time liabilities of pushing Israel into national elections; in all probability, it would involve a six-month hiatus in the peace-making process; it might prove fatal to the momentum that appeared to be so important. The period from the announcement of new elections until a new government would be in place, and capable of assuming its responsibility in the peace negotiations, would be six months—a gap Kissinger wanted to avoid.

Egypt also had little patience for any loss of momentum in Sinai. Sadat pressed hard for the priority of a second disengagement on the Israeli-Egyptian border. He had his own domestic pressures. Foreign Minister Ismail Fahmy and Gen. Mohammed Gamasy were unhappy with the limited concessions Egypt received in agreeing to Sinai I. After Sadat had carefully nurtured, domestically, the image of an Egyptian victory in the October War, he could ill afford to postpone acquiring another slice of the Sinai by waiting for time consuming Israeli elections. As if that wasn't enough, Sadat insisted it was futile to focus on the Jordanian option in view of the inevitably excessive demands the PLO would make.

In the meantime, in August, Nixon resigned and Ford became president. Kissinger made a special effort to keep foreign-policy initiatives flowing in order to present an international image of continuity in America's influence in the Middle East—an image of effectiveness not to be interrupted by the transition of power in Washington. [100]

Kissinger returned to Egypt to seek Sadat's support for Hussein at the forthcoming Arab summit. While in Cairo, the secretary of state announced efforts to secure another disengagement in Sinai. In part, the effort was intended as an incentive for Sadat to push for a pro-Jordan position at the Rabat conference in regard to any action it might take concerning the West Bank. Had American decision makers anticipated what the Arab leaders would agree to at the summit, even greater diplomatic efforts would have been made on behalf of King Hussein's role in a proposed West Bank solution.101

To Kissinger's dismay, the Rabat conference specifically decided in favor of the Palestine Liberation Organization. The PLO, not King Hussein, should be the sole legitimate representative of the Palestine people living in the West Bank. King Hussein felt pressured into publicly accepting this Arab League decision. At the time, the liability to the Kissinger strategy was not popularly recognized.

The prestige of the PLO was also enhanced at the international level when the PLO leader, Yasir Arafat, was invited to speak to the UN General Assembly soon after the Rabat decision. The Arab leaders had put the PLO at the center of the negotiating process dealing with the most vital and intractable aspect of the Arab-Israeli dispute—the West Bank and a future home for the Palestinian people.102

Henry Kissinger's step-by-step approach to the Arab-Israeli dispute would prove rewarding only if it led to a comprehensive settlement. The opposite was also true. If ameliorating the confrontation between Israel and one Arab state resulted in magnifying the conflict with other Arab states, it would be counterproductive. Sinai II, in retrospect, became the initial threat to an overall settlement. By the parties' failing to head off the (radical) PLO as the negotiating partner for a West Bank solution and, instead, adding another agreement to satisfy Egypt's interests against Israel, a comprehensive solution might well become less likely. At the time, however, a return to the Sinai focus seemed advisable.

By the end of 1974, Kissinger had gotten a good idea about each side's negotiating position. He knew the Egyptians wanted Israel to withdraw beyond the strategic Mitla and Gidi passes. Moreover, they wanted Israel to give up the oilfields of Abu Rudeis and Ras Sudr. They preferred to have the changes appear as a military transaction, not as a political deal, for Egypt did not want to develop the image of being isolated from the Arab world in its struggle against Israel. On the Israeli side, Kissinger knew Israel wanted Egypt to renounce the state of belligerence. Furthermore, it wanted to maintain a presence at the passes and keep the oilfields. The negotiations revealed the unwillingness of the Egyptians to compromise their position. Kissinger decided to advise Israel to accept something equivalent to nonbelligerency, such as the end of the economic boycott.

The Syrians and the Soviets, for their part, were unhappy with the Egyptian position. A second Israeli-Egyptian agreement would isolate Egypt from Syria and would leave the latter with the liability of having to threaten war unilaterally if negotiations with Israel failed. Assad was opposed to any further disengagement on the Egyptian front unless it was part of a comprehensive settlement.

The Soviets, realizing Kissinger's policy of weakening their influence in the Middle East, opposed a second accord on the Egyptian front. At the summit in Vladivostok in November 1974, Ford and Brezhnev added a discussion of the Middle East to their SALT agenda. The Soviets wanted the Middle East talks to be moved to Geneva, while Ford favored a continuation of the step-by-step approach as long as the regional parties supported it.[103]

The new American president agreed with Kissinger, who consistently opposed the Geneva forum as an actual negotiating medium. Geneva was to serve primarily a ratifying function for agreements already negotiated in the step-by-step diplomacy as conducted by the United States. Nevertheless, President Ford hinted to Brezhnev that the United States might resort to the Geneva option if there were no progress through the step-by-step approach. The Israelis got the message and sent Foreign Minister Yigal Allon to Washington for substantive talks in January, 1975. Allon brought with him a ten-point proposal that excluded the passes and the oilfields.[104] Ford and Kissinger were unhappy with the proposal.

To narrow the gap between both sides, the secretary of state left for the Middle East in early February for further exploratory talks. In Egypt, he found Sadat flexible, willing to accommodate certain Israeli concerns about security. Israel took a tough bargaining stance due to its domestic political situation and national security concerns.[105] Kissinger left the region on the assumption that he would return in March to resume his mission.

In March he returned to the Middle East, as he had promised. The Egyptians were again relatively flexible, but Israel maintained a hard bargaining position. To get an agreement, Kissinger kept the pressure on both sides. Eventually the gap was closed in terms of an agreement in principle. Israel would return the oilfields and pull back about 35 miles from the Suez Canal, with the new front lines being in the vicinity of the passes.[106] Now the haggling over the details began. Israel tightened its bargaining stance; concessions would have to be matched by Egyptian concessions. Ford and Kissinger understood the basic Israeli dilemma of having to give up tangible concessions for intangible ones—i.e., Arab changes of attitude in terms of elusive political commitments to peace; nonetheless, Kissinger was unhappy with Israel's stalling. Essentially, he thought Sadat's intangible concessions were real and an important development on the Arab side.[107] In his view, even a peace treaty between the parties was intangible; it would be highly unwise for Israel to let this negotiating opportunity pass without achieving an agreement. Equally important, he feared the United States would lose control of the diplomatic process if the negotiations failed.[108] Sadat knew the Ford administration was weak and still tainted by Watergate; this encouraged Israel to take a harder stand.

Under the circumstances, it was questionable whether Kissinger could mount enough pressure to cope with the Israeli strategy. 109 Perhaps a cooling-off period would help; Kissinger decided to suspend the negotiations for the time being, and on March 23 he went back to Washington.

The Ford administration was hardly in a mood to haggle with the Israelis in the light of other international problems such as the situation in Southeast Asia and the rising oil prices. To signal its displeasure, the administration, on March 24, announced it was "reassessing" its Middle Eastern policy; Israel should be made to understand America's displeasure with its negotiating position. This tactic, however, caused some consternation in Congress and in the American Jewish community. President Ford decided to stonewall the domestic pressure for the sake of keeping the peace process alive. Accordingly, he met with a representative of the Israeli-Jewish lobby, explaining his determination to continue the Middle East peace efforts in spite of the domestic opposition. Ford maintained it would be best for Israel to keep the momentum for peace going. 110 However indirectly, Jerusalem got the message.

On June 1, 1975, Ford and Sadat met in Salzburg, Austria, for talks on disengagement and other issues. At the meeting, Sadat complained about past Soviet behavior toward Egypt, especially in matters of arms supplies. Obviously he wanted to secure American economic and military aid. In fact, the question of military aid had been raised earlier during Kissinger's shuttle-diplomacy in 1974; but because of domestic opposition to the selling of arms to Egypt, Ford and Kissinger were more receptive to the idea of European arms supplies to Egypt. They did not want Egypt to rely solely on the United States for arms to replace Soviet weaponry; it would be best to diversify its arms sources. 111 In the political dimension, Sadat wanted to know about the latest Israeli proposal for disengagement; Ford said Israel had made no proposals. In the continuing dialogue with Sadat, the American president considered the situation unfortunate; if there were no progress in the peace process, pressures for renewing hostilities would increase. 112 Sadat, who shared Ford's assessment of the situation, came up with the idea of stationing American civilians in a buffer zone around the strategic passes; they could perform a vital surveillance role. Ford and Kissinger were receptive to the idea; perhaps it could break the diplomatic deadlock. 113 A few days later, when Rabin visited Washington, Ford presented Sadat's idea as an "American proposal." Rabin said he would submit the suggestion to his cabinet for closer examination. 114

The Israeli government, having realized the Ford administration's determination to ignore domestic pressures and move ahead with the peace process, was now ready to resume the talks. Against this background, Kissinger left for the Middle East on August 20 to pick up where he had left off in March. Before the talks got underway, Israel insisted on a memorandum of understanding with the United States on two points: Jerusalem should be notified beforehand of the direction of American policy in the region, and more American arms should be available to Israel. Even though the Pentagon expressed reservations about increased arms shipments, President Ford agreed to give Israel arms in excess of the Pentagon recommendations. This would make Israel feel more secure and, therefore, more willing to take "risks . . . for peace."[115]

In summary, the American-Israeli understanding made it easier for Israel to be more flexible. Both sides, the Egyptians and the Israelis, made some concessions, especially in regard to the strategic passes, and an agreement for another disengagement was reached; a force of approximately 200 American civilian technicians would be stationed in a buffer zone between the Egyptian and the Israeli military forces.

Kissinger's diplomatic efforts had produced another disengagement treaty, Sinai II, initialled September 1, 1975, and signed in Geneva on September 4. Associated with it was a series of "security blankets" involving American policy pledges and commitments.[116] Each side, somewhat precarious in its domestic power position, needed more-or-less unpublicized reassurances from the United States. For Kissinger this provided the opportunity for American policy to keep the Soviets out of the peace process.

Even though the treaty and the secret agreements that accompanied it entailed a heavy price for the United States in economic, political, and military terms, Ford and Kissinger considered it the best of all alternatives. Another war or another embargo could have disastrous consequences for the United States.

Sinai II provided for an Israeli territorial retreat. It was a trade-off; Egypt gained domestic political satisfaction by acquiring another slice of its Sinai territory plus the economic and prestigious benefit of the Abu Rudeis oilfields. Israel gained by reducing the bargaining threat of unified Syrian-Egyptian military action in the immediate future. In addition, Sinai II created the potential for serious inter-Arab divisiveness, which became actualized several years later (in 1977-79) in Sadat's moves to formally make peace with Israel. More specifically, the actual break in Arab ranks occurred during Sadat's three-step progression: the pilgrimage to Jerusalem on November 19, 1977; the Camp David Accords of September 17, 1978; and the Egyptian-Israeli peace treaty of March 26, 1979.

In Sinai II, Egypt formally agreed to forgo military force to resolve the Middle East conflict; avoid the threat of military force or a military blockade against Israel; allow nonmilitary Israeli shipping

through the Suez Canal; limit its military forces on the east side of
the canal; accept a UN-controlled buffer zone separating Israeli- and
Egyptian-controlled territories in Sinai; and welcome American civilian observers in the area of the crucial passes from which its own
military forces were still excluded. Egypt received the right to exploit
the Abu Rudeis oilfields but the area was closed to its military forces.

Israel had been unwilling to agree to even these limited Egyptian
gains without a number of assurances, understandings, and pledges on
the part of the United States. To appear evenhanded, Kissinger worked
out some assurances for Egypt also.

For Israel the primary concessions received from the United
States involved American civilian observers at the crucial passes;
assurances of diplomatic support—particularly vis-à-vis the PLO,
and in the United Nations, where Israel had taken a beating since the
Soviets turned against the Jewish state in the 1950s, and since the
explosion of UN membership as a result of the tidal wave of decoloni-
zation in the 1960s; and pledges of large-scale, sophisticated military
weapons in the context of a subsidized aid program.

Sinai II taxed even Kissinger's widely recognized diplomatic in-
genuity. Not only was he uneasy about pushing ahead with Egypt in the
peace process—magnifying the abyss caused by leaving the Jordanian-
Palestinian front without progress, and increasing the liabilities for
Syria in the status quo on the Golan Heights; he had to sell an entangling
American involvement to a Vietnam-embittered Congress under circumstances of a weak chief executive, Gerald Ford.

The administration knew that approval for the American civilian
technicians had to be secured from the Congress. Hopefully, all the
other understandings and commitments could bypass the Congress,
under the constitutional interpretations of presidential foreign-policy
authority and/or under various legislative acts already in the law books.

The various promises, interpretations, and commitments made
to Israel and Egypt were politically sensitive as each of the governments faced close scrutiny in the context of its domestic political
environment. The State Department hoped to maintain the confidential-
ity of these memorandums by making them classified documents while,
at the same time, requesting Congress for prompt action on the 200
American civilians.

Sinai II hearings in the Senate Foreign Relations Committee and
in the House Foreign Affairs Committee provided an outlet for the concern not only of sophisticated voices, but also for numerous groups
and personalities determined to vent their frustrations at American
foreign policy—from Vietnam, to the years of Middle East conflict,
and to the perils of détente with the Soviet Union.

In these hearings Kissinger's strategy, seeking prompt congressional approval via joint or concurrent resolutions, disintegrated due

to protracted haggling over concerns about treaty commitments versus executive agreements or joint action by both houses of Congress; the existence of secret executive agreements; and the legally binding nature of diplomatic commitments included in the classified memorandums of assurances considered an integral part of Sinai II.

Yet substantively, the most crucial issue raised in the hearings focused on the Kissinger step-by-step strategy in contrast to a comprehensive approach to a peace settlement in the Middle East. Foreign-policy veterans such as George Ball, Paul Warnke, and Charles Yost, in their testimony, focused on the benefits of Kissinger's step-by-step procedure versus a comprehensive final-settlement approach. They questioned whether the United States had paid too much in terms of diplomatic support, aid concessions, and sophisticated military weapons—especially to Israel—for only a limited step in reconciling Middle East tensions. Furthermore, the United States, they suggested, might well be buying counterproductive incentives to the supreme American interest in a comprehensive final settlement of the Arab-Israeli dispute.

The moderate Sadat, they said, should have an ameliorating role to play on the Arab side in bringing the Arab world to a satisfactory resolution of the conflict with Israel. To the degree Egypt found itself an outcast, how could the excessive demands of the Arab radicals be reduced to any acceptable compromise that Israel could be pressured into accepting?

Kissinger had his own doubts about the step-by-step procedure. Initially, it involved creating a cease-fire that could hardly be criticized as in advisable procedure. Beyond this, no previous attempt at an overall settlement had been successful after numerous wars and over a quarter-century of the conflict. Up to this time, the hard-line leaders had dominated the Arab approaches to a settlement. The oil-rich and conservative Arab states seemed to be unduly influenced by threats from the Arab radicals.

To Sadat, it didn't make sense to have the most powerful Arab state, Egypt, bear the brunt of international decisions made by lesser Arab nations. Egypt had the right to lead—at least act in its own national interests—rather than be dominated by policies not of its own making. Especially after the Rabat decision of October 28, 1974, to abandon probable progress on the Egyptian front, in favor of the Jordanian option, implied progress only on PLO terms—an exercise in futility since it would be anathema to Israel.

In summary, the step-by-step success in Sinai II did weaken Arab unity and reduced the likelihood that the United States would be able to pressure Israel into a final settlement, except on the latter's terms. In defense of Kissinger's moving ahead to consummate Sinai II, one notes it was in the interest of neither the United States nor the moderate Arab states, such as Saudi Arabia, Kuwait, Jordan, or Egypt, to settle on PLO terms. Kissinger felt it would be impossible to ignore a major Palestinian input, after the Rabat resolution, if one pushed ahead immediately for a final solution.

Sinai II created no irreparable split in the Arab front. Although "the jury was still out" as of mid-1983, those skeptical of Sinai II might more convincingly become critical of the moves President Sadat made after Kissinger left the administration, when Sadat took risks for peace by offering peace in Jerusalem, accepting the commitments of Camp David, and ratifying the formal peace treaty with Israel. It was this policy that carried the momentum beyond the accommodation capabilities of the other moderate Arab states. Whether or not this reduced the reality of a future comprehensive peace remains to be seen. Yet Sadat's actions after the Kissinger era were not inevitable and cannot be considered as mandated by the Kissinger strategy. They must be evaluated in the context of the Carter administration.

NOTES

1. Richard Nixon, RN: The Memoirs of Richard Nixon (New York: Grosset and Dunlap, 1978), p. 942.

2. Ibid.

3. Ibid., p. 1031.

4. Interview with a top Kissinger aide, Washington, D.C., July 13, 1977.

5. Interview with a former defense official in the Nixon administration, Washington, D.C., July 9, 1977.

6. U.S., Congress, House, Committee on International Relations, The Palestinian Issue in Middle East Peace Efforts, Hearings before the Special Subcommittee on Investigations of the Committee on International Relations, 94th Cong., 1st sess., 1975, p. 180.

7. William B. Quandt, Decade of Decisions: American Policy Toward the Arab-Israeli Conflict, 1967-1976 (Berkeley and Los Angeles: University of California Press, 1977), pp. 208-09.

8. William B. Quandt, "Kissinger and the Arab-Israeli Disengagement Negotiations," Journal of International Affairs 29 (Spring 1975): 39-40.

9. Quandt, Decade of Decisions, pp. 210-11.

10. Ibid., p. 216.

11. Ibid., pp. 214-15.

12. Ibid., p. 215.

13. Ibid.

14. Nixon, RN: The Memoirs of Richard Nixon, 942-43.

15. Quandt, Decade of Decisions, pp. 216-17.

16. Ibid., p. 217.

17. See Mohammed Heikal, "Discussion with Henry Kissinger," Al-Anwar (Beirut) November 9, 1973, pp. 1, 9; also see Bernard and and Marvin Kalb, Kissinger (Boston: Little, Brown and Co., 1974), p. 502.

18. Quandt, Decade of Decisions, pp. 217-18.

19. For details of the accord, see Matti Golan, The Secret Conversations of Henry Kissinger: Step-by-Step Diplomacy in the Middle East (New York: Quadrangle, 1976), p. 114.

20. Anwar el-Sadat, In Search of Identity: An Autobiography (New York: Harper and Row, 1978), p. 347.

21. Quandt, Decade of Decisions, p. 218.

22. Edward R. F. Sheehan, The Arabs, the Israelis, and Kissinger: A Secret History of American Diplomacy in the Middle East (New York: Reader's Digest Press, 1976), pp. 71-73.

23. Ibid.

24. Quandt, Decade of Decisions, p. 219; Golan, The Secret Conversations of Henry Kissinger, p. 119.

25. Golan, The Secret Conversations of Henry Kissinger, p. 120.

26. Quandt, Decade of Decisions, p. 220.

27. Golan, The Secret Conversations of Henry Kissinger, pp. 120-21.

28. Dayan, The Story of My Life, p. 548.

29. Quandt, Decade of Decisions, p. 221.

30. Quandt, Decade of Decisions, p. 220.

31. Ibid., p. 219.

32. Ibid., p. 220.

33. Ibid., pp. 220-21.

34. Ibid., p. 221; also see Sadat, In Search of Identity, p. 348.

35. Quandt, Decade of Decisions, p. 221.

36. Ibid., p. 223.

37. Bernard Reich, Quest for Peace: United States-Israel Relations and the Arab-Israeli Conflict (New Brunswick, N.J.: Transaction Books, 1977), p. 253.

38. Quandt, Decade of Decisions, pp. 221-22; Golan, The Secret Conversations of Henry Kissinger, pp. 125-26.

39. Quandt, Decade of Decisions, p. 222.

40. Ibid.

41. Kalb and Kalb, Kissinger, p. 527; see Sheehan, The Arabs, the Israelis, and Kissinger, p. 108, regarding the secret memorandum of understanding of December 20, 1973, between Kissinger and the Israelis.

42. Henry Kissinger, American Foreign Policy, 3d ed. (New York: W. W. Norton & Co., 1977), pp. 136-37.

43. Interview with Walter B. Smith II, Department of State, Washington, D.C., July 25, 1977.

44. Golan, The Secret Conversations of Henry Kissinger, p. 152.

45. Ibid., pp. 152-53.

46. Ibid., pp. 153-54.

47. Ibid., pp. 155-56.

48. Ibid., pp. 156-57.

49. Quandt, Decade of Decisions, 225-26; Sheehan, The Arabs, the Israelis, and Kissinger, pp. 108-9.

50. Quandt, Decade of Decisions, p. 226; Sheehan, The Arabs, the Israelis, and Kissinger, p. 107.

51. Kalb and Kalb, Kissinger, pp. 534-35.

52. Ibid.

53. Ibid., p. 535; Quandt, Decade of Decisions, p. 226.

54. Quandt, Decade of Decisions, pp. 226-28; Sheehan, The Arabs, the Israelis, and Kissinger, pp. 109-10; for details, see app. 6 in Sheehan, pp. 239-40.

55. Quandt, Decade of Decisions, p. 228; Sheehan, The Arabs, the Israelis, and Kissinger, pp. 111-12.

56. Nixon, RN: The Memoirs of Richard Nixon, p. 986.

57. Ibid., pp. 986-87.

58. Ibid., p. 987; also Quandt, Decade of Decisions, p. 231.

59. Quandt, Decade of Decisions, pp. 229-30.

60. Ibid., p. 230.

61. Interview with Harold Saunders, National Security Council, Washington, D.C., July 26, 1977; also see his statement to Committee on International Relations in Hearings, in The Palestinian Issue in Middle East Peace Efforts, pp. 178-80.

62. Quandt, Decade of Decisions, p. 230.

63. Ibid., p. 231.

64. Ibid., pp. 232-33.

65. Ibid.

66. Ibid.

67. Ibid.

68. Ibid., pp. 233-34.

69. Ibid., pp. 238-39.

70. Ibid., pp. 234-35.

71. Nixon, RN: The Memoirs of Richard Nixon, p. 987.

72. Quandt, Decade of Decisions, p. 236.

73. Ibid., pp. 236-37.

74. Ibid., p. 237.

75. Ibid.

76. Ibid., pp. 237-38.

77. Ibid., p. 240.

78. Golan, The Secret Conversations of Henry Kissinger, pp. 190-91.

79. Ibid., p. 196; also see Quandt, Decade of Decisions, pp. 240-41, especially n. 47 on p. 241.

80. Quandt, Decade of Decisions, p. 241, especially n. 50.

81. Ibid., p. 242.

82. Ibid., pp. 242-43.

83. Golan, The Secret Conversations of Henry Kissinger, p. 207.

84. Ibid., p. 208; also see Quandt, Decade of Decisions, p. 243.

85. Golan, p. 208; Quandt, p. 244.

86. Quandt, Decade of Decisions, p. 244; Sheehan, The Arabs, the Israelis, and Kissinger, p. 127.

87. See the statement of Alfred L. Atherton in U.S., Congress, House, Committee on Foreign Affairs, The Middle East, 1974: New Hopes, New Challenges, Hearings before the Subcommittee on Foreign Affairs, 93rd Cong., 2d sess., p. 133.

88. Nixon, RN: The Memoirs of Richard Nixon, pp. 1011-12.

89. Quandt, Decade of Decisions, p. 246.

90. Nixon, RN: The Memoirs of Richard Nixon, p. 1012.

91. Quandt, Decade of Decisions, pp. 247-48.

92. Nixon, RN: The Memoirs of Richard Nixon, p. 1016.

93. Golan, The Secret Conversations of Henry Kissinger, p. 216; also see Atherton's statement in The Middle East, 1974: New Hopes, New Challenges, p. 137.

94. Nixon, RN: The Memoirs of Richard Nixon, p. 1017.

95. Interview with Harold Saunders, NSC, Washington, D.C., July 26, 1977.

96. Stephen D. Hayes, "Joint Economic Commissions as Instruments of U.S. Foreign Policy in the Middle East," Middle East Journal 31 (Winter 1977).

97. Mohammed Hassanein Heikal, The Sphinx and the Commissar (New York: Harper and Row, 1978), p. 268.

98. Henry Kissinger, Years of Upheaval (Boston: Little Brown and Co., 1982), p. 1140.

99. Interview with Harold Saunders, July 26, 1977.

100. Kissinger was worried that the Watergate affair might undermine U.S. global and regional policies; see, for instance, Gerald Ford, A Time to Heal: An Autobiography (New York: Harper and Row, 1979), p. 121.

101. Interview with Harold Saunders.

102. See Richard Ullman, "After Rabat: Middle East Risks and American Roles," Foreign Affairs 53 (January 1975): 284-87.

103. Quandt, Decade of Decisions, p. 261.

104. Golan, The Secret Conversations of Henry Kissinger, pp. 229-30.

105. Ford, A Time to Heal: An Autobiography, pp. 245-46.

106. Ibid., p. 246; also see Quandt, Decade of Decisions, pp. 266-27.

107. Interview with a top Kissinger aide, Washington, D.C., July 13, 1977.

108. Quandt, Decade of Decisions, pp. 226-27.

109. Sadat, In Search of Identity: An Autobiography, p. 350.

110. Ford, A Time to Heal: An Autobiography, pp. 247-48.

111. Interview with Helmut Sonnenfeldt, Department of State, Washington, D.C., August 3, 1977.

112. Ford, A Time to Heal: An Autobiography, p. 290.

113. Ibid., pp. 290-91.

114. Ibid., pp. 291-92.

115. Ibid., pp. 308-9.

116. Quandt, Decade of Decisions, pp. 275-76; also see app. 8 in Sheehan, The Arabs, the Israelis, and Kissinger, pp. 245-57.

7

CONCLUSION

THE MIDDLE EAST IN THE KISSINGER GRAND DESIGN

Kissinger sought to end the Vietnam War without sacrificing important American interests in other areas such as the Middle East. Instead of dealing with foreign-policy problems in isolation, Kissinger saw the genius of a foreign secretary in his grand design—the ability to integrate and guide foreign policy in terms of a vision appropriate to both current global demands and future expectations. [1] The vision included a stable international setting in which the United States must play a central role. [2] The grand design included the Nixon Doctrine, détente with the Soviet Union and China, and the extension of this détente to other major powers. America's ability to maintain political stability and influence in regional politics could be an important factor in the grand design of global politics. [3]

Détente and the Middle East Conflict

Unlike the cold-war era, which assumed the maintenance of a relatively high tension, détente sought a conscious and deliberate reduction of tension at both the global and regional levels. [4] Negotiations and agreements in the context of the Nixon Doctrine were to replace "containment-through-confrontation" as emphasized in the cold-war era.

To Kissinger, détente was a continuing process, and not an obtainable condition. In his view, the overriding objective was the avoidance of a nuclear war, but détente could not escape some hard choices. A strong military force was essential to its success. Soviet expansion under the cover of détente had to be resisted. However, Kissinger realized détente would be impossible without benefits for both sides. [5]

The Middle East conflict involved, in part, local issues, yet the regional dynamics had to be accommodated to the overall American-Soviet détente.[6] Kissinger promoted two assumptions underlying an American Middle East policy: The key to a settlement of the Arab-Israeli dispute was to be found in Moscow as much as in the Middle East capitals; and the chief objective of détente—the avoidance of a total nuclear war—should be given priority over all regional concerns. Accordingly, the Kissinger Middle East strategy was mainly designed to save détente—which was almost shattered in the 1970 Jordanian civil war, and again in the 1973 war. It also was intended to solve the Arab-Israeli conflict (after the October War)—assuming the Arabs, Israelis, and Soviets were ready for such a settlement.

In 1969 and 1970, Nixon and Kissinger viewed the Middle East conflict as a contest of strength (via proxies) between the two super-powers, with Israel representing the American side, and the Arabs representing the Soviets. Given this view, it was not surprising that Nixon and Kissinger were unwilling to direct their efforts toward a solution until a new configuration of power and interests, resulting from the October War, had created a more fluid political situation.

There was, in all this, a nuance of difference between Nixon's and Kissinger's understanding of American strategy. At times Nixon went along with the "regional perspective" of State Department initiatives; at other times he soft-pedalled them; but in the end he usually leaned toward Kissinger's "geopolitical perspective," or long-term strategy.[7] Ultimately, Nixon agreed with Kissinger that the Middle East problem could only be tackled as part of the overall Soviet-American relationship.

The long-term strategy had several ambitious goals.[8] Nixon and Kissinger initially wanted to contain, and then reduce, Soviet influence in the Middle East. In their view, this could be achieved partly by separating Moscow's position from that of the Arabs. Kissinger sought to frustrate Moscow's policy by confronting the Arab leaders with the dilemma faced by the Soviets. Moscow was not in a position to deliver a peace settlement, because it lacked the leverage over both sides, nor was it willing to support a military solution, because it feared a confrontation with the United States. Kissinger also believed Moscow needed to be convinced that its support for worldwide regional crises could not undermine American influence either regionally or globally. Indeed, Kissinger, as a strategic thinker, noted how American behavior in one crisis would invariably affect Soviet behavior toward other crises; therefore, he stressed the need for American policy to appear tough during crises, as it did in regard to Cambodia, Cuba, Jordan in 1970, and the Indo-Pakistani war in 1971.[9] Kissinger also felt it was important to disengage from Vietnam in an orderly way so as to present the American withdrawal as an act of policy rather than as a collapse.[10] For Kissinger, the honorable abandonment of Vietnam required a policy involving three limiting parameters: a "decent interval" between an agreement and the North Vietnamese conquest of Saigon; no erosion of confidence in the United States as a "dependable ally" by alliance partners; and the avoidance of bitter domestic recriminations—charges of treason over who sold out the United States in Vietnam. In this way the Indochina policy would fit into the grand design. The idea was to counter inevitable charges of neoisolationism (to reassure Japan and our allies in Europe), and, at the same time, to enhance American credibility among the parties in the Middle East, who were watching the Vietnam negotiations and their outcome.

Another long-term goal was Kissinger's determination to have the Soviets behave responsibly in the Middle East, especially in crisis situations—to reward them when they did so. In reality, he used both rewards and sanctions for the purpose of achieving political objectives. In concrete terms, the strategy was to play on the Soviets' desire for Western trade and technology; the American government would decide when to reward or when to punish Soviet behavior; but the question was whether Congress would back the administration and give it a free hand to do "the fine tuning." As it turned out, many members of Congress wanted to make American trade and technology conditional upon the Soviets' willingness to liberalize their emigration policies, especially toward Soviet Jewry. This represented American ideological demands with an excessive cost factor that drained American "deposits in the Soviet bank" to the point where no assets were left to pay for much more important U.S. national interests. Kissinger knew the congressional emigration demands upon the Soviet Union were counterproductive; the United States would be much more effective by approaching the Soviets on emigration through confidential contacts.

The Soviets, for their part, were interested in détente and American trade and technology, but only at an acceptable price. In fact, they were exceedingly sensitive about outside interference in their internal affairs. In January of 1975, they cold-shouldered the trade agreement (and the Jackson Amendment to it) that linked the most-favored-nation status to the emigration rights of their citizens (Jews).[11]

Nevertheless, despite his reservations about the Jackson Amendment, Kissinger insisted international problems (high politics) could not be solved in isolation from each other; linkages of some sort were inevitable. As Kissinger noted: "Our approach proceeds from the conviction that in moving forward across a wide spectrum of negotiations, progress in one area adds momentum to progress in other areas."[12] In the conduct of foreign policy, Nixon and Kissinger sought to link the Salt negotiations to other areas of concern, including Vietnam and the

Middle East.[13] Nixon, in particular, had a notion about an American-Soviet trade-off involving Vietnam and the Middle East.[14] If the Soviets pressured North Vietnam to end the war, the United States, in turn, would make its Middle Eastern position more flexible. The Soviets, initially, were unenthusiastic about such a scheme; yet for the sake of a paramount issue like SALT, and in view of the desire for Western trade and technology, they were somewhat willing to discuss these problems in terms of the linkage approach.

Another aspect of linkage in international politics was the Kissinger emphasis on tripolar politics—the new relationship involving Moscow, Peking, and Washington. Even though the American-Chinese rapprochement had its own intrinsic significance, this new tripolar relationship was motivated in part by White House efforts to induce Soviet cooperation in regard to Vietnam and the Middle East.[15] Interestingly enough, President Nixon privately reassured the Chinese leadership about American determination to resist threats in the Middle East.[16] In addition, despite the initial shocks in Japan regarding the American-Chinese rapprochement, this new tripolar relationship would show American allies around the world, especially Japan and Western Europe, that détente was not a two-power (U.S.-Soviet) condominium at their expense.

Another long-term goal of American strategy was to develop some Soviet cooperation in the region. After the reduction of Soviet influence in the Middle East (e.g., after the expulsion of the Soviet military forces from Egypt in July 1972), Kissinger expected the Soviets to be more cooperative in regard to the area. Clearly, once he realized, at the May 1972 summit, that the Soviets were not going to change their basic orientation to the Middle East, Kissinger maneuvered the Soviets into a "holding pattern" with respect to both military and political expansion. Moscow's restraint was motivated largely by its reluctance to support an Arab military solution in the face of Israeli military power and, of course, by the need to avoid a direct confrontation with the United States.[17] As one American diplomat described the episode, "This took the Middle East out of the major power arena to some extent; . . . the major power factor in the equation certainly had been greatly reduced as a result of the events of 1972."[18] Politically, the 1972 summit proved to be a watershed in Soviet Middle Eastern policy. The Soviets were outwardly reluctant to accept any theory of détente which would be opposed by their local clients; but, in reality, Moscow's desire for détente with the United States, and for the apparent benefits that would be derived from it, exceeded regional concerns. As one Middle Eastern expert observed, "Moscow's interest in a global détente with the U.S. proved greater than its interests in capitalizing on the Egyptians' or other Arabs' helplessness."[19] Kissinger considered the 1972 summit a turning point in the Middle East situation because shortly thereafter, the moderate Arab leaders started to move in Washington's direction in search of a settlement.

All in all, the Basic Principles Agreement (of the May 1972 summit) and the Agreement on the Prevention of a Nuclear War (reached at the June 1973 summit) seemed to legitimize the process of détente between the United States and the Soviet Union. Though these agreements were not legally binding, Kissinger considered them standards of conduct (guidelines) for evaluating the progress in areas of concern involving the two countries. The Middle East was one such area of concern. In his view, these agreements marked the end of the cold war.[20] In fact, during the 1973 October War, Kissinger urged the Soviets to exercise restraint, reminding them of their responsibilities under these agreements.[21] However, the Soviets must have regarded the war itself as a vindication of their earlier warnings to American policy makers, in 1972 and 1973. Kissinger, nonetheless, regarded the 1973 war not as an example of the failure of détente, but as an indication of its limits.[22] As he saw it, even though the Soviets did not play a positive role in the Middle East conflict, Moscow could have made it harder for Washington to play a mediator's role in the postwar negotiations.[23]

The Nixon Doctrine and the Middle East Conflict

Conceptually, the Nixon Doctrine had its roots in previous foreign-policy experiences. These included Eisenhower's new-look defense program of the 1950s, Nixon's assessment of the Asian situation in the 1960s (the belief that the United States had a vital interest in the Pacific region), and domestic sentiments (public and congressional) against the Vietnam War.[24]

The strategy of the Nixon Doctrine (which Nixon and Kissinger preferred to call a "strategy for peace") was conceptualized in terms of strength, partnership, and negotiation.[25] These elements signalled a new pragmatic relationship between the United States and its regional allies. In short, regional allies were expected to share the burden of defense to a larger degree than was the case in the past. Kissinger placed less emphasis on formal alliances and more emphasis upon interest-based commitments.

The underlying assumption of the Nixon Doctrine was simple: American military technology and economic aid had become the substitute for direct American intervention in regional disputes. The doctrine was really not one of retrenchment; it did not support the no-more-Vietnams syndrome. Thus, in the future regional disputes, the emphasis would be on strategy and method rather than on objectives.[26]

Seen in this light, the aim of the doctrine was to sustain the American involvement in regional affairs through proxies and through tactical adjustments to changing circumstances. The doctrine, therefore, was far from reducing American commitments abroad or even redefining American interests—although it was cast in a phraseology conducive to good public relations toward a public soured on Vietnam. In reality, the doctrine was intended to put together an informal network of un-written alliances throughout the world.[27] For instance, countries like Israel, Iran, Jordan, Saudi Arabia, South Vietnam, and Ethiopia (later exchanged for Somalia) became advanced American positions within the framework of the doctrine.[28]

In a variety of ways, American Middle Eastern policy, after the June war of 1967, could be characterized as consistent with the under-lying principles of the Nixon Doctrine. Above all, there was a continu-ity in American support for Israel and also, of course, support for overall Middle East stability.[29] But after the 1967 war, the Soviets expanded their influence in the Middle East. That influence seemed to undermine the stability of the region and to exacerbate the Arab-Israeli conflict. In this context, the Nixon Doctrine was designed, in part, to discourage Soviet exploitation of regional conflicts. It amounted to a new containment of the Soviet Union at the regional level. In prac-tice, this meant the retaining of American predominance in the Middle East through proxies such as Israel, Iran, and Jordan.

Even though the doctrine was initially designed for application in Asia—i.e., it was used for Vietnamization and the containment of China—Kissinger hoped to use the Middle East (especially after the Jordanian civil war) as a model for other regions of the world. In ref-erence to the doctrine, Kissinger was prepared to help these countries that were willing to defend themselves against external and internal threats. Israel, therefore, qualified as a preeminent example because it needed only American economic and military aid, rather than Amer-ican forces, to defend its national security.[30] In this instance, how-ever, the premises of the doctrine coincided with American ethnic politics and with the moral foundations of the American ethnic political culture supporting democratic countries and Western values.

In the light of the doctrine, Kissinger was unwilling either to impose a settlement on Israel or to pressure it to accept a peace it considered harmful to its national security. He felt an imposed settle-ment of any kind would not contribute to the long-run stability of the region. It was easier, therefore, for the Nixon administration to re-main detached—provided Israeli security was preserved—than to favor a settlement under the auspices of the two superpowers, which would be opposed by Israel.[31] Israel, for its part, supported the Nixon Doc-trine as a counteraction to Soviet threats, because its security in the long run depended upon the willingness of the United States to be glob-ally involved.[32]

Clearly, the Nixon Doctrine was based on the overriding assumption that local clients needed a high degree of stability in order to protect themselves and American interests at the same time. In the Middle East, the outcome of the Jordanian civil war seemed to convince Kissinger of Israel's importance as a bulwark against radical ideology (including communism) and as a strategic ally against Soviet advancements in the region. American aid to Israel was thus justified on two grounds: to preserve the security of Israel and to insure the stability of the region (in the sense of perpetuating the status quo). Nevertheless, an American partnership with the moderate Arab states of the region was also considered important. In summary, the Kissinger policy sought to devise a strategy in which the political, economic, military, and psychological (ideological) components were combined in an effectively integrated policy. [33]

Because the status quo of the Middle East was shattered, the October War can be seen as a failure of the Nixon Doctrine. Yet the net result of the war and its aftermath demonstrated the relative success of the doctrine in several ways. First, American predominance was preserved in the Middle East, especially with the decrease of Soviet influence. To Kissinger, local predominance was essential for the survival of détente in an unstable area like the Middle East.

Second, the American commitment to Israel increased as a result of the war. The American airlift during the war (albeit somewhat belated) and the subsequent aid after the disengagement agreements highlighted the special relationship that has existed since 1948. Israel, realizing its great dependence on the United States during the October War, placed a great deal of emphasis on the military and economic aspects of the Nixon Doctrine. By contrast, Kissinger put more stress on the political dimension of the doctrine, especially during the post-October War negotiations; after all, the Israeli emphasis on the military aspect had failed to guarantee either the status quo or the overall stability of the region.

Finally, even though the American commitment to Israel increased after the war, American influence and prestige remained intact in most of the Arab world. In addition to its use in the Arab-Israeli conflict, Kissinger tried to promote the Nixon Doctrine in the Persian Gulf area, with its vital oil resources. This emphasis on regionalism and self-reliance through arms transfers and economic ties might not, however, guarantee American interests in the long run. [34] International politics are much too complicated to be controlled by the magic of aid alone. Threatened or actual use of American military power might well be necessary at times.

THE KISSINGER MIDDLE EAST STRATEGY—A SUMMARY

Kissinger sought to develop a Middle Eastern strategy appropriate to global détente with the Soviet Union, yet the strategy should include elements specifically tailored to the needs of the particular region. To elaborate, the Middle East policy should be set within the constraints of the Nixon Doctrine, including the preservation of American predominance in the area.

Immediately upon taking office on January 20, 1969, President Nixon initiated a review of American foreign policy, including Middle East policy as well as the global perspective. The State Department promptly presented its policy proposals to President Nixon. It proposed the continuation of the Jarring mission in the context of UN Resolution 242 (of November 22, 1967). The Johnson administration had placed considerable faith in the mission's ability to accommodate the Arab-Israeli dispute. Now the State Department also supported the idea of big-power talks on the Middle East—four-power and two-power talks. These talks were intended, first, to augment the Jarring mission and, at the same time, to provide a framework within which the Arabs and the Israelis could negotiate a settlement. Secretary of State William Rogers supported these various efforts, in the belief that the process itself might create its own momentum for peace. In his view, nothing would be lost if the United States acted as a mediator between the Arabs and the Israelis. By the end of 1969, however, the gap between Israel and the Arabs had shown no movement. Clearly, neither the big-power talks nor the Jarring mission produced meaningful negotiations, especially in the light of the on-going war of attrition at the Suez Canal.

Therefore, on December 9, 1969, the State Department presented a comprehensive American plan—known later as the Rogers Plan— based on Resolution 242. It was announced as a "balanced" solution to the conflict. Essentially, the Rogers Plan called for an Israeli withdrawal from the occupied territories in exchange for a genuine peace with the adjacent Arab states. The Arabs were unenthusiastic about the plan; worse still, the Soviets and the Israelis rejected it.

With the failure of the Rogers Plan, the State Department reverted back to the Jarring mission; but by the beginning of 1971, this mission too had reached an impasse. Yet the State Department continued to support the mission, largely for tactical purposes: to encourage the Egyptians to extend the cease-fire that was due to expire in February. There was little reason to believe Israel would accept the Jarring mission, since Jarring's substantive ideas were similar to the Rogers Plan, already rejected a year earlier.

Kissinger was frankly skeptical about the State Department's policy, since it assumed the road to peace in the Middle East lay rather exclusively in Washington's pressuring of Israel to return to the June 4, 1967, boundaries. [35] Kissinger felt there were severe liabilities in this kind of pressure on Israel. In part, it involved reasons of American domestic politics; there was already enough national divisiveness over Vietnam, without adding the Middle East. Kissinger also opposed the anti-Israel policy because he was unwilling to press Israel as long as the Soviets and the Arabs refused to modify their positions. The logic of the situation dictated a militarily strong Israel that could avoid the necessity of American intervention (the Nixon Doctrine) on its behalf. [36] In brief, Kissinger resisted imposing a settlement on Israel.

The Nixon administration had little confidence in the United Nations' ability to effect a solution. Before the October War (1973), Kissinger, and to some degree the president, saw little opportunity for a settlement. Positions were simply too irreconcilable, unless a crisis occurred, to change the status quo. Neither the Soviets nor the local parties were ready, according to Kissinger, for a comprehensive settlement of the Arab-Israeli dispute at this time. Yet just such a crisis to break the status quo was produced by Anwar Sadat in the October War.

By 1970, Nixon and Kissinger were more concerned about a Soviet exacerbation of the Arab-Israeli conflict than they were about finding a comprehensive solution to it. The Soviet Union had now escalated the shipments of military weapons to Egypt. The expanded aid included sophisticated weapons such as SAM-2s and SAM-3s. Even more worrisome, Moscow had begun to send its own personnel to operate these weapons. In short, the modern military technology and the Soviet military presence in Egypt—including now the movement of SAMs into the forbidden standstill zone of the Suez Canal—created a mood of pessimism in the White House.

Given these considerations, the Jordanian civil war of September 1970 seemed to convince Kissinger that the Middle East conflict was essentially a microcosm of the larger East-West conflict. In his view, the favorable outcome of the war, as well as the Israeli-American cooperation during the war, demonstrated to the Soviets and their local clients the relative success of the Nixon Doctrine strategy. But in reality, the White House overemphasized the Soviet role in the civil war. This overemphasis, in turn, led to a faulty assessment of the situation: that the American-Israeli strategic unity, newly coalesced during the Jordanian civil war, could preserve the status quo almost indefinitely. The October War demonstrated the error of this assessment.

Thus, in the period between the Jordanian civil war and the 1973 October War, White House efforts were aimed at preserving the stability of the region. Only in this context could Kissinger support the

State Department's efforts at trying to promote an interim agreement on the Israeli-Egyptian front. Henry Kissinger felt it would be a mistake to try to link the State Department's 1971 interim initiative to a comprehensive peace treaty. He supported the initiative because he felt it would reduce the Soviet military presence in Egypt. As it turned out, both the Egyptians and the Israelis were not ready for even a limited agreement.

While President Nixon supported the State Department's initiative at first, he gradually abandoned that position and moved to support Kissinger's long-term strategy to split the Soviet-Arab unity and drastically reduce Soviet influence in the Middle East. Seen in this light, the moderate Arab states clearly held the key to the Kissinger strategy. After neutralizing the Soviet position, it was important to induce the Arabs to look toward Washington for a solution.

The 1972 and 1973 summits gave Nixon and Kissinger the opportunity to freeze the situation in the Middle East. In effect, this amounted to the incorporation of the Arab-Israeli conflict into the overall Soviet-American process of détente. From this emerged the Kissinger strategy for influencing the Soviet Union (through the incentives of arms limitation [SALT], Western technology, and expanded trade credits) to act with restraint and be cooperative in relation to the United States in the Middle East. It was a strategy of détente based upon linkage and "the-concert-of-great-powers" idea.

The American challenge was to induce Moscow toward greater Soviet-American cooperation; this implied some replacement of Soviet influence with American influence, to create an acceptable great-power role for the United States in the Middle East.

Sadat realized that the White House's pro-Israel stance in the Arab-Israeli conflict was directly linked to the Soviet military presence in Egypt. He decided to remove this obstacle to the improving of relations with the United States; this was done in July 1972 (as previously discussed). Next, President Sadat set out to further modify the international politics of the Middle East. He found the no-war, no-peace situation of the status quo to be intolerable, and he was determined to change it. The situation would have to be changed either through the diplomatic route (e.g., Ismail met with Kissinger in 1973), or by resort to the military option. Interestingly enough, Kissinger himself had similar thoughts on the Arab-Israeli conflict. Whether in Vietnam or in the Middle East, Kissinger believed both sides of the regional conflict needed a "brutal episode of battle" before meaningful negotiations could start. [37] A Middle East war was considered almost indispensable in order to break the stalemate; after all, with some luck, a regional war could be manageable under the umbrella of détente. [38]

Given this assessment, the October War of 1973 created the political fluidity necessary for the Kissinger strategy. Indeed, Kissinger's efforts, after the war, were designed to produce a situation in which the local disputants could feel secure about their ability to make concessions. Essentially, he wanted to conduct the substantive negotiations under American auspices, while keeping Moscow out of the negotiating process until an Arab-Israeli agreement was at hand. The Soviets' cooperation would be necessary in this American endeavor, and their "hands-off" cooperation would have to be paid for—with luck, it could be purchased—by the promise of prestige resulting from a highly publicized, highly visible, jointly sponsored U.S.-USSR conference that would formally approve the Arab-Israeli peace agreement negotiated by the United States. If the price for cooperation were inadequate, additional "funds" would have to be found in détente—the carrot of trade credits, agricultural products, Western technology, etc.

As far as the United States was concerned, Kissinger's Middle East efforts, after the October War, should be considered in the context of saving détente while striving to resolve the Arab-Israeli conflict under American auspices. In this context, Kissinger's step-by-step approach attempted to break the psychological barriers between the disputants. The negotiations avoided, for the time being, a discussion of the central issues: final borders, Jerusalem, the Palestinians, etc. Despite the convening of the Geneva conference under UN sponsorship and under joint Soviet-American cochairmanship, the actual disengagement talks were conducted under American auspices. Kissinger, of course, kept the Soviets informed about the negotiations so as to keep them "in the Middle East game."

In negotiations with the Arabs, Kissinger articulated the American position: The United States was the only country that could influence Israel to make concessions; another war was possible but should be kept out of the disengagement talks. In the negotiations with Israel, Kissinger noted that absolute security for one country meant absolute insecurity for all other countries; Israel needed to look for long-term security interests rather than short-term military considerations. Israel would have to enlarge its perspective to consider American global concerns, such as détente and the energy crisis, in assessing its negotiating position. Kissinger talked to Israel about the importance of stable, regional economic relationships. He projected Middle East economic commissions that would include Israel. Kissinger felt the development of economic ties was an important complement to the politics of conflict resolution.

AMERICAN POLICY: ITS STRENGTHS

The Nixon-Kissinger era (or, to use Stanley Hoffmann's phrase, the "Kissinger cycle") coincided with a major transformation in American policy, triggered by the Vietnam War. Conceptually, Nixon and Kissinger sought to develop an American world policy that harmonized immediate concerns with long-term goals. In practice, they wanted to end the war in Vietnam and, at the same time, retain American credibility, both globally and regionally.

Unlike previous American diplomacy, which was highly blended with ideology, moralistic principles, and legalistic formulations, the Kissinger approach rested on interests and power. This approach made it easier for the Nixon administration to deal with regimes like those of the Soviet Union and China. Following this approach, for instance, Kissinger was able to end Chinese isolation from international politics in 1971 and 1972—an isolation stemming from China's revolutionary ideology. He was also successful in reducing America's isolation from the international community due to the American involvement in Vietnam.

Overall, the Kissinger approach to foreign policy introduced political appreciation and understanding to the strategic nuclear equation between the United States and the Soviet Union. These were embodied in the 1972 and 1973 summit agreements. Kissinger hoped that a détente based upon linkage would have a spillover effect on other areas of concern to the two countries, especially in an unstable area such as the Middle East. He considered the survival of détente in the Middle East as a test for détente in other areas around the world. Whether during the Jordanian civil war of 1970, the Cuban crisis over Soviet intentions to build a submarine base in Cuba in 1970, or the October War of 1973, he believed the relative restraint in Soviet behavior was achieved through a détente-oriented foreign policy. Even though each superpower rallied behind its local clients during the 1973 October War, the two superpowers did cooperate inside and outside the United Nations to end the hostilities.

After the October War, Kissinger's step-by-step diplomacy succeeded in convincing both the Arabs and the Israelis of its integrity. The United States could be an honest broker in the disengagement talks without endangering the basic security interests of either side. Indeed, Kissinger's diplomacy eased each side's psychological inhibitions which had characterized the history of the Arab-Israeli conflict. Kissinger managed to keep the negotiations under American auspices. In addition, his concentrated Middle East diplomacy, after the hostilities, improved Arab-American relations to the point of terminating the Arab oil embargo against the United States.

AMERICAN POLICY: ITS WEAKNESSES

In the settlement after World War II, the United States favored a basic restoration of the prewar situation in the Middle East. A quarter-century later, the Nixon-Kissinger grand design was again a renewed effort, via political realism, to preserve the international status quo while denying Moscow's objective of a pro-Soviet modification of that status quo.

Henry Kissinger's strategy in pursuing the grand design of détente via the Nixon Doctrine conformed to the time-honored practice of political realism—policy based on interest and power. Though the approach was an improvement over the crusades of the cold war, it lacked the comprehensive adequacy to deal with the total milieu of world politics making its demands upon the leadership role to which the United States aspired. For example, the U.S. allies in Western Europe and the Asian ally, Japan, became skeptical about the possible consequences of the détente policy with respect to their own possibilities for self-assertion—especially where their unilateral interests diverged from those of the United States. U.S.-USSR détente might well appear to America's allies as superpower collusion designed to dominate world politics.

Also, the Kissinger grand design experienced competition between regional and global objectives in a crucial range of challenges. For instance, the effort to achieve regional predominance could be pushed to a point where it threatened global equilibrium. A case in point was the October War, where détente between the two superpowers was almost shattered. Furthermore, Kissinger's preoccupation with "high politics" and global stability diverted attention from the pressing problems of the Third World. [39]

In spite of Kissinger's frequent reference to the statesman's need for vision and a sensitivity to the movement of history, his grand design was basically pessimistic and inadequate as a long-range conceptualization of international politics. Not only was it unable to restore the domestic consensus on foreign involvement that had been shattered by the Vietnam War; it was also criticized for being "power effective" in a kind of Bismarckian mold—with all the limitations that policy implied. The idea here implied that Kissinger was effective in manipulating a power balance to acquire valid U.S. national interests, yet the pursuit of national self-interests against the self-interests of other states had, as its logical conclusion, the self-destruction of the very international system that was to be preserved. What was lacking in this ultimately self-defeating policy was a conceptualization of dimensions promising more than zero-sum payoffs in regard to political problems in the global society. The Kissinger politics of secretive manipulation lacked the vital long-range imperatives of a society's soul. Viewed analytically, power, as in the Weltanschauung of "political realism," needs to be complemented by a sense of shared values lest the "law of the jungle" ("might makes right") become a rational behavior model. What is it that gives the citizen meaning and purpose—

roots? What is it that stimulates the citizenry, through common purposes, to a sense of common achievement worthy in terms of something to live by? A national society without community values is hardly a community worth defending—or, for that matter, capable of defending itself. Kissinger's grand design emphasized Realpolitik to preserve the status quo but was weak in building national motivation and voluntary support for common values that made national survival worthwhile.

Developing meaning and purpose in the life of a society, Kissinger may perhaps correctly affirm, is not the responsibility of a statesman. In Bismarckian terms, it may well be praiseworthy to note his heroic task of containing the law of the jungle (the very purpose of civil society)—and, equally commendable, the deflation of righteous crusades. But who, then, will fill the role of developing meaning and aspirations in the national society—so that we can have something worthwhile to defend in national security terms? In fairness to Kissinger, he did, on occasion, address the issue.[40]

In line with the above discussion, critics pointed out various other weaknesses in the Kissinger foreign policy. They charged, with considerable validity, that too little attention was devoted to an effective and sustained policy toward the Third World's claims of economic injustice; toward promoting a more equal status relationship and greater shared political values among the Western powers; and toward the threatened malaise of Western society itself—e.g., the "strange spiritual emptiness,"[41] arising simultaneously with the rise of Western material affluence and scientific development, by which man destroys his humanness through his subconscious self-conversion into a machine, via engineering, to promote material productivity.

With regard to Israel and the Arab world, the Nixon administration had no coherent policy toward the Arab-Israeli conflict from 1969 until late 1971 (when Nixon authorized Kissinger to take a more active role in Middle East affairs). The reason for this was simple: Nixon and Kissinger were restraining the State Department from actively pursuing its initiatives in the area. This restraint undermined the authority of American diplomats (including Rogers and Sisco) to deal with the Arab and Israeli leaders. In fact, by 1972 all the important diplomatic transactions regarding negotiations in the Middle East were conducted by Nixon and Kissinger from the so-called White House back channel rather than from the normal channel of the State Department. The White House back-channel approach reflected Kissinger's priority on global policy over regional policy when the two seemed to overlap; centralization of decision making brought efficiency and integration to global foreign policy. Nixon and Kissinger were more concerned about the Soviet influence in the Arab-Israeli conflict, and (until mid-1972) the continued Soviet military presence in Egypt, than they were about finding a diplomatic resolution for the Arab-Israeli conflict.

This overriding concern with Soviet influence almost invariably overshadowed the dynamics of the regional conflict. Whereas Rogers saw the Middle East problem as an American predicament that needed the harmonizing of Soviet-American differences for the sake of a settlement, Kissinger considered the problem a Soviet difficulty that could be magnified so as to split the Soviet-Arab position. Accordingly, Nixon and Kissinger were unwilling to make compromises with the Soviets because they feared Moscow would win the acclaim of the Arab world if its Middle East policy succeeded, and it became the successful champion of the Arabs. Furthermore, the Soviets would be seen as instrumental in pressuring the United States toward a more pro-Arab policy—a development Kissinger found intolerable.

Kissinger's back-channel preemption of Middle East policy can also be seen in the way the White House ignored the Soviet warnings, in 1972 and 1973, of a renewed war in the Middle East. The White House similarly dismissed the State Department's repeated concerns about war in the Arab-Israeli dispute. The long-standing view of the State Department was that, sooner or later, war would break out if there were no progress on the diplomatic front. The October (1973) War vindicated the Soviets' as well as the State Department's assessment of the situation.

After the October War, Kissinger pursued a Middle East policy known as step-by-step diplomacy, in coping with the exceedingly unstable cease-fire that had left Israelis on the west bank and Egyptians on the east bank of the Suez Canal. Kissinger's step-by-step diplomacy had serious liabilities. First, it was never conceptualized as the initial step in the pursuit of an overall peace settlement; rather, it was a policy designed to cope with the present threat of renewed hostilities. Viewed from this angle, Kissinger, ironically, was implementing the essential provisions of the now-defunct Rogers Plan—the step-by-step emphasis, the very same thing he opposed in 1969-70.

Second, Kissinger's step-by-step diplomacy, being a highly personalized effort, was effective only when it involved a bilateral setting such as the case with Egypt and Israel; however, it was ineffective when the number of actors increased. [42] In a highly complex situation such as the Middle East conflict, Kissinger's diplomacy proved inadequate for the multilateral dimensions of the Arab-Israeli dispute. In addition, the diplomacy produced a paradox in American policy: On the one hand, Kissinger urged the Israelis to take a long view of the international situation; on the other hand, he concentrated on the short-term advantages for the United States—emphasizing the immediate arrangements while deemphasizing the long-term goals. [43]

Third, Kissinger's step-by-step diplomacy was somewhat unrealistic in trying to isolate the Soviet Union and Western Europe from the substance of the negotiations. It should be noted, however, that the

Soviets themselves underestimated the timely confluence of interests that occurred between the Arab states and the United States after the October War. The Soviets hinted vaguely about participating in guarantees for a final settlement, while, at the same time, waiting for the Arabs to become disillusioned by Kissinger's diplomacy. Yet the Soviets could have created added difficulties for Kissinger's Middle East diplomacy had they chosen to do so. Certainly, Nixon and Kissinger were continually aware of the necessary Soviet participation in any final peace settlement—an insurance policy to keep the Kremlin leadership from negating the American peace effort.

Finally, Kissinger's step-by-step diplomacy avoided the central issues of the Arab-Israeli conflict. Quite obviously, Nixon and Kissinger recognized the impossibility of finding a meaningful and lasting settlement for the Middle East dispute unless the Palestinian problem were resolved, yet they consistently rejected any contacts with the PLO. It was not until November 1975 that one of Kissinger's top Middle East aides admitted the obvious: "In many ways, the Palestinian dimension of the Arab-Israeli conflict is the heart of the conflict."[44] Kissinger, like most Washington foreign-policy decision makers before and since, maintained that the Palestinian problem should be dealt with in the context of a Jordanian-Israeli settlement. In his view, the Israel-Jordan peace settlement should come first. Once this were achieved, the Palestinians should then settle their differences with the Jordanian regime, not with Israel. It was a very attractive solution, however utopian, to resolve the Palestinian issue via the moderate, pro-Western government of Jordan. In effect, Kissinger wanted to transform the Palestinian problem from an international problem to an intra-Arab one. Yet it was a game both sides could play. The Kissinger strategy suffered a severe blow when the Arab League, meeting in Rabat on October 29, 1974, unanimously agreed to make the Palestine Liberation Organization "the sole legitimate representative of the Palestinian people on any liberated Palestinian territory." Jordan felt compelled to publicly affirm its support for this resolution.

In conclusion, any critical evaluation of Kissinger would be incomplete without touching two bases: the chronic occupational hazard of any political practitioner—the problem of morality, including deception; and the nihilistic nature of responses to conflicts of will and interests in any semianarchical situation such as international politics.

No foreign-policy decision maker can survive over time without giving a certain priority to the defense of the national interest. Henry Kissinger frequently came under attack for his willingness to utilize national power in the attainment of national interests. Similarly, he was criticized for his excessive determination to achieve results, even to the extent of sacrificing personal integrity, i.e., deception.

In this journey of the statesman, how can the guideposts of morality be affirmed? What is morality in international affairs? Answers are perilously difficult, and respondents frequently become the victims of public predation. Yet we can posit the following standard: Foreign policy cannot validly be judged directly by absolute or eternal moral injunctions. Rather, a policy is moral if it maximizes the net results of all relevant values measured in terms of both ends and means, and available alternatives based on available information. We shall, however, accept one qualification: In system-overload situations where severe cases of individual moral agony threaten the very personal integrity of the individual's subjective self, Western Judeo-Christian culture has tended to allow for a "backup system" of "checking out" of political reality and into "inner spirituality."

Thus, for serious students of international affairs, the issues related to (1) some kind of theoretical guidance as to the optimum "sugar-vinegar" mix in international confrontations and (2) a theory of political deception demand a response. Let us examine the second issue first.

Kissinger defended his numerous incidents of behind-the-scenes maneuvering as justifiable action to achieve comprehensive results. This is not unusual, for it is frequently pointed out how interpersonal interaction, even in the intimate relations between spouses, is stabilized by sensitivity to the other's particular mental-emotional and/or value status; unessentials are best left unsaid if they threaten the stability of the relationship. Yet at what point do behind-the-scenes diplomatic assurances and deliberately created impressions, lacking in verity, become morally intolerable deceptions—or a fatal flaw in developing trust upon which détente was to be built?

The basic Kissinger genius in working out disengagements in Sinai and in meeting the expectations of King Hussein on the Jordanian front involved, for instance, personal assurances that omitted very important information to the respective parties. Kissinger's model for avoiding the disaster of total nuclear war focuses on this very point. He emphasized that an expansionist state should be confronted with an incentive to become a "legitimate" state, by being offered respect for its legitimate interests in the international community. The respect would emphasize trust and integrity.

Henry Kissinger prided himself (and justifiably so) in developing President Sadat's trust in him ("my friend Henry") in the Sinai disengagement negotiations. Yet, when he felt Moshe Dayan was willing to make concessions to Egypt beyond those that, Kissinger had indicated to Sadat, Israel was willing to make, he waffled. He cautioned Dayan to retract some of his concessions in order to give Egypt the impression (deception) of more determined U.S. efforts to get concessions for Egypt from Israel. In Years of Upheaval, Kissinger makes numerous references to deceptions of this kind in U.S.-USSR diplomatic contacts. One cannot charge such behavior as being a priori, immoral since each side suspected the other was somewhat aware of what was going on. Yet trust should have some common meaning if it is to play the Kissinger-designated role.

In an address to the Senate Foreign Relations Committee,[45] Kissinger noted the importance of "modes of conduct that extend beyond the letter of agreements to the spirit of relations as a whole." In essence, he again stressed the important role envisioned for trust in the easing of international tensions. But we look in vain for transcendental values or meaning by which national decision makers assume a trusting role in their national leadership positions. It is difficult to avoid the conclusion that, for Kissinger, trust in international diplomacy is an exceedingly illusive concept that all too often evolves into an act of prudence for the prevailing moment.

A second basic issue raised by the Kissinger legacy concerns some kind of theoretical guidance for an optimum sugar-vinegar mix of policy in any confronting situation. How does one change the enemy's mind—or, for that matter, how does the enemy change one's own mind in the matter of an excessive definition of "legitimate" national interests or "just demands" of one's own state? Karl von Clausewitz reminds us of the intractable dimension of the answer by his axiom that war is a continuation of diplomacy by other means.

Presumably, what the world demands of political scientists, or perhaps wise men sophisticated in political reality, is to avoid the supreme holocaust—World War III. In this context we look at Kissinger's Middle East diplomacy for clues to the vital priority question of guidance in optimizing the sugar-vinegar mix. To illustrate what is at stake, we can look at the foreign-policy choices of any state, yet the case is most obvious if we take Israel as an example. Israel's national interest will not be maximized by either depending on goodwill and entirely renouncing the use of force in its policy toward the Arabs; or by relying exclusively on a hard line (vinegar), i.e., no compromise—the objective of unconditional surrender of all Arab armies.

An optimum policy is based upon an optimum mix, and that mix decision has all too often been based on a hunch or a fleeting feeling far removed from objective theoretical considerations. What did Kissinger contribute to the sugar-vinegar dilemma of foreign-policy analysis? If it is true, as Peter Dickson's elaborate analysis concludes, that "Auschwitz made it impossible for Kissinger to believe in . . . universal moral principles and eternal values . . . " and that he "was unable to find an ultimate value or purpose in historical process because he considered death final,"[46] is there any possible conclusion except that of political nihilism? Does anomie prevail broken only by the impact of the challenge-capitulation dilemma in which "might makes it right," or the verdict in the dispute is decided in favor of the state most successful in exploiting the reluctance of the other to go to war? The development of a carrot-stick (sugar-vinegar) trade-off theory is impossible without some kind of knowable pattern of expectations and responses in international confrontations.

In one of his most memorable speeches to the Senate Foreign Relations Committee, [47] Kissinger presented the outlines of his own theory of an optimum sugar-vinegar mix in foreign policy—at least as it was relevant to the United States in the mid 1970s. The context of a U.S.-USSR confrontation is not appropriately characterized by anomie or anarchy in the sense of the challenge-capitulation dilemma, i.e., the Soviet Union being guided by an attempt to exploit goodwill and gain from the reluctance of the United States to resort to a violent confrontation. Kissinger projected a reciprocal Soviet response to ease tensions resulting from a U.S. détente initiative. The sugar portion of the American foreign-policy mix ought to include providing the Soviet Union with a substantial enrichment of its national interests in terms of the most-favored-nation treatment in trade, technology, etc.; and avoiding American interference in the Soviet Union's internal affairs as it related to Jewish emigration, internal civil-rights policies, etc.—at least not by public pressures. The vinegar portion of the American policy mix involved a cancellation of the above Soviet interests (a retraction of American détente policy) if the USSR attempted to interfere in our defense alliances; if crises were used to achieve unilateral gains; if the Soviet Union failed to cooperate in arms-limitation agreements; and "if it does not contribute to progress toward stability." [48]

Optimistically, Kissinger projected a movement "from competition to cooperation" and the development of habits of prior "consultation"; an expanding of the network of relationships between the United States and the USSR; increasing "collaboration between East and West"; [49] and even the developing of more harmonious national policies in international organizations, leading to a greater sense of world community. The result would be one of essentially changing each state's priorities from developing war capabilities associated with a state's responsibility for national security to the tasks more commonly associated with the domestic political order.

We have here a Kissinger at his optimistic best. In this moment of semieuphoria, Kissinger's theory of the optimum sugar-vinegar policy mix is not anomic indeterminism, but an orderly response scenario in which gradual increments in a sugar policy, while force is kept in reserve (vinegar policy), elicit a more or less reciprocal sugar response evolving eventually, if one may extrapolate somewhat, into a vast stable network of legitimized responsibilities and obligations resembling a stable domestic political system.

Whether Kissinger actually believed this or whether he simply developed the fine art of public relations, telling the public what it wanted to hear, the reader must judge for himself.

NOTES

1. Dan E. Caldwell, "American-Soviet Détente and the Nixon-Kissinger Grand Design and Grand Strategy" (Ph.D. diss., Stanford University, 1978), pp. 147-56.

2. David Landau, Kissinger: The Uses of Power (Boston: Houghton Mifflin, 1972), p. 7.

3. J. L. S. Girling, "Kissingerism: The Enduring Problems," International Affairs 51 (July 1975): 341.

4. Coral Bell, The Diplomacy of Détente: The Kissinger Era (New York: St. Martin's Press, 1977), pp. 1-2.

5. U.S., Congress, Senate, Committee on Foreign Relations, United States Relations with Communist Countries, Hearings before the Committee on Foreign Relations, 93d Cong., 2nd sess., 1974, pp. 248-49.

6. Interview with Helmut Sonnenfeldt, NSC and State Department, Washington, D.C., August 3, 1977.

7. Henry Kissinger, White House Years (Boston: Little, Brown and Co., 1979), pp. 898-99.

8. Interview with Morton Halperin, NSC, Washington, D.C., March 16, 1977.

9. Kissinger, White House Years, p. 897.

10. Interview with a top Kissinger aide, Washington, D.C., July 13, 1977.

11. Caldwell, "American-Soviet Détente and the Nixon-Kissinger Grand Design and Grand Strategy," pp. 240-41.

12. See Kissinger's statement on détente in United States Relations with Communist Countries, p. 249.

13. Caldwell, "American-Soviet Détente and the Nixon-Kissinger Grand Strategy and Grand Design," pp. 166-67.

14. Kissinger, White House Years, p. 559.

15. Landau, Kissinger: The Uses of Power, p. 106.

16. Richard Nixon, RN: The Memoirs of Richard Nixon (New York: Grosset and Dunlap, 1978), p. 574.

17. Kissinger, White House Years, p. 1297.

18. Alfred LeRoy Atherton, Jr., "The Nixon Administration and the Arab-Israeli Conflict," in The World Balance and Peace in the Middle East: Reality or Mirage?, ed. Seymour M. Finger (London: Associated University Presses, 1975), p. 203.

19. Malcolm H. Kerr, "Nixon's Second Term: Policy Prospects in the Middle East," Journal of Palestine Studies 2 (Spring 1973): 28.

20. Kissinger, White House Years, p. 1250; Caldwell, "American-Soviet Détente and the Nixon-Kissinger Grand Design and Grand Strategy," pp. 260-62.

21. Caldwell, "American-Soviet Détente and the Nixon-Kissinger Grand Design and Grand Strategy," p. 444.

22. Nixon, RN: The Memoirs of Richard Nixon, p. 941; also see Kissinger's Statement on détente in United States Relations with Communist Countries, p. 267; and Bell, The Diplomacy of Détente, chap. 5.

23. Nixon, RN: The Memoirs of Richard Nixon, p. 1038; also see Kissinger's statement on détente in United States Relations with Communist Countries, p. 263.

24. Melvin Gurtov, "Security by Proxy: The Nixon Doctrine and Southeast Asia," in Conflict and Stability in Southeast Asia, eds. Mark Zacker and R. Stephen Milne (Garden City: Anchor Books, 1974), p. 208.

25. Walter F. Hahn, "The Nixon Doctrine: Design and Dilemmas," Orbis 16 (Summer 1972): 363.

26. Gurtov, "Security by Proxy: The Nixon Doctrine and Southeast Asia," p. 233.

27. See Naseer Aruri, "The Nixon Doctrine and the Mideast," New York Times, May 20, 1972, p. 33.

28. Ibid.

29. Seymour M. Finger, "The Nixon Doctrine and the Middle East," in The World Balance and Peace in the Middle East: Reality or Mirage?, ed. Seymour M. Finger (London: Associated University Press, 1975), p. 210.

30. Shlomo Slonim, United States-Israel Relations, 1967-1973: A Study in the Convergence and Divergence of Interests, Jerusalem Papers on Peace Problems, No. 8 (Jerusalem: The Leonard Davis Institute for International Relations, Hebrew University of Jerusalem, 1974), p. 37.

31. Kerr, "Nixon's Second Term: Policy Prospects in the Middle East," p. 25.

32. Aruri, "The Nixon Doctrine and the Mideast," p. 33.

33. Stephen R. Graubard, Kissinger: Portrait of a Mind (New York: W. W. Norton and Co., 1972), p. 96.

34. Guy J. Pauker et al., "In Search of Self-Reliance: U.S. Security Assistance to the Third World Under the Nixon Doctrine," Rand Memorandum, R-1092-ARPA, June 1973, pp. 7-12.

35. Kissinger, White House Years, p. 357.

36. Ibid., p. 371.

37. Cited in Roger Morris, Uncertain Greatness, Henry Kissinger and American Foreign Policy (New York: Harper and Row, 1977), p. 253.

38. Ibid., pp. 253-54.

39. William Fulbright, "Basic Aspect of the National Interest," in The Nixon-Kissinger Foreign Policy: Opportunities and Contradictions, ed. Fred Warner Neal and Mary Kersey Harvey (Santa Barbara: Center for the Study of Democratic Institutions, 1974), pp. 36-37.

40. See, for instance, Henry Kissinger, "Détente with the Soviet Union: The Reality of Competition and the Imperative of Cooperation," The Department of State Bulletin 71, no. 1842 (October 14, 1974), 505-19.

41. Zbigniew Brzezinski, "U.S. Foreign Policy: The Search for Focus," Foreign Affairs 51 (July 1973): 717-18.

42. George W. Ball, "The Looming War in the Middle East and How to Avert It," The Atlantic Monthly 235 (January 1975): 10-11; also see George Ball, "Kissinger's Paper Peace: How not to handle the Middle East," The Atlantic Monthly 237 (February 1976): 41-49; George Ball, Diplomacy for a Crowded World: An American Foreign Policy (Boston: Little, Brown and Co., 1976).

43. Interview with Walter B. Smith II, Department of State, Washington, D.C., July 25, 1977.

44. U.S., Congress, House, Committee on International Relations, The Palestinian Issue in the Middle East Peace Efforts, Hearings before the Special Subcommittee on Investigations of the House Committee on International Relations, 94 Cong., 1st sess., 1975, p. 178.

45. Kissinger, "Détente with the Soviet Union: The Reality of Competition and the Imperative of Cooperation," p. 519.

46. Peter W. Dickson, Kissinger and the Meaning of History (New York: Cambridge University Press, 1978), p. 8.

47. Kissinger, "Détente with the Soviet Union: The Reality of Competition and the Imperative of Cooperation," p. 505-19.

48. Ibid., pp. 516-19.

49. Ibid., p. 509.

8

EPILOGUE

Looking back from the vantage point of mid-1983, Kissinger's impact on the Middle East comes into sharper focus. He created the foundation for at least a major resolution of the Arab-Israeli dispute. The PLO's disaster in Lebanon could not have happened as it did in the summer of 1982 without the prior stabilization of the Israeli-Egyptian front. Henry Kissinger's role in Middle East policy indeed created a foundation for the political stabilization of the Middle East—the goal of American foreign policy since 1948. "It was Kissinger who built the foundation for Camp David and the peace treaty; Kissinger is the real scoundrel," a sophisticated Palestinian lamented to us in Amman (November 1981).

Detaching Egypt from the irreconcilable Arab front seems, in turn, to have been impossible without Nasser's death in 1970 and the October War of 1973. Much of the controversy surrounding Kissinger's foreign-policy leadership centered, as already discussed, on his role related to the 1973 war.

Memoirs share great events from a personal perspective. An array of such autobiographies, related to this era of the Middle East, adds depth to the crises of the Kissinger legacy. National leaders of that tragic period who have now completed their memoirs give an account of the war as seen through their uniquely tinted lenses. As Alexander Pope once quipped, "All looks yellow to the jaundiced eye." Or, as has been more recently observed, The substance of the scholar's objectivity is a bias of his culture. In any case, a synoptic examination of memoirs makes a fascinating commentary on the October War, the springboard from which Kissinger applied the wedge for a resolution of the Arab-Israeli conflict.

EXAMINING THE MEMOIRS

Mahmoud Riad

"Memoirs inevitably channel events through honorable perspectives." With this in mind, let us examine the memoirs by beginning with Mahmoud Riad and his account of the 1973 war. Riad spent a decade as Egypt's foreign minister under Nasser and Sadat. He was secretary general of the Arab League during the war.

Riad attributed Egypt's defeat in the October War (the Arabs call it the Ramadan War) to a failure in Egyptian military strategy—the Egyptian invasion force should have driven to "the Sinai passes" (which, he said, could have been achieved at the time of initial military superiority over Israel), instead of stopping "ten kilometers east of the canal"; to its failure to maintain "reserve forces" on the western side of the canal; and to the lack of a "commander at the front," instead of the battle field operations being directed from Cairo.[1] In addition, there was the inevitable Arab citing of U.S. military aid to Israel, especially the wartime airlift, as the ultimate explanation for the defeat.

Kissinger's peace efforts were seen by Riad as a public deception to erode the Arab position. "The image of Kissinger constantly shuttling between capitals of the region was superimposed over the action in the form of a heroic drama, . . . a written drama, produced and played by Kissinger himself. The role he was anxious to project was that of the great peace-maker; in fact, he was sowing the seeds of discord and friction, . . . deliberately aborting opportunities for a real peace. . . . His devious step-by-step policy . . . was confined to those steps which Israel permitted."[2]

Anwar Sadat

When Anwar Sadat's memoirs were published in 1977, Egypt's defeat in the 1973 October War became an Egyptian victory. His memoirs, In Search of Identity, affirmed Egypt's victory over Israel—a success due to his own leadership. In the words of the president, he signed the Aswan armistice agreement, formally ending hostilities, to maintain "the real magnitude of my territorial victory. . . ."[3]

Sadat took strong issue with the Western conclusion that only the "emergency cease-fire" saved the Egyptian military forces from utter disaster resulting from the brilliant Israeli Deversoir strike across the canal. "By concentrating vast forces at Deversoir," writes Sadat, "the Israelis hoped to frighten me into believing that they posed a threat to Cairo! . . . I was fully confident that the [Israeli] countercrossing was a naive, though reckless, operation and that it was doomed to failure. If I proceeded with the military plan we had laid down, . . . Israel would have lost 400 tanks and suffered 10,000 casualties, killed and wounded. This result wasn't merely possible or probable: it was a definite certainty."[4] Why, then, didn't the Egyptians launch the attack against the Israelis' Deversoir bulge? To quote Sadat: "Because it would have meant more bloodshed, more 'bad blood' and hatred."[5]

If Egypt was winning the war, why did he accept the October 19 unfavorable cease-fire in place? Accepting this arrangement included accepting strong Israeli armored forces, on the West Bank of the canal, with an open road to Cairo. Sadat anticipated the question; he said the cease-fire was necessary because: "For the previous ten days I had been fighting—entirely alone—against the Americans with their modern weapons. . . ."[6]

Anwar Sadat relates an interesting dialogue that occurred during a meeting with Henry Kissinger on December 11, 1973. He asked Kissinger what the United States would do if Egypt moved militarily against the Israeli military forces, on the West Bank of the canal, that had encircled the Egyptian Third Army and were threatening the supply line to the Second Army when the cease-fire occurred. Sadat records in his memoirs that Kissinger told him the United States would attack Egypt "if you attempt to liquidate the Israeli pocket."[7]

Mohammed Hassanein Heikal

Mohammed Heikal is best known as a long-time close associate of Nasser and as editor-in-chief of the semiofficial Egyptian newspaper, Al Ahram. He was minister of information for a short time under Presidents Nasser and Sadat. His relations with Anwar Sadat were quite good early in Sadat's presidency (including the period of the 1973 war). Later these relations cooled significantly—especially after the Sinai I Agreement. On September 4, 1981, Sadat had Heikal arrested and imprisoned along with over 1,500 other journalists, opposition political leaders, and religious activists. After Sadat's assassination on October 6, 1981, the new Egyptian president, Hosni Mubarak, freed Heikal in November.

Heikal may well be Egypt's most sophisticated and knowledgeable journalist and political observer. He first became a recognized Egyptian journalist while with the Egyptian army in Palestine in 1948.

Plans for the 1973 war, he insisted, began in "the immediate aftermath of the 1967 defeat."[8] The results of the October War were presented not as an Israeli victory, but as a standoff between the Arab and Israeli armies, in which the superpowers preempted the course of the war. The United States, as he saw it, had defeated the Soviet Union in the political confrontation after the superpowers had brushed aside the Middle East belligerents and preempted control of the events.

Kissinger's worldwide alert for U.S. military forces was the moment of truth symbolizing Heikal's conclusion.

In terms of military operations, Egypt's biggest mistake of the war was a "failure in communication."[9] Heikal notes that Prime Minister Golda Meir spoke to the Knesset on October 16 (Tuesday) about the Israeli army, "now fighting," in Meir's words, "east and west of the Suez Canal"; Egypt's President Sadat, Heikal notes, insisted it was only "Israeli psychological warfare"; local Egyptian forces would wipe out, Sadat told Heikal, the "three infiltrating Israeli tanks" that "managed to cross the canal."[10] When the Egyptian command got a more accurate picture of the Israeli thrust across the canal, it was too late. On Wednesday and Thursday, the Soviets showed Sadat aerial photographs of some 270 Israeli tanks and armored vehicles on the west bank of the canal.[11]

How could Egypt have let this happen? Heikal explained the success of the Israeli bridgehead by citing five factors. First, Egyptian reserves had inadvisedly been sent across the canal to aid the drive toward the Sinai passes.[12] Israel found a gap of "about forty kilometers between the two Egyptian armies" that was virtually "unguarded at that time."[13] Third, at the point of crossing, there was still an Israeli-held fort at the Bar Lev Line that Egypt had failed to capture; this position gave "great assistance to the crossing Israeli troops."[14] Fourth, "Egypt's forces remaining west of the canal had been stripped of their anti-tank missiles for the benefit of the units which had crossed."[15] Finally, the inevitable Arab response: It was impossible to defeat the United States (referring to the U.S. airlift to Israel).[16]

In direct contradiction to Premier Meir's clear affirmation that it was the Arabs who were the first to violate the October 22 cease-fire, Heikal categorically said that "Israel never had any intention of respecting the cease-fire." "No Arab politician or commander had any excuse for being surprised." After the cease-fire was effected, Israel "immediately . . . began to break it."[17]

In contrast to Moshe Dayan's memoirs, which calculated the Soviet military supplies to the Arab side of the war at three times the amount Israel received from the United States,[18] Mohammed Heikal insisted the aid to each side was approximately equal: "When the airlifts were finally halted it was found that the amount of arms which America had supplied to Israel almost exactly balanced, ton for ton, the amount which the Soviet Union had supplied to Egypt and Syria."[19] Apparently Heikal did not count the Soviet military equipment other Arab states contributed to the Syrian and Egyptian military fronts, as Dayan did when he calculated (see below) that superpower aid to each side in the war was approximately equal.

Mohammed Heikal was not optimistic about the results of the October War. He was especially critical of Henry Kissinger, who, he felt, had ignored the justice of Middle East causes by being preoccupied with the relations between the United States and the Soviet Union. Heikal was indeed very pessimistic concerning the bloody 1973 Middle East conflict. Kissinger, as "the main architect of the truce," had failed to tackle the roots of the problem; the war ended in a precarious cease-fire. "The only conclusion to be drawn" from the war, said Mohammed Heikal, "is that another war is inevitable."[20]

Golda Meir

In contrast to Sadat's In Search of Identity, Israel's prime minister referred to the October War (the Yom Kippur War) as the "fifth to be forced on Israel" by the Arabs since Israel's creation.[21]

Although Israel "neither wanted nor started the Yom Kippur War," writes Premier Meir,"we . . . won it, and we had a war aim of our own—peace."[22] "In their hearts the political and military leaders of both Syria and Egypt know that they were defeated again, despite their initial gains."[23] Israel bowed to American pressure on October 21 and agreed to a cease-fire which spared Egypt and Syria another humiliating total collapse. Meir related how desperate the situation had indeed become for the two Arab states by October 21: "North of Ismalia we were pressing hard on the Egyptian Second Army. South of Suez, we were completing the encirclement of the Egyptian Third Army. On the Golan Heights, the Syrian positions on Mount Herman had fallen. . . . We had complete supremacy on both fronts. . . ."[24] The UN Security Council Resolution 338 was passed "with such indecent speed," she said, "to avert the total destruction of the Egyptian and Syrian forces by us . . ."[25]

"Although the Egyptians declared their acceptance, they did not stop shooting on October 22. The fighting went on, and we completed the encirclement of the Third Army and gained control of parts of the city of Suez."[26] Golda Meir insisted Egypt was the first to violate the October 22 UN cease-fire agreement. Kissinger was inclined to believe the Egyptians and the Russians in their charge that Israel deceptively violated its pledged cease-fire in order to surround the Egyptian force. Israel's Ambassador Dinitz, in Washington, when confronted by Kissinger's accusation in this matter, finally got Premier Meir on the telephone in Jerusalem. Meir noted her reply to Kissinger: "You can say anything you want about is, but we are not liars. The allegations are not true."[27]

In the shuttle diplomacy, Kissinger also made a courtesy call on King Feisal in Riyadh. According to Meir, King Feisal impressed upon Kissinger that "the Jews had created the communist movement in order to conquer the world."[28] King Feisal gave Kissinger a copy of (the forged) Protocols of the Elders of Zion, but the American secretary of state refused to accept the gift.

Historically, the United States and Israel defined their national interests complementarily across a broad policy range (helped along by an effective pro-Israel interest group in American domestic politics), but the encompassing circle of American national interests and the configuration of Israeli national interests were never coterminous. Kissinger recognized this and had the courage to pressure Israel, when convinced of its necessity, and to accept the resulting wrath, from both officialdom and the grass roots of pro-Jewish groups. Golda Meir related her exasperation with Kissinger's role in the delay of arms shipments to Israel. He had warned Israel not to attack first, even to refrain from mobilization; now Israel was paying a frightful cost and Washington seemed irresponsibly slow in sending military aid. Yet despite the intermittent conflict of interests between the two states, Meir characterized Kissinger as "an outstanding personality in the Middle East, . . . whose efforts on behalf of peace in the area can only be termed super-human."[29]

Golda Meir's memoirs conclude with a conviction concerning Israel—the essence of the historical Arab-Israeli conflict—as it relates to the ultimate orientation of both Arabs and Jews. To the Arabs, Israel has been viewed as an outpost of Western colonialism carved out of the Arab homeland. Arabs find it very difficult to empathize with Meir's ringing justification for the existence of Israel: We "know that for Jewish people to remain a people, it is essential that there be a Jewish state where Jews can live as Jews, not on sufferance and not as a minority. . . . Israel is a Jewish state that has come into existence as the result of the longing, the faith and the determination of an ancient people. We in Israel are only part of the Jewish nation, and not even its largest part, but because Israel exists Jewish history has been changed forever."[30] At this dimension of the human predicament, the Israeli leader seemed to express excessive optimism about what could be done permanently. It was Renaissance liberal thought expressed in terms of historical progress—something Henry Kissinger could not accept and could only consider dangerous to the political stability of the Middle East. On the other hand, Kissinger was sophisticated enough to avoid the characteristic American trap of a legal solution. He correctly assessed the Israeli will to survive: Human wills cannot necessarily be changed or explained by resort to law or reason.

Moshe Dayan

Moshe Dayan, Israel's defense minister during the Yom Kippur War, confirmed the failure of American military aid to reach Israel during the first week of the war. He also saw it as a deliberate political move to restrain Israel's response capability against the Arab attack.[31]

Confirming Premier Meir's statement, Moshe Dayan attributed the October 22 cease-fire violation to the duplicity of President Anwar Sadat. At 2:30 P.M., October 22, "Radio Cairo announced that President Anwar Sadat had accepted the cease-fire,"[32] which was to be effected at 6:38 P.M. the same day. However, according to Dayan, "both that night and the next day, the Egyptian Air Force maintained its attacks on our troops. . . . Apparently this was done because Syria had rejected the cease-fire. The local Egyptian commanders, both senior and junior, ordered their units to advance and seize Israeli positions, and they did indeed try. As for us, if the Syrians, or even the Egyptians alone, had halted the fighting, we would surely have ceased fire and frozen our lines. We would have done so despite our military advantage."[33]

In Story of My Life, Dayan said it was he who suggested the new cease-fire deadline, of 7:00 A.M. on October 24, to the commander of the UN Observer Force, who, in turn, contacted Cairo for confirmation. Since the Egyptian military positions were becoming more precarious by the hour, Sadat's government radioed back an anxious "agree, agree, agree."[34]

Two days earlier (October 22), Dayan had met Kissinger in Jerusalem. To Kissinger, the Israeli defense minister expressed concern about Israeli prisoners held by the Arabs: "No prisoner exchange, no cease-fire!" Kissinger agreed to try; he requested the Russians to help in facilitating the prisoner exchanges. Kissinger mentioned how important it was to nail down the cease-fire immediately: "If the war went on and the Arab armies were utterly routed, the Soviet Union was likely to take extreme measures to save her allies from collapse."[35]

Dayan spoke of Kissinger with considerable eloquence: "I am very much impressed by his wisdom, his broad-ranging knowledge his prodigious capacity for work, and his ability to set things in perspective." However, "his greatness stems primarily from his knowledge of how to use the powerful lever of the United States to exert pressure and to retaliate, to influence and to promise guarantees."[36]

Nevertheless, Dayan pointed out some dangers Kissinger posed to Israel; he would not hesitate to go against Israel "if forced to choose between aid to Israel" and "grave suffering for America." In that case, American foreign policy would reach "agreement with the Arabs, even at our expense." "I was by no means certain that an improvement in America's relations with the Arab states and the lifting of the oil embargo would not be bought—at least partly—with Israeli currency, namely through pressure exerted on us for Arab benefit."[37]

In Israel's political struggles with the United States, none was more important than the effort to obtain military weapons—an effort that had become a perennial struggle for Israel but that became crucial in the October War. According to Dayan, the Soviets had delivered to the Arab states (both via sea and air) 300,000 tons of military supplies, while the United States had made less than one-third of this available to Israel[38]—a conclusion in sharp contrast to Sadat's pronouncements.

There are other sharp contradictions between the memoirs of Sadat and of Dayan. Sadat's In Search of Identity affirmed an Egyptian victory in the October War. Dayan presented a very different conclusion. In the struggle for a ceasefire, wrote Dayan,

> President Sadat was in fact anxious to reach an arrangement with us. The main reason was his distressing military predicament. . . . The one thing of which Sadat was certain was that his armed forces were powerless to break the Israeli siege.
>
> His official spokesmen, and therefore the Egyptian press, kept declaring that it was our forces on the west bank of the Canal who were trapped. But the Egyptian army commanders knew the true situation. They were aware that in order to push us back, or isolate us, their Second and Third Armies would have to link up and thereby sever our bridgehead. But they had not the slightest chance of being able to do that. The Third Army was cut off, with little food and water, and above all without ammunition and weapons. It was almost completely exposed to our Air Force, for the SAM batteries which had given it cover had either been destroyed by our troops or withdrawn. As for Egypt's Second Army, it was strong as long as it remained in its entrenched positions, with anti-tank defenses and protection from the air by an umbrella of SAM batteries. But any attempt to move out and proceed southward to link up with the Third Army would have left it open to bombing by our aircraft and ambush by our armor. The Second Army would have been wiped out, as had happened to the Egyptian 25th Brigade earlier in the war when it moved toward our bridgehead in an effort to destroy it and lost fifty tanks in the attempt, without the loss of a single tank by our forces. Sadat understood that his achievements in this war were all behind him, and he had to end it, even at the cost of concession and compromise.[39]

Abba Eban

Abba Eban, Israel's foreign minister during the Yom Kippur War, freely admitted the cataclysmic shock the war created in Israel's national life. Eban arrived in New York in September 1973 for the regular UN General Assembly meeting. Secretary of State Kissinger invited him to the American UN mission headquarters for a routine meeting on October 4 (two days before the war). Kissinger mentioned to Eban the upcoming Israeli elections and then summarized the Middle East political situation: "In any case, nothing dramatic is going to happen in October."[40]

The Arab strike against Israel succeeded in deceiving both the U.S. and Israeli intelligence organizations. The latter detected the planned Arab attack with only ten hours of warning time—and then with a four-hour error.[41] Eban saw the war as a vindication of his policy position, which turned out to be a minority one that was therefore never accepted by the government. Although always tactful and generous in relating to colleagues, Eban was more critical of Dayan than of Kissinger. By early 1973, according to Eban's memoirs, Dayan had abandoned the need to search for a compromise with the Arabs, including the necessity of trading territories to the Arabs for the sake of peace. Now, lamented Eban, the Israeli defense minister spoke in terms of Israel's eternal claim to the West Bank; Dayan now spoke of "the Israel Government extending from the Jordan to the Suez Canal."[42] "In all these statements," said a pantothenate Eban, "Israel's armed strength and expanded boundaries figured as the only components of national security. There was silence about the idea of peace, and nothing was said about any of the nonmilitary ideals or values that Israel was born to serve."[43]

The defense minister also received relatively harsh treatment in Eban's memoirs concerning the former's refusal, after Israeli intelligence had categorically concluded the Arabs would attack in a matter of hours, to support the request by the chief of staff, General Elazar, for "general mobilization." According to Eban, Dayan approved the mobilization of only two divisions, "one division for each of the north and south commands."[44] Dayan disputes this statement in his own memoirs by saying he supported mobilization of all the troops that General Elazar felt the situation required.[45]

Eban credited a junior Israeli intelligence officer, Lt. Benjamin Tov, with having submitted accurate intelligence conclusions, on October 1, 2, and 3, that the Egyptian and Syrian "maneuvers" were, in fact, meticulously created deceptions to cover a carefully planned war initiated against Israel with all the advantages of a preemptive strike.[46]

The October War, in Eban's view, vindicated his own dovish reputation among the Israeli cabinet members.

Henry Kissinger, in contrast to Moshe Dayan, received rather generous treatment in Abba Eban's memoirs. In general, Israel's political leadership was sophisticated enough to know the rewards of good public relations—i.e., public compliments for American political leaders. Eban could play this role most eloquently in defending Kissinger. Two examples are classic.

Firstly, with regard to the controversial role Kissinger played in demanding that Israel refrain from a preemptive strike, Eban masterfully soothed the postwar tempest by calling attention to Kissinger's statement during the Eban-Kissinger conversation in the early hours of October 6 (after the certainty of the impending Arab attack became known). As recorded by Eban in his memoirs, Kissinger mentioned the message from Jerusalem that said Premier Meir had decided against preempting the Arab attack. Kissinger "wanted to put on record with me [Eban] that this was an Israeli decision conveyed to the United States after it had been taken. He [Kissinger] believed it to be the right decision, but the United States had no need to give advice on an issue Israel had already determined for herself."[47]

Secondly, Eban ingenuously calmed the controversy surrounding Kissinger's image of deceptively withholding military aid to Israel in the desperate first week of the war: "Since we were telling Washington that the Egyptian and Syrian advances were going to be crushed in a few days," wrote Eban, "there was not yet any solid reason for Washington to prepare for an emergency supply operation. . . . By the fourth day of the war, Israel's losses both in first-line planes and in tanks were so heavy that our commanders were inhibited from throwing further forces into new attacks. . . . It was now essential to ask the United States for immediate reinforcement of lost material."[48] Israel was now in a crisis situation. Kissinger had always felt another Arab-Israeli war would probably be required to make the parties sufficiently predisposed for the necessary compromises. Now, with the Israelis hard pressed and desperately in need of supplies, Kissinger used his bargaining position to push Israel into the concession of a cease-fire in place. "I was surprised," recalled Eban, "when I received a cable from . . . the Prime Minister's office, saying that the Cabinet had decided to acquiesce in a cease-fire 'in place'. . . ."[49]

Yet the military supplies promised were not forthcoming. Israeli Ambassador Dinitz and Eban arranged for a very urgent meeting with Kissinger Saturday morning (October 13). In spite of the hard bargaining in Israel's difficult situation, Eban remained magnanimous toward Kissinger. At the Saturday meeting, wrote Eban, "Kissinger agreed that the slowness in conveying supplies to Israel was disturbing and he would now go to the White House where there would be a decisive meeting."[50] Eban returned to New York. In the evening of that same Saturday, Kissinger called him from Washington to say that 60 major transport aircraft were already airborne and would be arriving in Israel sometime within the next 24 hours.[51]

Richard Nixon

The October War pushed President Nixon into a "system over-load." In August 1973 (two months before the war), Attorney General Elliot Richardson sent Vice President Spiro Agnew the fateful letter; the Justice Department had officially launched an investigation of bribery, extortion, conspiracy, and tax-fraud allegations against him. On September 25, less than two weeks before the war, Agnew's case took a turn for the worse, as the president learned from his meeting with the vice president that day. The Agnew people were upset; in their opinion, the president should be giving his dedicated supporter and vice president more public support as the public charges against Agnew deepened. Yet Nixon realized he was in enough Watergate trouble without the additional risk of supporting Spiro Agnew—a risk that could be very damaging if later, the charges against the vice president proved true. With the deepening of the Watergate allegations against the president himself, there was little time for a review of American Middle East policy.

Richard Nixon was concerned about the Soviet Union's role in the October War. There seemed to be no obvious opportunity for American action to contain the crisis. A few days after the outbreak of hostilities, a pro forma, low-keyed response was made by requesting a meeting of the UN Security Council. In the absence of a better alternative, there would be the standard procedure of a Security Council resolution calling for a cease-fire. Nixon knew, of course, that effectiveness in the United Nations depends upon the determination and unity of the superpowers. In this case, wrote Nixon, "the Soviets . . . clearly thought . . . the Arabs would win on the battlefield if they had enough time to secure their early victories. The French and the British . . . were trying to stay at arm's length; . . . they knew that Arab oil was at stake in this confrontation. . . . I saw no point in trying to impose a diplomatic cease-fire that neither side wanted or could be expected to observe."[52] The best chance for negotiating the end of hostilities would occur after the result of a trial by combat had imposed itself on the situation—perhaps even an "equilibrium of mutual exhaustion."[53] There was a danger, of course, that the Soviets would try to reap benefits from the conflict. If Israel administered another decisive defeat on the Arabs—i.e., no battlefield stalemate developed—the Soviets might be determined to send their own military units to avoid another humiliating defeat like the one in the 1967 war. There was a precedent for this when the Soviet military forces actually operated the sophisticated SAMs and flew combat missions in Egypt during the war of attrition in 1969-70. Such a development might well necessitate American troops being sent to the Israeli side, creating an extremely dangerous situation conducive to an escalatory showdown between the superpowers.

On Tuesday, October 9, Nixon said he realized the expected quick victory for Israel was much too optimistic. He had "no doubt or hesitation about what we must do."[54] In spite of his concern about an Arab oil embargo, he told Kissinger (on October 9) to work out the logistics for replacing all the Israeli equipment lost in the war.[55]

In the Nixon memoirs, the controversial "Schlesinger slowdown" comes into focus—although not the slightest mention is made of what the critics charged was a public-relations, "Mutt and Jeff" deception in restraining aid to Israel to make the Jewish state more amenable to an American peace settlement in the Middle East. According to Nixon, on October 10 (Wednesday), Kissinger met him to complain that "Defense [under James Schlesinger] is putting up all kinds of obstacles."[56] The reference was, in part, to the demand that Israel's planes stop first in New York to have "their tail markings painted over." President Nixon notes in his memoirs: "It was unthinkable that Israel should lose the war for lack of weapons while we were spraying paint over the Stars of David. 'Tell Schlesinger to speed it up,' I told Kissinger."[57]

By Friday (October 12) the military-supply operation had literally not gotten off the ground. The Defense Department had asked Israel to use chartered American civilian planes, but this didn't work because insurance companies would not accept the risk of flying into the war zone. There was also a plan for turning the supplies over to Israel on the Portuguese Azores. Portugal initially refused permission, and the proposal had other even more important liabilities.

After the order was given to use U.S. military planes, there was disagreement within the Pentagon over which kinds of planes should be used.[58] Edward Sheehan quotes Secretary of Defense Schlesinger as, later, admitting the use of public deception in national policy; Schlesinger reportedly said: "There was a cover story in that period—that the source of resistance [to the airlift] was to be the Pentagon. This story was basically to protect the realities of national policy."[59]

According to President Nixon's account, it was on Friday (October 12) that he issued the order commanding the Air Force to deliver the supplies "now."[60] The first group of 30 C-130's arrived in Israel on Sunday, October 14—after the tide of battle had already turned in Israel's favor.

As mentioned above, the presidency had to deal with two decision-making crises simultaneously. During the three weeks of the Middle East war, with its potential for triggering World War III, the constitutional crises of domestic politics also deepened. Vice President Agnew resigned on October 10; and "the Saturday night massacre" (the firing of Watergate Special Prosecutor Archibald Cox after the resignations of Attorney General Richardson and his deputy, William

Ruckelshaus, who refused to accept the president's directive in this matter) occurred on October 20. The event was duly exploited by the press and by various public figures whose public image needed to benefit from righteous indignation. Nixon recalled Ralph Nader charging that the president was "acting like a madman, a tyrant, or both." Nixon noted that Senator Robert Byrd "said the Cox firing was a 'Brownshirt operation' using 'Gestapo tactics.'"[61] A weak presidential personality could not have functioned under these pressures. The showdown on the incriminating Watergate tapes had to be faced on October 23-24.

Simultaneously (on October 24), Nixon "received information that seven Soviet airborne divisions, numbering 50,000 men, had been put on alert; and eighty-five Soviet ships, including landing craft and ships carrying troop helicopters, were now in the Mediterranean."[62] In this volatile situation, Egypt's President Sadat publicly requested both the Soviet Union and the United States to send military forces to Egypt to cope with what he charged were Israeli violations of the ceasefire. President Nixon had already informed Brezhnev that "Egypt was the first party to violate the cease-fire" on October 22.[63]

At 10:00 P.M. (on October 24), Nixon received a crucial threat from the Soviet Union that requested joint military intervention in the Middle East. Brezhnev threatened unilateral intervention if the United States refused. In the midst of intense pressure from both the Middle East and the domestic situation, Richard Nixon asked Kissinger to order the worldwide alert of American conventional and nuclear forces in the early hours of October 25.[64]

"Just as a crisis in one area seemed to be settling down," the president concluded in his memoirs, "it would be overtaken by a crisis in another area, until all the crises reached a concerted crescendo as we neared the brink of nuclear war."[65]

Henry Kissinger

Years of Upheaval, the second volume of his memoirs, is political writing "in its finest hour." Again, it is important to remember that "memoirs inevitably channel events through honorable perspectives." There is no law against some selectivity in recreating a story. The "sins of omission," unless excessive, are an accepted tradition in memoirs, although a nagging problem for the aspirations of scholarship in the social sciences.

Reading the Kissinger story on the October War is both delightful and arresting. The reader is well advised to maintain a sense of caution mixed with a little skepticism. It is easy to be lulled into an uncritical acceptance by the beauty of its exquisite prose. In truth, reality just doesn't fall into place quite so accommodatingly. Only the master storyteller is able to interlock the mortise and tenon joints of existential events so smoothly; one is troubled by what this generation of Americans refers to as "Monday-morning quarterbacking."

Militarily, Israel won the October War: "Israel . . . had prevailed militarily; it ended up with more Arab territory captured than lost."[66] However, Kissinger was quick to point out the perils of victory. By October 18 "the Egyptian army was now in serious difficulties. But it was not in our interest that the war end with Egypt's humiliation. We had wanted to prevent a victory of Soviet arms. We did not want to see Sadat overthrown or Egypt radicalized by total defeat."[67] By this time, with Israeli units sweeping effectively from the Deversoir beachhead on the west bank of the canal and the Russians beginning to press the panic button on behalf of their client Arab states, Kissinger saw the need for the United States "to take charge of the process of negotiation, to gain a little more time for Israel's offensive, and then to settle so that we could start the postwar diplomacy in the best setting."[68] As Karl von Clausewitz had written a century and a half earlier, war, when not in the service of political objectives, becomes senseless slaughter. For Kissinger, the most crucial reality of the October War was that it created new opportunities, as well as dangers, for American foreign policy. The old Arab-Israeli stalemate had been replaced by a new, politically fluid situation.

After the Middle East peace had been shattered, the American secretary of state sought to influence the battle to facilitate a resolution of the Arab-Israeli dispute; reduce the Soviet presence in the Middle East and replace it with American influence; keep from unnecessarily alienating the Arab world, with its threat of an oil embargo; manage American domestic politics to avoid serious internal divisiveness eroding American influence in world affairs; maintain the survivability of Richard Nixon in office; save détente, if possible; and preserve the unity of NATO.

Kissinger called a meeting of the Washington Special Action Group at 9:00 A.M. on October 6 (one hour, Washington time, after the war broke out); yet intelligence at this time still reported its conclusion that no major, coordinated Arab attack would take place. American intelligence failed, not because of "background noise" in which it is hard to pick out relevant from irrelevant facts, but, rather, because of faulty political analysis. The intelligence failure "resulted from the misinterpretation of facts available for all to see."[69] In retrospect, Kissinger saw primarily a failure to comprehend the personality and mentality of Anwar Sadat: "Sadat fought a war not to acquire territory but to restore Egypt's self-respect and thereby increase its diplomatic flexibility. . . . Rare is the statesman who at the beginning of a war has so clear a perception of its political objective; rarer still is a war fought to lay the basis for moderation in its after-math."[70]

Kissinger's glowing tribute to Sadat is not and cannot be supported objectively. One must frankly acknowledge that the tribute has its roots in the desire to praise Sadat, plus having the dimension of hindsight woven into a beautiful story created by a superb memoirs writer. It would have been entirely possible, in the absence of U. S. restraint, for Israel to have destroyed the Egyptian Third Army; in that case Sadat's position would have been quite similar to Nasser's situation after the 1967 war. The pressure for a broader destabilization would have increased, but, whether or not Israel had destroyed the encircled Egyptian army at Suez would not have changed America's inherent superpower obligation to oppose the Soviet threat of intervention—only the pressure would have been increased.

Objectively, without the benefit of hindsight and the ability to tell a good story, the most convincing case for Sadat's motivation in the October War was no more and no less than President Nasser's motivation for the 1969–70 war of attrition: to shatter the Arab-Israeli stalemate (a deadlock benefitting Israel and an unacceptable liability to Arabs) via an action maximizing Arab advantages and Israeli disadvantages in the context of a minimum risk to the very survival of Egypt.[71] As Mohammed Hassanein Heikal noted in outlining Egypt's predicament, the unacceptable bias in favor of the status quo was provided by the Israeli military presence on the East Bank of the Suez Canal. On the basis of each side's prevailing frame of political reference, the dispute was irreconcilable. Egypt could realize its minimum demands only by having at least some success in war. Starting a war was not an unacceptable risk for Egypt because Israel could not readily conquer all of Egypt and maintain the conquest by occupation. On the other hand, Egypt's military success would not require a conquest of Israel; it would only require keeping Israel militarily mobilized, or having the ability to inflict sustained significant casualties on the Israeli forces without having to absorb greatly disproportionate Egyptian casualties or disproportionate Egyptian material destruction.[72] This was Nasser's conceptualization of the problem and there is no evidence, except in hindsight, that Sadat had any alternative scenario. Sadat acknowledged that he had no image of how the war would end. "It was impossible, as I have always said, for the United States (or, indeed, any other power) to make a move if we ourselves didn't take military action to break the deadlock. The drift of what Kissinger said to Ismail [at a back-channel meeting in Paris in 1973] was that the United States regrettably could do nothing to help so long as we were the defeated party and Israel maintained her superiority."[73]

Years of Upheaval provides the opportunity to search Kissinger's own account of events for clues concerning the critics' crucial charges of duplicity. In brief, responsible scholars have charged Kissinger with demanding that Israel accept the serious liability of an Arab first strike in the October War; then pressuring Israel, when it was reeling under the heavy casualties and the defensive disadvantage caused by the Arab first strike, to accept on October 12 the liability of a cease-fire in place as a condition for essential military supplies from the United States; and deception, in the delaying of promised military supplies, to weaken Israel, thereby insuring greater dependence on, and greater subservience to, the United States in its postwar role of mediating a peace settlement.

As a response to these charges, Years of Upheaval is an adventure in subtleties. The book is written with a pro-Israeli, pro-moderate-Arab readership favorably in mind. It is less necessary to be deferential to, for example, the sensitivities of a pro-Soviet reader. In this context, note the various incidents relevant to our concern.

Kissinger summarized overall American objectives after the war broke out: We would seek to thwart "the military designs of the side armed by the Soviets," yet try "to win Arab confidence." This would put us in a position to "both emerge as mediator and demonstrate that the road to peace led through Washington."[74] In reference to "Arab confidence," the objective was to support the moderate Arab leaders against the radical Arabs. Under the cover of using a joint approach with the Soviet Union to pass a cease-fire resolution in the Security Council, Kissinger sought to keep the issue out of the General Assembly, where American control of the action would be impossible; to "keep Moscow from harassing us with its own proposals";[75] and to work cooperatively in the Security Council with the Soviet Union and thereby "separate Moscow from its Arab clients"[76]—the Arabs would see it as Moscow giving preference to its ties with Washington over its support of Arab interests. Furthermore, if Washington could pull off its "cooperative" policy with Moscow, "this would cool the ardor of our European allies who might be tempted to rush in with more one-sided [pro-Arab] approaches."[77]

Kissinger then proceeded to implement the strategy. He contacted Dobrynin at 9:35 A.M. (Washington time on October 6) to warn the Soviets not to act "irresponsibly." "We would have no choice," Kissinger told Dobrynin, but "to let nature take its course . . . [and] await the inevitable Israeli victory."[78] (At this time Washington still expected a quick Israeli victory.) To continue playing out the created scenario, Kissinger told Dobrynin we would defer to the Soviet Union in our cooperative efforts and take no further diplomatic initiatives while awaiting its reply. Kissinger then elaborated the American strategy, noting that "our first need was to gain time." Yet "we had played our little game" with the Soviets.[79] "So long as Moscow was hinting at coordination, we were relieved of the danger that it would mount a political assault against us at the United Nations."[80]

Kissinger presents a classic discussion of what is relevant—what is at the core of the critics' charges of duplicity and deceptions (referred to previously). He described the crucial wartime relationship with the Israeli ambassador in Washington, Simcha Dinitz. Each of them, he wrote, resorted to the device of blaming someone else for the "painful decisions" each had to make in being true to that primary consideration of every national leader, namely, to promote one's national interest even in the range of the inevitable conflict of interests. "Dinitz was brilliant at mobilizing media and Congressional pressures but much too wise to make his prowess explicit. Listening to him, one could only be astonished how it had happened that so many normally individualistic Americans had come spontaneously to the conclusion that we were not doing enough for Israel. In turn, when I had bad news for Dinitz, I was not above ascribing it to bureaucratic stalemates or unfortunate decisions by superiors. Neither of us fooled the other."[81]

The evidence supports what the critics verbalized as Kissinger's duplicity in the three actions described above—although no overt support for them can be found in Kissinger's memoirs, with perhaps the exception of this last quoted passage. Nevertheless, statesmen have to operate within the range of available options measured, ultimately, against realistically projected results. Certainly, resolving the seemingly intractable Arab-Israeli dispute (involving decades of bloodshed and destruction of material necessities) and avoiding World War III (sparked in the Middle East) are tremendous moral achievements.

That Kissinger superbly played the diplomat's game—i.e., what the critics charge as duplicity—there can be little doubt. Examples are amply presented in his own memoirs; only they are skillfully presented to avoid unnecessarily alienating those publics that must not be offended. Note the following examples of duplicity or of the superb skills of a brilliant statesman—the choice depending upon two factors. First, how is the diplomat's action to be measured: directly by absolute moral principles or by the morality of results, i.e., morality identified by net results based on pragmatically defined, available alternative courses of action. Second, the measure of morality must take into account the statesman's task of defining which public he is committed to serve. The particular public to be served establishes the parameters of communication and tact (a speech must be tailored to fit the audience).

Note carefully these two variables of morality in the following two examples chosen from Kissinger's own testimony.

The first:"But on October 10, whatever our perception of the resupply problem, we had to delay the diplomacy until there was a change on the war front. We thought the optimum military circumstance for the postwar diplomacy we were planning was if Israel could restore the prewar situation or perhaps go slightly beyond it. This would demonstrate that the military option backed by Soviet arms was an illusion; that diplomatic progress depended on American support."[82]

Note a second example: Late in the afternoon of the same day (October 10), the American diplomatic objective was still one of delay. Kissinger told Dobrynin that the U.S. still "had not had time to consider" the Soviet request for joint action to maintain inaction in the Security Council.[83]

Four hours later, Kissinger notes, "I called Dobrynin again: 'Anatoly, we won't be able to give you an answer till tomorrow.' Dobrynin, who understood very well what I was doing, responded with affable menace: 'You are playing quite well. Don't overplay the theme of Russian irresponsibility.'"[84]

Still later the same night, the American secretary of state, as he recorded in Years of Upheaval, "reviewed the day's events and our progress. . . . Our aim was to slow down diplomacy without appearing obstructionist, to urge a speedup of [Israeli] military operations without seeming to intervene, and then force a cease-fire before the impatience and frustration of the parties [the threat of Soviet military intervention] or unforeseeable events [another shattering defeat of the Arab armies by Israel] could rip the whole finely spun fabric to smithereens."[85]

Kissinger praised the Shah of Iran for his pro-Western contribution during the October War and the accompanying Arab oil policy. Mohammed Reza Pahlavi was smart enough to recognize the long-run interests of Iran in the U.S. proposals. A militarily strong Iran would serve both American and Iranian interests. Iran would be a blocking pad deterring Soviet attraction to the world's greatest oil reserves. It would deter radical Iraq from dominating the fertile crescent and threatening the moderate, oil-rich states of the Persian Gulf area.

While America's NATO allies allowed Soviet overflights to supply the Arab armies during the October War, Iran refused the same Soviet request. The Shah resisted Arab pressures to embargo oil and curtail production. He was willing to pay the political price for refusing determined Arab demands to stop oil shipments to Israel. Iraq was kept off balance as an Israeli enemy during the war by the Shah's support for the Iraqi Kurds in their smoldering civil war with Baghdad and by the positioning of powerful Iranian forces on Iraq's eastern border.

From the perspective of 1982 (when his memoirs were published), Henry Kissinger attributed the Shah's demise primarily to his successful policy of modernization. Antimodernization, anti-Western groups succeeded in overthrowing the public order to establish the new Khomeini government in Iran. Modernization produced a rootless class in the wave of peasant migrations from the villages to the cities—especially to Teheran. Development also created a voiceless bureaucratic and entrepreneurial middle class. Together with those deprived of their status in the traditional religious structure, the confluence of opposition groups overthrew the Shah's government "in an orgy of retribution and vengefulness."[86] Those who criticize U.S. policy in Iran, said Kissinger, would be better advised to direct their criticism at the Western failure in achieving a valid liberal development model.

Jimmy Carter's policy toward the Shah appalled Kissinger: "America and its allies shamed themselves by their later behavior toward him [the Shah], abandoning a friend not only politically . . . but also humanly, when he was adrift without refuge and required succor."[87]

Conclusion

From the perspective of mid-1983, Israel appeared to have delivered a shattering blow against the threat from the PLO in Lebanon—a serendipity from the peace settlement with Egypt that, in turn, had its roots in the post-October War era orchestrated by Henry Kissinger. The decisive strike into Lebanon might have provided a bonus of long-run stability for Israel, although it was a disaster for the Palestinians. The scenario could not have been predicted even a decade ago. Crucial components of the 1982 situation included the Israeli peace treaty with a reasonably stable Egypt; the stabilization of the Lebanese frontier, with the militant PLO gone; the Soviet faltering in the Arab Middle East; and an ideologically oriented Iran now attacking Iraq. The new configuration of political forces may prove to be the demise of what earlier seemed an endlessly threatening and seemingly unresolvable Arab-Israeli dispute. A word of caution, however, is in order. History has a way of making foolish the perspectives of the present.

Yet in reflection on the Kissinger era, certain events are worthy of note. Sadat's pilgrimage to Jerusalem (November 1977), the Camp David accords (September 1978), the Egyptian-Israeli peace treaty (March 1979), the complete Israeli withdrawal from Sinai (April 1982), and the events in Lebanon (summer, 1982) would all be inconceivable without the foundation built by Henry Kissinger during and after the October War.

Kissinger's effectiveness was in part a chance occurrence in history that he utilized effectively to concentrate foreign-policy control in himself. By the fall of 1973, President Nixon's authority was being eroded by the Watergate charges (the so-called Saturday night massacre and the crucial White House tapes controversy occurred during the October War). Vice President Agnew resigned four days after the war broke out when the battles were going badly for Israel and Washington was locked in the resupply controversy.

Kissinger had succeeded in replacing William Rogers only two weeks before the Arab attack. As the new secretary of state, he managed to retain (for quite some time) the position of national security advisor to the president—allowing for an enhanced concentration of foreign-policy power as Watergate further distracted the president's attention. Henry Kissinger added to this fortuitous circumstance his own genius for gaining a favorable press and securing domestic public support for his foreign policy. By the use of secrecy and a ruthless courage to bypass the bureaucracy, he effectively utilized the immense power of the United States to pursue his foreign-policy goals.

Kissinger's Middle East legacy created, during the Nixon-Ford years, a foundation upon which the succeeding Carter administration could build the miraculous, if tenuous, Egyptian-Israeli peace treaty. Yet at least until after the Israeli invasion of Lebanon in mid-1982, the frailties of men still demonstrated the failures and follies of their efforts at stabilizing the Middle East political order. Successfully resolving the antagonism between only two parties to the Arab-Israeli dispute magnified the antagonism at the comprehensive level. The Carter administration failed, in the end, to achieve results—there was too little vision at the Gestalt level and too much vacillation at the policy level.

Until mid-1982, the Reagan administration also failed in the comprehensive perspective of Henry Kissinger. In this early period of Ronald Reagan's presidency, rhetoric substituted for policy. It was difficult to perceive where the Reagan administration wanted to go in international affairs. Domestic issues seemed to preempt a realistic grasp of the international system's demands on the United States.

During the Haig tenure, foreign policy was publicly cast in a generalized, anti-Soviet mold. To some it seemed to resurrect the cold-war rhetoric of the McCarthy era. The administration's public relations was in danger of molding foreign policy, instead of utilizing public-relations opportunities to promote foreign-policy objectives. Conducting foreign policy by public relations has an excessive cost factor for a major power. The United States experienced this in its Middle East policy—especially in its so-called anti-Soviet strategic consensus. It was never clear whether the Reagan-Haig policy evolved from an ideological base of personal convictions; from the need to keep the Republican right happy (primarily domestic political considerations); or from assumptions about the pragmatic advantages of a harder line against the Russians. In reference to the last alternative, one assumes that political behavior is influenced by a mix of threats and rewards from the environment—the problem of a sugar-vinegar mix. Did the Reagan administration simply assume more could be gotten from the Russians by a hard line than by a détente policy? At least through 1982, the evidence seems to indicate a more ideological orientation in President Reagan's foreign-policy assumptions—we ought to do it because it is right in some ultimate sense. On the other hand, the same kind of anti-Soviet rhetoric rested on a more pragmatic, hard-line emphasis in Haig's case (the hard-line-weighted optimum mix). In a Haig-Kissinger comparison, the question is whether, for instance, the Soviets would be more likely to leave Afghanistan by threats (Haig), or via a more reward-oriented mix—a mix publicly referred to as a strategy of negotiation within the framework of détente (Kissinger).

George Shultz succeeded Alexander Haig as secretary of state during the Israeli military operations in Lebanon (July 1982). In contrast to the Haig style, the new member of Reagan's cabinet deliberately kept a low profile during his initial months in office.

In retrospect, Kissinger's contribution becomes more evident in his comprehensive vision of international affairs, and in the steady course of foreign policy he followed (with some exceptions) to realize that vision. Public relations served policy objectives—not the other way around. In the partisan context of the 1980 presidential campaign, Kissinger provided, in truth, a fitting commentary on his strengths as compared to lesser men: "If you don't know where you are going, any road will take you there."

Henry Kissinger may well have been second to none as a foreign-policy leader in American history. Yet a true hero is a believer. Unfortunately, the Harvard professor turned statesman never seems to have found transcendent values as related to human destiny—the foundation from which greatness evolves or from which the hero emerges. Without meaning in some ultimate sense, foreign-policy objectives lose the quality of morality and, at best, lapse into the realm of prudence. Kissinger's enemies found the Achilles' heel all too quickly. Thus, while his Middle East diplomatic accomplishments struck the attentive public as a brilliant flare of genius, the spark seemed always to fade rapidly and the true hero image of Kissinger, even among his would-be worshippers, evaporated. It was difficult for Americans to become true believers in Kissinger's brilliant moves when his own Weltanschauung was void of ultimate meaning or moral destiny for individuals or society or was void of faith in progress (history).

Nevertheless, while the hero's role was elusive, he spared American national life the painful liabilities of the crusader so generously represented, for example, by his predecessor, under Eisenhower, John Foster Dulles.

NOTES

1. Mahmoud Riad, The Struggle for Peace in the Middle East (London: Quartet Books, 1981), pp. 255-61.

2. Ibid., p. 285.

3. Anwar Sadat, In Search of Identity (New York: Harper & Row, 1977), p. 270.

4. Ibid., p. 290.

5. Ibid., p. 291.

6. Ibid., p. 263.

7. Ibid., p. 269.

8. Mohammed Heikal, The Road to Ramadan (New York: Quadrangle/New York Times Book Co., 1975), p. 12.

9. Ibid., p. 231.

10. Quoted in ibid.

11. Ibid., p. 246.

12. Ibid., pp. 226-29.

13. Ibid.

14. Ibid., p. 230.

15. Ibid., p. 258.

16. Ibid., pp. 238-39.

17. Ibid., p. 240.

18. Dayan, pp. 550-51.

19. Heikal, p. 256.

20. Ibid., p. 7.

21. Golda Meir, My Life (London: Weidenfeld and Nicolson, 1975), p. 353.

22. Ibid., p. 368.

23. Ibid., p. 353.

24. Ibid., p. 369.

25. Ibid., pp. 369-70.

26. Ibid., p. 370.

27. Quoted in ibid., p. 375.

28. Ibid., p. 374.

29. Ibid., p. 372.

30. Ibid., pp. 386-87.

31. Moshe Dayan, Story of My Life (New York: William Morrow and Co., 1976), pp. 511-13.

32. Ibid., p. 535.

33. Ibid.

34. Ibid., p. 537.

35. Quoted in ibid., p. 538.

36. Ibid., p. 537.

37. Ibid., p. 538.

38. Ibid., pp. 550-51.

39. Ibid., p. 547.

40. Abba Eban, Abba Eban, an Autobiography (New York: Random House, 1977), p. 498.

41. Ibid., p. 509.

42. Quoted in ibid., p. 487.

43. Ibid.

44. Ibid., p. 509.

45. Dayan, p. 460.

46. Eban, p. 510.

47. Ibid., p. 502. This was Eban's way of ameliorating some of the harsh criticism leveled against Kissinger for the high casualties suffered by Israel due to Kissinger's demand that Israel not carry out preemptive hostilities against the Arabs.

48. Ibid., p. 512.

49. Ibid., p. 515.

50. Ibid., p. 516.

51. Ibid., p. 517.

52. Richard Nixon, RN: The Memoirs of Richard Nixon (New York: Grosset & Dunlap, 1978), p. 921.

53. Ibid.

54. Ibid., p. 922.

55. Ibid.

56. Quoted in ibid., p. 924.

57. Ibid.

58. Ibid., p. 927.

59. Quoted in Edward Sheehan, The Arabs, Israelis, and Kissinger (New York: Thomas Crowell Co., 1976), p. 33.

60. Nixon, p. 927.

61. Quoted in ibid., p. 935.

62. Ibid., p. 937.

63. Ibid., p. 936.

64. Ibid., pp. 938-39. Sheehan is in error here. The alert was ordered before midnight, October 24.

65. Ibid., p. 922.

66. Henry Kissinger, Years of Upheaval (Boston: Little, Brown and Co., 1982), p. 561.

67. Ibid., p. 541.

68. Ibid.

69. Ibid., p. 459.

70. Ibid., p. 460.

71. Mohammed Hassanein Heikal, in Al Ahram, March 1969.

72. Ibid.

73. Anwar Sadat, In Search of Identity (New York: Harper & Row, 1977), p. 238.

74. Kissinger, pp. 470-71.

75. Ibid., p. 471.
76. Ibid.
77. Ibid.
78. Ibid.
79. Ibid., p. 472.
80. Ibid., p. 473.
81. Ibid., p. 485.
82. Ibid., p. 502.
83. Ibid., pp. 498-99, 502.
84. Ibid., pp. 502-03.
85. Ibid., p. 503.
86. Ibid., p. 671.
87. Ibid., p. 667.

Bibliography

BOOKS

Acheson, Dean. Present at the Creation: My Years in the State Department. New York: W. W. Norton & Co., 1969.

AlRoy, Gil Carl. The Kissinger Experience: American Policy in the Middle East. New York: Horizon Press, 1975.

Atherton, Alfred LeRoy, Jr. "The Nixon Administration and the Arab-Israeli Conflict." In The New World Balance and Peace in the Middle East: Reality or Mirage?, edited by Seymour Maxwell Finger, pp. 196-205. London: Associated University Presses, 1975.

Badeau, John. The American Approach to the Arab World. New York: Harper and Row, 1968.

Bader, William B. The United States and the Spread of Nuclear Weapons. New York: Pegasus, 1968.

Ball, George W. Diplomacy for a Crowded World: American Foreign Policy. Boston: Little, Brown and Co., 1976.

Bell, Coral. The Diplomacy of Détente: The Kissinger Era. New York: St. Martin's Press, 1977.

Bergsten, Fred C. Toward a New International Economic Order: Selected Papers of C. Fred Bergsten, 1972-1974. Lexington, Mass.: D.C. Heath and Co., 1975.

Brandon, Henry. The Retreat of American Power. New York: Doubleday and Co., 1973.

Brecher, Michael. Decisions in Israel's Foreign Policy. New York: Yale University Press, 1975.

Campbell, John C., and Caruso, Helen. The West and the Middle East. New York: Council on Foreign Relations, 1972.

Chase, James. A World Elsewhere: The New American Foreign Policy. New York: Charles Scribner's Sons, 1973.

Cooley, John K. Green March, Black September: The Story of the Palestinian Arabs. London: Frank Cass and Co., 1973.

Cottrell, Alvin. "The Politico-Military Balance in the Persian Gulf Region." In The Energy Crisis and U.S. Foreign Policy, edited by Joseph S. Szyliowicz and Brad E. O'Neal, pp. 125-37. New York: Praeger, 1975.

Destler, M. I. Presidents, Bureaucrats and Foreign Policy: The Politics of Organizational Reform. Princeton, N.J.: Princeton University Press, 1972.

Draper, Theodore. Israel and World Politics: Roots of the Third Arab-Israeli War. New York: Viking Press, 1968.

Evan, Rowland, Jr., and Novak, Robert D. Nixon in the White House: The Frustration of Power. New York: Random House, 1971.

Evron, Yair. The Middle East: Nations, Super-Powers and Wars. London: Elek Books, 1973.

Finger, Seymour Maxwell. "The Nixon Doctrine and the Middle East." In The New World Balance and Peace in the Middle East: Reality or Mirage?, edited by Seymour Maxwell Finger, pp. 209-216. London: Associated University Presses, 1975.

Ford, Gerald R. A Time to Heal: The Autobiography of Gerald R. Ford. Harper and Row Publishers and Reader's Digest Press, 1979.

Freedman, Robert O. Soviet Policy Toward the Middle East Since 1970. New York: Praeger, 1975.

Fulbright, William. The Crippled Giant: American Policy and Its Domestic Consequences. New York: Random House, 1972.

George, Alexander L., and Smoke, Richard. Deterrence in American Foreign Policy: Theory and Practice. New York: Columbia University Press, 1974.

Gilpin, Robert. "Three Models of the Future." In World Politics and International Economics, edited by C. Fred Bergsten and

Lawrence Krause, pp. 37–60. Washington, D.C.: Brookings Institution, 1975.

Golan, Galia. Yom Kippur and After: The Soviet Union and the Middle East Crisis. London: Cambridge University Press, 1977.

Golan, Matti. The Secret Conversations of Henry Kissinger: Step-by-Step Diplomacy in the Middle East. New York: Quadrangle, 1976.

Graubard, Stephen R. Kissinger: Portrait of a Mind. New York: W. W. Norton and Co., 1972.

Gurtov, Melvin. The United States Against the Third World: Anti-nationalism and Intervention. New York: Praeger, 1974.

_____. "Security by Proxy: The Nixon Doctrine and Southeast Asia." In Conflict and Stability in Southeast Asia, edited by Mark Zacker and R. Stephen Milne, pp. 203–36. Garden City, N.Y.: Anchor Books, 1974.

Heikal, Mohammed. The Cairo Documents. Garden City, N.Y.: Doubleday and Co., 1973.

_____. The Road to Ramadan. New York: Quadrangle, 1975.

_____. The Sphinx and the Commissar: The Rise and Fall of Soviet Influence in the Middle East. London: William Collins Sons and Co., 1978.

Hoffmann, Stanley. Primacy or World Order: American Foreign Policy Since the Cold War. New York: McGraw-Hill Book Co., 1978.

Holzman, Franklyn D., and Legvold, Robert. "The economics and politics of East-West relations." In World Politics and International Economics, edited by C. Fred Bergsten and Lawrence B. Krause, Washington, D.C.: Brookings Institution, 1975.

Hunter, Robert. The Energy Crisis and U.S. Foreign Policy, Headline Series, No. 216. New York: Foreign Policy Association, June 1973.

Isaak, Robert A. American Democracy and World Power. New York: St. Martin's Press, 1977.

Jabber, Fuad. Israel and Nuclear Weapons: Present Options and Future Strategies. London: Chatto and Windus, 1971.

_____. "Petrodollars, Arms Trade, and the Pattern of Major Conflicts." In Oil, the Arab-Israeli Conflict and the Industrial World, edited by J. C. Hurewitz, pp. 149-64. Boulder, Colo.: Westview Press, 1976.

Johnson, Lyndon B. The Vantage Point: Perspective of the Presidency. New York: Holt, Rinehart and Winston, 1971.

Jones, Alan., ed. U.S. Foreign Policy in a Changing World: The Nixon Administration, 1969-1973. New York: David MacKay Co., 1973.

Kalb, Bernard, and Kalb, Marvin. Kissinger. Boston: Little, Brown and Co., 1974.

Kamath, V. M. Kissinger: The Incomplete Diplomat. Bombay: Jaico Publishing House, 1975.

Kennan, George F. Memoirs, 1925-1950. Boston: Little, Brown and Co., 1967.

Kerr, Malcolm H., ed. The Elusive Peace in the Middle East. Albany: State University of New York Press, 1975.

_____. The Middle East Conflict. Headline Series, No. 191. New York: Foreign Policy Association, 1968.

_____. The Arab Cold War: Gamal Abd Al-Nasir and His Rivals, 1958-1970. 3d ed. London: Oxford University Press, 1970.

Kinter, William R., and Foster, Richard B. eds. National Strategy in a Decade of Change: An Emerging U.S. Policy. Lexington, Mass.: D. C. Heath and Co., 1973.

Kissinger, Henry A. White House Years. Boston: Little, Brown and Co., 1979.

_____. American Foreign Policy. 3d ed. New York: W. W. Norton and Co., 1977.

_____. "The Nature of the National Dialogue on Foreign Policy." In The Nixon-Kissinger Foreign Policy: Opportunities and Contradictions, edited by Fred Warner Neal and Mary Kersey Harvey, pp. 6-17. Santa Barbara: Center for the Study of Democratic Institutions, 1974.

_____. "Bureaucracy and Policy-making: The Effect of Insiders and Outsiders on the Policy Process." In Bureaucracy Politics and Strategy, edited by Henry Kissinger and Bernard Brodie, pp. 1-14. Los Angeles: University of California, 1968.

Klebanoff, Shoshona. Middle East Oil and U.S. Foreign Policy/With Special Reference to the U.S. Energy Crisis. New York: Praeger, 1974.

Kohler, Foy D.; Goure, Leon.; and Harvey, Mose L. The Soviet Union and the October 1973 Middle East War: The Implications for Détente. Miami: University of Miami Press, 1974.

Kolkowicz, Roman. "The Soviet Policy in the Middle East." In The U.S.S.R. and the Middle East, edited by Michael Confino and Shimon Shamir, pp. 77-97. New York: John Wiley and Sons, 1973.

Lake, Anthony, ed. The Vietnam Legacy: The War, American Society and the Future of American Foreign Policy. New York: New York University Press, 1976.

Landau, David. Kissinger: The Uses of Power. Boston: Houghton Mifflin Co., 1972.

Laqueur, Walter. Confrontation: The Middle East and World Politics. New York: Quadrangle, 1974.

Liska, George. Beyond Kissinger: Ways of Conservative Statecraft. Baltimore: John Hopkins University Press, 1975.

Mackintosh, Malcolm. "Soviet Mediterranean Policy." The Atlantic Papers. Vol. 2. Lexington, Mass.: Lexington Books, 1972.

Mazlish, Bruce. Kissinger: The European Mind in American Policy. New York: Basic Books, 1976.

McLaurin, R. D. The Middle East in Soviet Policy. Lexington, Mass.: D. C. Heath and Co., 1975.

Meir, Golda. My Life. New York: G. P. Putnam's Sons, 1975.

Morris, Roger. Uncertain Greatness: Henry Kissinger and American Foreign Policy. New York: Harper and Row, 1977.

Newhouse, John. Cold Dawn: The Story of SALT. New York: Holt, Rinehart and Winston, 1973.

Nixon, Richard. RN: The Memoirs of Richard Nixon. New York: Grosset and Dunlap, 1978.

Nutter, Warren G. Kissinger's Grand Design. Washington, D.C.: American Enterprise Institute for Public Policy Research, 1975.

Osgood, Robert, ed. Retreat From Empire? The First Nixon Administration. Baltimore: Johns Hopkins University Press, 1973.

Owen, Henry, ed. The Next Phase in Foreign Policy. Washington, D.C.: Brookings Institution, 1973.

Peretz, Don. "Energy: Israelis, Arabs and Iranians." In The Energy Crisis and U.S. Foreign Policy, edited by Joseph S. Szyliowicz and Brad E. O'Neil, pp. 89-96. New York: Praeger, 1975.

Pfeffer, Richard M., ed. No More Vietnams? The War and the Future of American Foreign Policy. New York: Harper and Row, 1968.

Polk, William R. The United States and the Arab World, rev. ed. Cambridge: Harvard University Press, 1969.

Pranger, Robert J. American Policy For Peace in the Middle East, 1969-1971: Problems of Principle, Manoeuver and Time. Washington, D.C.: American Enterprise Institute for Public Policy Research, 1971.

Pranger, Robert, and Tahtinen, Dale R. Nuclear Threat in the Middle East. Washington, D.C.: American Enterprise Institute for Public Policy Research, 1975.

Quandt, William B. Decade of Decisions: American Policy Toward the Arab-Israeli Conflict, 1967-1976. Berkeley and Los Angeles: University of California Press, 1977.

_____. "Domestic Influences on United States Foreign Policy in the Middle East: The View From Washington." In The Middle East: Quest for an American Policy, edited by Willard A. Beling, pp. 263-85. Albany: State University of New York Press, 1973.

_____. "U.S. Energy Policy and the Arab-Israeli Conflicts." In Arab Oil: Impact on the Arab Countries and Global Implications, edited by N. A. Sherbiney and Mark A. Tessler, pp. 279-94. New York: Praeger, 1976.

Quandt, William B.; Jabber, Fuad; and Lesch, Mosely Ann. The Politics of Palestinian Nationalism, Berkeley and Los Angeles: University of California Press, 1973.

Reich, Bernard. Quest for Peace: United States-Israel Relations and the Arab-Israeli Conflict. New Brunswick, N.J.: Transaction Books, 1977.

Rostow, Eugene V. Peace in the Balance: The Future of American Foreign Policy. New York: Simon and Shuster, 1972.

Rostow, Eugene V., ed. The Middle East: Critical Choices for the United States. Boulder, Colo.: Westview Press, 1976.

Rostow, Walt W. The Diffusion of Power: An Essay in Recent History. New York: Macmillan Co., 1972.

Sadat, Anwar. In Search of Identity: An Autobiography. New York: Harper and Row, 1978.

Safran, Nadav. From War to War: The Arab-Israeli Confrontation 1948-1967. New York: Pegasus, 1969.

Sankari, Farouk A. "The Character and Impact of Arab Oil Embargoes." In Arab Oil: Impact on the Arab Countries and Global Implications, edited by N. A. Sherbiney and Mark A. Tessler, pp. 265-78. New York: Praeger, 1976.

Sheehan, Edward R. F. The Arabs, Israelis, and Kissinger: A Secret History of American Diplomacy in the Middle East. New York: Reader's Digest Press, 1976.

Stoessinger, John C. Henry Kissinger: The Anguish of Power. New York: W. W. Norton and Co., 1976.

Szulc, Tad. The Illusion of Peace: Foreign Policy of the Nixon Years. New York: Viking Press, 1978.

The Pentagon Papers. Vol. 1 (Senator Gravel ed.). Boston: Beacon Press, 1971.

Vincent, R. J. "Kissinger's System of Foreign Policy." The Year Book of World Affairs. Vol. 31. London: Stevens and Sons, 1977.

Whetten, Lawrence L. The Canal War: Four-Power Conflict in the Middle East. Cambridge: Massachusetts Institute of Technology Press, 1974.

Zumwalt, Elmo R. Jr. On Watch: A Memoir. New York: Quadrangle, 1976.

ARTICLES IN JOURNALS AND MAGAZINES

Abu-Lughod, Ibrahim. "Altered Realities: The Palestinians since 1967." International Journal 27 (Autumn 1973): 648-69.

Aikens, James E. "The Oil Crisis: This Time the Wolf is Here." Foreign Affairs 51 (April 1973): 462-90.

Anabtawi, Samir. "The Palestinians and the 1973 Middle East War." Middle East Information Series 25 (Winter 1973-74): 38-41.

Arbatov, G. A. "American Foreign Policy on the Threshold." Orbis 15 (Spring 1971): 134-53.

Aron, Raymond. "Richard Nixon and the Future of American Foreign Policy." Deadalus 101 (Fall 1972): 1-24.

Aruri, Naseer, and Hevener, Natalie. "France and the Middle East, 1967-68." Middle East Journal 23 (Autumn 1969): 484-502.

Ball, George W. "Kissinger's Paper Peace: How not to handle the Middle East." The Atlantic Monthly 237 (February 1976): 41-49.

_____. "The Looming War in the Middle East and How to Avert It." The Atlantic Monthly 235 (January 1975): 6-11.

_____. "Slogans and Realities." Foreign Affairs 47 (July 1969): 623-41.

Bechtoldt, Heinrich. "Middle East between Kissinger and Geneva." Aussen Politik 26 (2d Quarter, 1975): 127-36.

Bell, Coral. "Kissinger in Retrospect: The Diplomacy of Power-Concert?" International Affairs 53 (April 1977): 202-16.

_____. "The October Middle East War: A Case Study in Crisis Management During Détente." International Affairs 50 (October 1974): 531-43.

Brandon, Donald. "A New Foreign Policy for America." World Affairs 138 (Fall 1975): 83-107.

Brandon, Henry. "Jordan: The Forgotten Crisis (I): Were We Masterful?" Foreign Policy 10 (Spring 1973): 158-70.

Brenner, Michael J. "The Problems of Innovation and the Nixon-Kissinger Foreign Policy." International Studies Quarterly 17 (September 1973): 255-94.

Brzezinski, Zbigniew. "U.S. Foreign Policy: The Search for Focus." Foreign Affairs 51 (July 1973): 708-27.

_____. "The State of Nixon's World: Half Past Nixon." Foreign Policy 3 (Summer 1971): 3-21.

_____. "The Balance of Power Delusion." Foreign Policy 7 (Summer 1972): 54-59.

Buchan, Alastair. "The Irony of Kissinger." International Affairs 50 (July 1974): 367-79.

Campbell, John C. "Middle East Oil: American Policy and Super-Power Interaction." Survival 15 (September/October 1973): 210-17.

_____. "The Soviet Union and the United States in the Middle East." The Annals of the American Academy of Political and Social Science 401 (October 1970): 51-59.

Chace, James. "The Five-Power World of Richard Nixon." New York Times Magazine, February 1972, pp. 14-47.

Chaliand, Gerard. "Kissinger's Diplomacy." New Outlook 18 (March/April 1975): 11-18.

Cline, Ray. "Policy Without Intelligence." Foreign Policy 17 (Winter 1974-75): 121-35.

Crabb, Cecil V., Jr. "The Energy Crisis, The Middle East, and American Foreign Policy." World Affairs 136 (Summer 1973): 48-73.

Draper, Theodore. "Détente." Commentary 57 (June 1974): 25-47.

Dulles, John Foster. "Challenge and Response in United States Policy." Foreign Affairs 36 (October 1957): 25-43.

El-Sadat, Anwar. "Where Egypt Stands." Foreign Affairs 51 (October 1972): 114-23.

Evron, Yair. "A Nuclear Balance of Deterrence in the Middle East." New Outlook 18 (July/August 1975): 15-19.

Fallaci, Oriana. "Kissinger." The New Republic 167 (December 1972): 17-22.

Ferrell, Robert H. "American Policy in the Middle East." The Review of Politics 37 (January 1975): 3-19.

Flapan, Simha. "Nuclear Power in the Middle East: The Critical Years." New Outlook 17 (October 1974): 34-40.

Forsythe, David P. "The Soviets and the Arab-Israeli Conflict." World Affairs 134 (Fall 1971): 132-42.

Garrett, Stephan A. "Nixonian Foreign Policy: A New Balance of Power—or a Revised Concer? Polity 3 (Spring 1976): 389-421.

Gelb, Leslie. "The Coming New/Old Faces in the Middle East." Bulletin of the American Association For Peace in the Middle East 2 (January 1973): 1-2.

Girling, J. L. S. "Kissingerism: The Enduring Problems." International Affairs 51 (July 1975): 323-43.

_____. "The Guam Doctrine." International Affairs 46 (January 1970): 48-62.

Graebner, Norman A. "Henry Kissinger and American Foreign Policy: A Contemporary Appraisal." The Australian Journal of Politics 22 (April 1976): 7-22.

Hahn, Walter F. "The Nixon Doctrine: Design and Dilemmas." Orbis 16 (Summer 1972): 361-76.

Harbottle, Michael. "The October Middle East War: Lessons for U.N. Peacemaking." International Affairs 50 (October 1974): 544-53.

Hassner, Pierre. "The State of Nixon's World (2): Pragmatic Conservatism in the White House." Foreign Policy 3 (Summer 1971): 41-61.

Hayes, Stephen D. "Joint Economic Commissions As Instruments of U.S. Foreign Policy in the Middle East." Middle East Journal 31 (Winter 1977): 16-30.

Herzog, Haim. "Kissinger, Heikal, and Israel." Jerusalem Post Week-End Magazine, March 1969, p. 14.

Hodes, Aubre. "Implications of Israel's Nuclear Capability." The Wiener Library Bulletin 22 (Autumn 1969): 2-8.

Hoffmann, Stanley. "A New Policy for Israel." Foreign Affairs 53 (April 1975): 405-31.

_____. "Will the Balance Balance at Home?" Foreign Policy 7 (Summer 1972): 60-68.

Hoffmann, Stanley. "France, the U.S., and the Middle East." Middle East Information Series (December 1972): 2-15.

Howard, Harry. "Recent American Policy in the Middle East." Middle East Forum 47 (Summer 1971): 13-22.

_____. "The Development of United States Policy in the Near East, 1945-1951." Department of State Bulletin 25 (November 1951): 839-43.

Hudson, Michael C. "Towards a Critique of U.S. Middle East Policy." Middle East Forum 47 (Summer 1971): 25-29.

_____. "The Palestinian Arab Resistance Movement: Its Significance in the Middle East." The Middle East Journal 23 (Summer 1969): 291-307.

Hunter, Robert. "In the Middle In the Middle East." Foreign Policy 5 (Winter 1971-72): 137-50.

Ibrahim, Saad. "American Domestic Forces And the October War." Journal of Palestine Studies 4 (Autumn 1974): 55-80.

Indyk, Martin. "Détente and the Politics of Patronage: How the October Middle East War Started." The Australian Outlook 30 (August 1976): 171-96.

Ismael, Tareq I. "The Palestinians' Emergence and U.S. Foreign Policy." Middle East Forum 46, nos. 2 & 3 (1973): 65-71.

Jabber, Fuad. "The Arab regimes and the Palestinian Revolution, 1967–1971." Journal of Palestine Studies 2 (Winter 1973): 79–101.

_____. "Israel's Nuclear Options." Journal of Palestine Studies 1 (Autumn 1971): 21–38.

Kaplan, Morton A. "Kissinger and Foreign Policy." Commentary 57 (February 1974): 11–15.

Kattenburg, Paul M. "The Nixon 'New Look' in Foreign Policy." World Affairs 135 (Fall 1972): 115–27.

Kennan, George F. "After the Cold War: American Foreign Policy in the 1970s." Foreign Affairs 51 (October 1972): 210–17.

Kerr, Malcolm H. "Nixon's Second Term: Policy Prospects in the Middle East." Journal of Palestine Studies 2 (Spring 1973):14–29.

Kinter, William. "Political Implications of the Soviet Withdrawal from Egypt: II." Bulletin of the American Academic Association For Peace in the Middle East 2 (January 1973): 6–8.

_____. The Middle East in Soviet Global Strategy." Middle East Information Series 13 (Fall 1970): 9–11.

Klare, Michael T. "The Nixon/Kissinger Doctrine and America's Pacific Basin Strategy." Bulletin of Concerned Asian Scholars 7 (April/June 1975): 3–14.

Kohl, Wilfred. "The Nixon-Kissinger Foreign Policy System and U.S.-European Relations: Patterns of Policy-Making." World Politics 27 (October 1975): 1–43.

Kristol, Irving. "The Doctor's Dilemma." International Journal 1 (Spring 1974): 6–12.

Laqueur, Walter. "Kissinger and the Politics of Détente." Commentary 56 (December 1973): 42–52.

Leacacos, John P. "Kissinger's Apparat." Foreign Policy 5 (Winter 1971–72): 3–27.

Levy, Walter J. "An Atlantic-Japanese Energy Crisis." Foreign Policy 2 (Summer 1973): 159–90.

Lewis, Bernard. "Conflict in the Middle East." Survival 17 (June 1971): 192-98.

Love, Kenneth. "The Dangerous Middle East Double Standard." Middle East Forum 47 (Summer 1971): 31-38.

Luttwak, Edward, and Laqueur, Walter. "Kissinger and the Yom Kippur War." Commentary 58 (September 1974): 33-40.

Mark, Max. "United States Foreign Policy in the Middle East." New Outlook 15 (March/April 1972): 48-64.

Medzini, Meron. "China and the Arab-Israeli Conflict." International Problems 13 (January 1974): 323-33.

Meir, Golda. "Israel in Search of Lasting Peace." Foreign Affairs 51 (April 1973): 447-61.

Morgenthau, Hans J. "The New Diplomacy of Movement." Encounter 43 (August 1974): 52-57.

_____. "Henry Kissinger, Secretary of State." Encounter 3 (November 1974): 57-61.

Nes, David G. "The Soviets in the Middle East." Military Review 62 (June 1972): 81-85.

Noer, Thomas J. "Henry Kissinger's Philosophy of History." Modern Age 19 (Spring 1975): 180-89.

Oppenheim, V. H. "Why Oil Prices Go Up: I, The Past: We Pushed Them." Foreign Policy 25 (Winter 1976-77): 24-57.

Penrose, Edith. "Origins and Development of the International Oil Crisis." Journal of International Studies 3 (Spring 1974): 37-43.

Peretz, Don. "The United States, the Arabs, and Israel: Peace Efforts by Kennedy, Johnson, and Nixon." Annals of the American Academy of Social Science 401 (May 1972): 116-25.

Perlmutter, Amos. "Crisis Management: Kissinger's Middle East Negotiations, October 1973-June 1974." International Studies Quarterly 19 (September 1975): 316-43.

Pfaff, Richard C. "Perceptions, Politicians, and Foreign Policy: The U.S. Senate and the Arab-Israeli Conflict." Middle East Forum 47 (Summer 1971): 39-49.

Quandt, William B. "Kissinger and the Arab-Israeli Disengagement Negotiations." Journal of International Affairs 29 (Spring 1975): 33-48.

_____. "The Middle East in U.S. Strategy, 1970-71." Journal of Palestine Studies 1 (Autumn 1971): 39-52.

Ravenal, Earl C. "The Nixon Doctrine and Our Asian Commitments." Foreign Affairs 49 (January 1971): 201-17.

Reich, Bernard. "The Jarring Mission and the Search for Peace in the Middle East." The Wiener Library Bulletin 26 (New Series 1972): 13-20.

_____. "United States Policy in the Middle East." Current History 70 (January 1976): 1-4, 42.

_____. "United States-Arab Relations since the June War." The Wiener Library Bulletin 24 (New Series 1970): 1-8.

Reich, Bernard. "United States Policy in the Middle East." Current History 60 (January 1971): 1-6.

Rogers, William. "A Lasting Peace in the Middle East: An American View." Department of State Bulletin 62 (January 1970): 7-11.

Rosecrance, Richard. "Kissinger, Bismarck, and the Balance of Power." Journal of International Studies 3 (Spring 1974): 45-52.

Rostow, Eugene V. "The Middle East Crisis in the Perspective of World Politics." International Affairs 47 (April 1971): 275-88.

_____. "America, Europe, and the Middle East." Commentary 57 (February 1974): 7-9.

_____. "Where Kissinger Went Wrong: A Basis for Peace." The New Republic 172 (April 1975): 12-17.

_____. "Israel and Détente." The American Zionist 65 (November 1974): 7-9.

Safran, Nadav. "The War and the Future of the Arab-Israeli Conflict." Foreign Affairs 52 (January 1974): 215-36.

_____. "Arab Politics, Peace and War." Orbis 18 (Summer 1974): 377-426.

Said, Edward. "U.S. Policy and the Conflict of Powers in the Middle East." Journal of Palestine Studies 2 (Spring 1973): 30-50.

Salinger, Pierre. "Secretary Kissinger on Foreign Policy from 1969 to 1975." Department of State Newsletter 168 (May 1975): 17-19.

Sayigh, Yusif A. "Arab Oil Politics: Self-Interest versus International Responsibility." Journal of Palestine Studies 4 (Spring 1975): 59-73.

Schiff, Gary S. "Beyond Disengagement: Conflict Resolution in the Middle East since the 1973 War." World Affairs 137 (Winter 1974-75): 195-205.

Schoenbaum, David. "Jordan: The Forgotten Crisis (2) or Lucky?" Foreign Policy 10 (Spring 1973): 171-81.

Seere, Francoise de la. "Europe's Nine and the Arab-Israeli Conflict." International Journal of Politics 1 (Spring 1975): 85-97.

Sherabi, Hisham. "The Middle East Conflict." Lo Spettore Internazionale 10 (April/June 1975): 103-09.

Sheehan, Edward R. F. "The United States, the Soviet Union, and Strategic Considerations in the Middle East." Naval War College Review 23 (June 1971): 22-30.

Sisco, Joseph J. "The United States and the Arab-Israeli Dispute." The Annals of the American Academy of Political and Social Science 384 (July 1969): 66-72.

Slonim, Shlomo. "The United States, the Big Four, and the Middle East." The American Zionist 60 (February 1970): 20-26.

_____. "American-Egyptian Rapprochement." The World Today 31 (February 1975): 47-57.

Smart, Ian. "Oil, The Super-Powers and the Middle East." International Affairs 53 (January 1977): 17-37.

Smolansky, Oleg M. "Strategic Implications of the Soviet Withdrawal from Egypt: I." Bulletin of the American Academic Association For Peace in the Middle East 2 (January 1973): 5-6.

Stephen, Robert. "The Great Powers and the Middle East." Journal of Palestine Studies 2 (Summer 1973): 3-12.

Sus, Ibrahim. "Western Europe and the October War." Journal of Palestine Studies 3 (Winter 1974): 65-83.

Szulc, Tad. "Behind the Vietnam Cease-Fire Agreement: How Kissinger Did it." Foreign Policy 15 (Summer 1974): 21-69.

Thee, Mark. "Détente and Security in the Aftermath of the Fourth Middle East War." Bulletin of Peace Proposal 5 (1974): 88-95.

Trice, Robert. "Congress and the Arab-Israeli Conflict: Support for Israel in the U.S. Senate, 1970-1973." Political Science Quarterly 92 (Fall 1977): 443-63.

Time, May 1969, p. 17.

Ulam, Adam B. "Détente Under Soviet Eyes." Foreign Policy 24 (Fall 1976): 145-59.

Ullman, Richard. "After Rabat: Middle East Risks and American Roles." Foreign Affairs 53 (January 1975): 284-96.

Veruth, Heinz. "Kissinger's Foreign Policy System." Aussen Politik 24 (4th Quarter, 1973): 363-76.

Watt, D. C. "American Foreign Policy After Vietnam." The Political Quarterly 44 (July/September 1973): 271-82.

Yizhar, Michael. "Origins of the American Involvement in the Middle East." International Problems 13 (January 1974): 335-46.

_____. "The United States Middle East Resolution As Viewed by Foreign Powers." International Problems 12 (June 1973): 59-81.

UN DOCUMENTS

United Nations. Security Council, Resolutions and Decisions of the Security Council, 1967. New York: Security Council, Official Records, 1968.

_____. Security Council, Official Records. Supplement for January, February, and March 1971. <u>Report of the Secretary-General on the activities of the Special Representative to the Middle East,</u> Documents S/10070 and Add. 1 and 2. New York: Security Council, 1972.

_____. Security Council, <u>Resolutions and Decisions of the Security Council, 1973</u>. New York: Security Council, Official Records, 1974.

U.S. GOVERNMENT DOCUMENTS

U.S., President. <u>U.S. Foreign Policy For the 1970's: A New Strategy For Peace: A Report to Congress by Richard Nixon, President of the United States,</u> February 18, 1970. Washington, D.C.: Government Printing Office, 1970.

_____. <u>U.S. Foreign Policy For the 1970's: Building For Peace: A Report to the Congress by Richard Nixon, President of the United States,</u> February 25, 1971. Washington, D.C.: Government Printing Office, 1971.

_____. <u>U.S. Foreign Policy for the 1970's: The Emerging Structure of Peace: A Report to the Congress by Richard Nixon, President of the United States,</u> February 9, 1970. Washington, D.C.: Government Printing Office, 1972.

_____. <u>U.S. Foreign Policy For the 1970's: Shaping a Durable Peace: A Report to the Congress by Richard Nixon, President of the United States,</u> May 3, 1973. Washington, D.C.: Government Printing Office, 1973.

_____. <u>Public Papers of the President of the United States</u>. Washington, D.C.: Government Printing Office, 1971. Richard Nixon, 1969.

_____. <u>Public Papers of the President of the United States</u>. Washington, D.C.: Government Printing Office, 1971. Richard Nixon, 1970.

U.S. Department of State. <u>United States Foreign Policy, 1969-70: A Report of the Secretary of State to Congress</u>. Department of State Publication No. 8575, March 1971. Washington, D.C.: Government Printing Office, 1971.

_____. United States Foreign Policy, 1971: A Report of the Secretary of State to Congress. Department of State Publication No. 8634. Washington, D.C.: Government Printing Office, 1972.

U.S., Congress. Senate. Committee on Foreign Relations. Briefings By the Secretary of State William Rogers, Hearings before the Senate Committee on Foreign Relations, 91st Cong., 1st sess., 1969.

_____. Committee on Foreign Relations. Nomination of Henry A. Kissinger to be Secretary of State, Hearings before the Senate Committee on Foreign Relations, 93d Cong., 2d sess., 1973.

_____. Committee on Foreign Relations. United States Relations with Communist Countries, Hearings before the Senate Committee on Foreign Relations, 93d Cong., 2d sess., 1974.

U.S., Congress. House Committee on Foreign Affairs. The Near East Conflict, Hearings before the Subcommittee on the Near East and South Asia of the House Committee on Foreign Affairs, 91st Cong., 2d sess., 1970.

_____. Committee on Foreign Affairs. Soviet Involvement in the Middle East and Western Response. Joint hearings before the Subcommittee on Europe and the Subcommittee on the Near East and South Asia of the House Committee on Foreign Affairs, 92d Cong., 1st sess., 1971.

_____. Committee on Foreign Affairs. The Middle East 1971: The Need to Strengthen the Peace. Hearings before the Subcommittee on the Near East and South Asia of the House Committee on Foreign Affairs, 92d Cong., 1st sess., 1971.

_____. Committee on Foreign Affairs. Approaches to Peace in the Middle East. Hearings before the Subcommittee on the Near East of the House Committee on Foreign Affairs, 92d Cong., 2d sess., 1972.

_____. Committee on Foreign Affairs. U.S. Interests In and Policy Toward the Persian Gulf. Hearings before the Subcommittee on the Near East of the House Committee on Foreign Affairs, 92d Cong., 2d sess., 1972.

_____. Committee on Foreign Affairs. United States-Europe Relations and the 1973 Middle East War. Hearings before the Subcommittee on the Near East and South Asia and the Subcommittee on Europe of the House Committee on Foreign Affairs, 93d Cong., 1st and 2d sess., 1974.

_____. Committee on Foreign Affairs. Détente. Hearings before the Subcommittee on Europe of the House Committee on Foreign Affairs, 93d Cong., 2d sess., 1974.

_____. Committee on Foreign Affairs. The Middle East, 1974: New Hopes, New Hopes, New Challenges. Hearings before the Subcommittee on the Near East and South Asia of the House Committee on Foreign Affairs, 93d Cong., 2d sess., 1974.

_____. Committee on Foreign Affairs. U.S. Foreign Policy and the Export of Nuclear Technology to the Middle East. Hearings before the Subcommittee on International Organizations and Movements and the Subcommittee on the Near East and South Asia of the House Committee on Foreign Affairs, 93d Cong., 2d sess., 1974.

_____. Committee on Foreign Affairs. A Sino-Soviet Perspective in the Middle East. Hearings before the Subcommittee on the Near East and South Asia of the House Committee on Foreign Affairs, 92d Cong., 2d sess., 1972.

_____. Committee on International Relations. The Palestinian Issue in the Middle East Peace Efforts. Hearings before the Special Subcommittee on Investigations of the House Committee on International Relations, 94th Cong., 1st sess., 1975.

_____. Declaration for Peace in the Middle East. 91st Cong., 1st sess., April 22 to May 1969. Congressional Record. Vol. 115.

Government Periodicals

Congressional Quarterly Weekly Report, 1968.

Department of State Bulletin, 1969-73.

NEWSPAPERS AND POLLS

Al-Ahram, 1955-1970.

Al-Anwar, 1973.

Current Digest of the Soviet Press, 1955.

Gallup Opinion Index, 1969.

Jerusalem Post, 1955-70.

Jerusalem Post Week-End Magazine, 1969-1973.

New York Times, 1969-1974.

OTHER SOURCES

Becker, S. A., and Horelick, A. L. "Soviet Policy in the Middle
    East, 1955-1969." Rand Memorandum, R-504-FF (September
    1970): 1-115.

Caldwell, Dan Edward. "American-Soviet Detente and the Nixon-
    Kissinger Grand Design and Grand Strategy." Ph.D. disserta-
    tion, Stanford University, 1968.

Falk, Richard. "What's Wrong with Henry Kissinger's Foreign
    Policy." Center of International Studies, Policy Memorandum
    No. 39, Princeton, N.J.: Princeton University, 1974.

Hartley, Anthony. American Foreign Policy in the Nixon Era. In
    Adelphi Papers, No. 110. London: International Institute for
    Strategic Studies, 1974/75.

Horelick, Arnold. "Moscow's Rift with Sadat: Implications For Soviet
    Middle East Policy." Rand Memorandum, P-5666 (May 1976).

Itayim, Faud. "Strengths and Weaknesses of the Oil Weapon." In
    The Middle East and the International System: Security and the
    Energy Crisis, pp. 17-24. Adelphi Papers, No. 115. London:
    International Institute For Strategic Studies, 1975.

Kerr, Malcolm. "Regional Arab Politics and Conflict with Israel."
    Rand Memorandum, RM-5966-FF (October 1969): 1-50.

Ma'oz, Moshe. "Soviet and Chinese Relations with Palestinian Organi-
    zations." Jerusalem Papers on Peace Problems, No. 4. Jeru-
    salem: Leonard Davis Institute for International Relations,
    Hebrew University, 1974.

Momoi, Makoto. "The Energy Problem and Alliance Systems: Japan."
In The Middle East and the International System: Security and
the Energy Crisis, pp. 25-31. Adelphi Papers, No. 115.
London: International Institute For Strategic Studies, 1975.

Quandt, William B. "Soviet Policy in the October 1973 War." Rand
Memorandum, R-1864-ISA (May 1976).

_____. "United States Policy in the Middle East: Constraints and
Choices." Rand Memorandum, RM-5980-FF (February 1970):
1-86.

Reich, Bernard. "New Directions in U.S. Middle East Policy."
Research Analysis Corp., RAC-P-47 (January 1969): 1-22.

Slonin, Shlomo. "United States-Israel Relations, 1967-1973: A Study
in the Convergence and Divergence of Interests." Jerusalem:
Leonard Davis Institute for International Relations, Hebrew
University, 1974.

Index

About the Authors

ISHAQ I. GHANAYEM has a B.A. and an M.A. from San José State University, and a Ph.D. in Political Science from the University of California, Santa Barbara. He is a private researcher in the fields of American foreign policy, international political economy, and Middle Eastern politics. He has conducted research in Washington, D.C., and in the Middle East, and has also contributed to Alden Voth's book, <u>Moscow Abandons Israel for the Arabs: Ten Crucial Years in the Middle East</u>.

ALDEN H. VOTH received a B.A. from Bethel College (Kansas), an M.A. from Iowa State University, and a Ph.D. in International Relations from the University of Chicago.

In 1945-46 he worked for the United Nations Relief and Rehabilitation Administration in a short-term, war-relief project in Europe. From graduate school he received an appointment as Chairman of the Social Sciences Division, Upland College (California). Dr. Voth has taught in the Middle East for several years and is currently Professor of Political Science at San José State University.

He has served on the staff of numerous conferences, including the National Council of Churches' World Order Conference (Cleveland, 1958), the United Nations (New York), and at "Church and State" conferences in Washington, D.C.

Dr. Voth is the author of <u>Moscow Abandons Israel for the Arabs</u> and has published numerous articles in various professional journals.